CW00516927

# A Thousand Hills

## A Story of Crisis in Rwanda

**Tom Mullarkey**

**Ballintava Books**

A Thousand Hills
Published in Great Britain by Ballintava Books Ltd, 2000
100 Ack Lane East, Bramhall, Cheshire, SK7 2BH, UK


Copyright © Tom Mullarkey, 2000

The moral right of the author has been asserted

A CIP catalogue record for this book is available from the
British Library


ISBN 0-9540051-0-4


Printed and bound in Great Britain by Unity Print Ltd

# A Thousand Hills

A Story of Crisis in Rwanda

iii

For The Banyarwanda

# Introduction

It is rare for a soldier to write a good book. There are too many confidences to be respected, too many reputations to be protected and too many pages written under the intimidating influence of the chain of command. Most military literature is written by civilians - the soldiers' poet, after all, is Rudyard Kipling - or by soldiers who by leaving the service have gained the freedom to write about it.

Tom Mullarkey is just such an ex-soldier. A major with the Royal Artillery who in 1994 sought a discharge and a career in the City, he was assigned to a paper-pushing job to mark time in his last six months. Through a combination of guile and energy he managed to exchange this for a tour of duty as SO2 (Plans) with the headquarters of the troubled UN force in Rwanda.

SO2 (Plans) is nowhere near the top of the military pecking order. It is an unregarded desk job helping a colonel advise the Force Commander on various contingencies that might arise, almost all of them unpalatable.

Most officers would have gone with the flow. Tom Mullarkey chose not to. He used his talents, and a commandeered Chinese Jeep, to exceed his remit close to the point of insubordination. He put together a comprehensive plan - codenamed Op RETOUR - which offered Rwanda an escape from its nightmare and a constructive way forward following the genocide of its recent past. He argued for this proposal in Kigali and Geneva, and tactfully presented it as the work of others. It saved lives which would have been lost without it. If ever an MBE was earned the hard way, it was the one he later received at Buckingham Palace.

The obstacles were daunting and in some cases insuperable. These included the competing agendas of the international aid agencies, the obstructions of the Rwandan government, the institutionalised inertia of the UN force and the self-serving mentality of the bureaucracy that went with it. Within days of Tom Mullarkey's return to the United Kingdom, the bloodletting resumed. He could only watch it in despair on television.

*A Thousand Hills* is a horror story twice over. It is a soldier's story through and through. It is told, nonetheless, with humour and humanity. It is required reading for anyone who has experienced, or is interested in, the problems of peace-keeping in the collapsed nation states of the new world disorder, in Africa and elsewhere. It avoids the usual Eurocentric perspectives. It sets out the need for a tougher and more robust UN presence, for a force which will not flinch from its rules of engagement, and for the use of African troops in an African setting.

It should certainly occupy a place of honour in the 'Lessons Learned Department' at UN Headquarters. There actually is one. And following the debacle in Rwanda, there surely needs to be.

Martin Bell
MP for Tatton

# Preface

I started writing this book in 1995. It was an idea sparked off by Ambassador Khan, just before I left Rwanda and became part of my personal rehabilitation plan. There was little time to write during those first months of a civilian career, so I started by jotting a paragraph on the train from High Wycombe to London every morning and a second on the way home at night. If I had the energy, I would type them and a third into the computer in the evening, sometimes after midnight. And so it inched closer and closer to a first draft.

The biggest battle, bigger even than what subsequently seemed to be a mere skirmish with the UN, was the struggle with the publishing establishment. First, a well-known agent who courted his budding author with serious intensity, advising and recommending changes until, two years later, he abandoned me without a phone call or letter. Then a seemingly endless round of disappointments as I discovered how aspiring authors sell their books the hard way. Over 30 rejections, delivered in series, since that is what you have to do, led to my final determination to go it alone another 18 months later. Many of these publishers were complimentary about the work and explained their commercial conundrum with gratifying honesty. The first problem was the subject. It was not military history, international relations or current affairs in order to fit a niche; nor was it sufficiently juicy in the horrible and exposé stakes, to make it a mass-market book. But the brutal truth, explained by one of Britain's foremost publishers, was that the days of the new author are nearly over: 'Unless a book involves sport, TV tie-in or celebrity auto/biography, we will no longer publish it.' So it seems you have to be famous to have a book published nowadays, a contradiction which we can only hope, will not lead to the demise of the medium entirely.

I do not claim that I saw all of Rwanda during that time. My experience could not take in every essential component of the crisis and some readers may feel that I have got it wrong or missed important issues. If that is the case, then I can only say that what you read here happened to me and these are my thoughts about it. I have recorded what I saw and did and this book, in itself, is just a summary of that.

For me, the most important thing is that story is told. The world should not have to go through countless crises, each time re-inventing the creaky humanitarian wheel, when it is so obvious what went wrong, and when so little needs to be done to put it right. Since I left the Army, I have never been contacted by anyone 'official' to give my perspective or write a review, except for the BBC who turned me into one of their 'experts'. So this is it for me, a little later than I would have liked - my post-operation report.

Tom Mullarkey  
Manchester  
December 2000

# Acknowledgements

It seems hardly enough to thank those many people who were a critical part of Op RETOUR and who, but for reasons of space, would have been woven into the story. At the IOC, Ray Torres from UNICEF, who orchestrated the plan for 'unaccompanied minors', Paul Howard, whose International Organisation for Migration (IOM) trucks ground on, delivering people to the Home Communes; Dr Antoine, from the World Health Organisation who ran the Health Cell; Leon Haguma also from the WHO who coordinated the Food, Seeds and Tools programme; Steve Lawrence from UNICEF who looked after the Water and Sanitation programme; Adam Amberg from UNICEF who wrestled with land issues and ran the Shelter Cell; Marie-Jose Torres from UNHCR who organised the Open Relief Centre Cell and led the charge on Human Rights and Justice issues, supported by Major Mark Cuthbert-Brown; Major Don MacNeil and Captain Andre Demers, both UNAMIR officers from Canada, who worked hard on civil-military liaison; and in the centre, helping Mark Frohardt, Barney Mayhew and Margaux van de Fliert from UNREO, were Jean-Luc Stallon from UNICEF, and in pursuit of Barney's constant aim to involve Rwandese in the management process, Antoine Sendama, M. Lazar, Innocent Ngango, Evode Ntagwera and Beatrice Mukantwari from the Ministry of Rehabilitation; Major Fidelis Mhonda (Zimbabwe) and Captain Adam Mohammed Adamu (Nigeria), who are both mentioned in the text, were the constant UNAMIR presence, supported by Majors Steve and Andy Moore from Australia.

More widely, I must praise Anita Menghetti and Elizabeth Stanic, from UNREO, for their fortitude; Colonel Shiva (India) the Chief of Staff at UNAMIR whose arrival added a breath of fresh air and the Commanding Officer of the 1st Gurkhas of INDBATT, Colonel Singh, whose good-mannered professionalism was always a great boon. The team at

*Canadian Helicopters*, so hospitable and skilled, were a pleasure to work with. Within UNAMIR, Carole Harris, ever full of fun, was excellent for morale.

In the prologue, I have gathered information from many sources, not least *The Lonely Planet Guide to East Africa* and Fergal Keane's *Season of Blood*. For the opening sequence of the book, I have leant heavily on the work of Alison Des Forges *et al* (*Leave None to Tell the Story*), Linda Melvern (*The Ultimate Crime*), The Belgian Parliamentary Senate Report on Rwanda, African Rights (*Death, Despair and Defiance*) and comments from David Rawson, former US Ambassador to Rwanda.

In the preparation of this book, there are many to thank - Martin Bell for his Introduction, Martin Stephen, High Master at The Manchester Grammar School, Fergal Keane from the BBC and Lester Crook, at I B Taurus, all of whom encouraged me when publication looked a dim and distant prospect. Also Mark Cuthbert-Brown and Barney Mayhew whose comments have added detail and accuracy where my memory failed. John Neate, Sarah Parker and Keith Smith at *Access Advertising* in Manchester, for their help with the cover and the maps. Most of all, Rory and Patrick who were neglected while I wrote and above all others, for her faith, determination and excellent editorship, Sue, my wife.

For inspiration, I must thank T E Lawrence and from fiction, the honourable exemplar, Guy Crouchback, created by Evelyn Waugh. In my own career, I learnt to challenge the orthodoxy of traditional thinking with the encouragement of several mentors along the way - Edmund Burton, Tony Bleakley, Brendan Kavanagh, both Doug Briscoe and Ken Hague in Canada, Cedric Delves, Sam Cowan, Rupert Smith, Nick Hill-Norton. They all, in different ways, recognised the power of youthful optimism and let it take its course. It was their example which gave me the courage and the confidence to act when there was nobody there to give advice.

# List of Abbreviations

| | |
|---|---|
| BRITCON | British Contingent |
| DCOS (Ops) | Deputy Chief of Staff (Operations) - Col Jan Arp (Canada) |
| DCOS (Sp) | Deputy Chief of Staff (Support) - Col Kieran O'Kelly (UK) & Col Kelvin Tutt (UK) |
| DFC | Deputy Force Commander - Brigadier General Anyidoho (Ghana) |
| FC | Force Commander - Maj Gen Guy Claude Tousignant (Canada) |
| FRAFBATT | French African Battalion |
| GHANBATT | Ghanaian Battalion |
| IDP | Internally Displaced Person (a refugee within home borders) |
| IOC | Integrated Operations Centre |
| MOD | Ministry of Defence |
| MSF | Médecins Sans Frontières |
| NGO | Non Governmental Organisation |
| RGF | Rwanda Government Forces (Army of former regime) |
| RPA | Rwanda Patriotic Army |
| RPF | Rwanda Patriotic Front (later became RPA) |
| SRSG | Special Representative of the Secretary General - Ambassador Shaharyar Khan |
| UNAMIR | United Nations Assistance Mission in Rwanda [you-na-mere] |
| UNHCR | United Nations High Commissioner for Refugees |
| UNICEF | United Nations Children's Fund [you-ni-seff] |
| UNREO | United Nations Rwanda Emergency Office [un-ree-oh] |
| ZAMBATT | Zambian Battalion |

# The Author

Tom Mullarkey was born in Dunmore, Co. Galway, Ireland in 1957 and his family emigrated to Britain a year later. He was educated at Maidstone Grammar School. He joined the Army in 1975, prior to university at Lancaster, and was commissioned into the Royal Artillery. An unusually colourful career, which took in the management of several sporting and cultural events and an Arctic expedition, included postings to Germany and Northern Ireland and substantial command experience. He was twice selected to represent the UK as an Exchange Officer, firstly in Canada where he commanded a Battery and secondly to the Indian Staff College where he completed a post-graduate degree in Defence Studies. He was then selected to be the personal staff officer to the Deputy Chief of Defence Staff in Whitehall, which is where this story begins.

On leaving the Army in 1995, he worked for 18 months in a merchant bank in the City of London and is now a Director of the XVII Commonwealth Games, to be held in Manchester in 2002.

Tom is married to Sue and they have two boys - Rory and Patrick - aged 13 and 11. His interests include walking in the hills and riding a rusty *Enfield Bullet*.

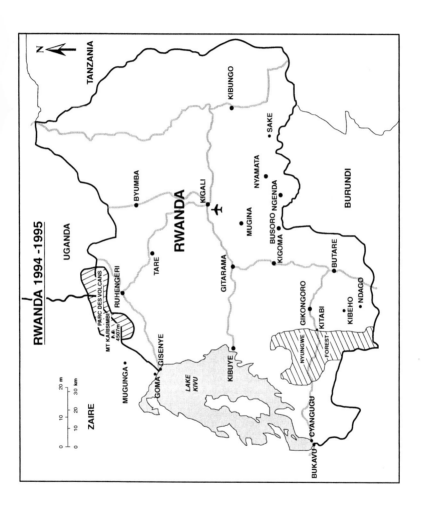

RWANDA 1994 -1995

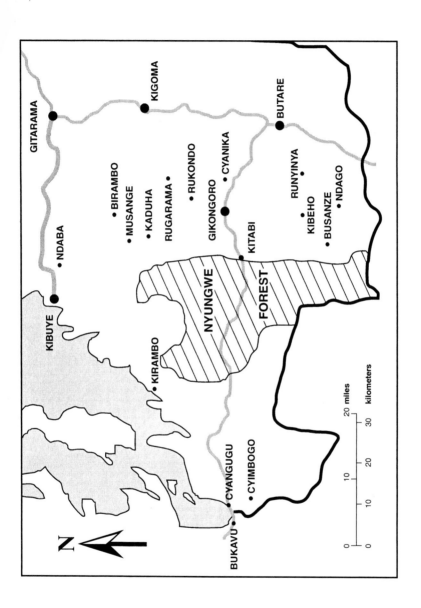

# Prologue

I know I was completely astounded to learn that a million people had died in just 100 days in the summer of 1994. I am not sure when I learnt this fact - it was certainly after I had arrived in Rwanda in September that year. Blurring into that almost incomprehensible statistic was the word 'genocide'. It seems impossible to understand that even then, the UN had not uttered the word that nobody else dared to utter whilst it was happening. But now it is a matter of fact. Genocide was committed in the summer of 1994, just as it had been in Cambodia, and before that in Nazi-occupied Europe. But of all the horrendous crimes of the twentieth century, the Rwandese genocide stands out for me as something especially horrible. The first reason is obviously that I was involved in the aftermath, saw the corpses for myself, heard the stories of the slaughter and met some of the extraordinarily resilient people who survived it by hiding or by playing dead. But there is something about the statistic itself which bears consideration. One million killings in 100 days require, on average, 10,000 to be killed every day. Given the tiny population of Rwanda - seven million in 1994 - the sheer scale and system required to butcher 10,000 a day for 100 days seems incomprehensible. In proportion to the British population, it would involve the murder of around 86,000 people per day, every day for 100 days. In the USA, it translates into about 357,000 people per day, every day for 100 days. This extrapolation serves only to illustrate that the enormity of the crime could not have been perpetrated without the knowledge or complicity or the personal involvement of practically everybody else in the country. And there were no gas chambers and few machine-guns - it was nearly all done face to face, eye to eye, by machete. The fact of the killing is an experience shared now by the majority of Rwandese, in a deeply ingrained and highly personal way which we in the West can never begin to understand.  The guilt is there for everyone to see and it will never go away.

But overlaid on this guilt is a strangely balancing tendency towards forgiveness and reconciliation.  They have been here before, these people, and it is foolish and idealistic to expect that they will never go there again.  For them, this is a pendulum which has swung with a somnolent regularity, out of peaceful co-existence into bloody conflict, the one side gaining an ascendancy which the other, as surely as the pendulum swings, will seek to take away by force.  In the interim, they somehow seem to have mastered the knack of uneasy truce at the political level, underpinned by some exceptionally strong relationships at the personal.  There really is no good and evil, no right and wrong, no established order of absolute morality.  Instead, there seems to be this uncanny ability to recognise the crimes of the past and to live with them and within them, until the pendulum swings again.

It goes back at least 1,000 years, so long that our own European squabbles come into perspective and, in Britain, our own most intractable saga of unending hatred - Northern Ireland - seems but a recent invention.  In central Eastern Africa, in the area now described as Rwanda and Burundi, the Twa Pygmies, living a simple life of foraging subsistence, were gradually displaced by nomadic tribesmen of the Bantu peoples - the Hutu - who established a system of intensive agriculture and loose political cohesion based on local organisation and a community-based society.  This system was no match for a tribe which descended from the North (often erroneously described as being of Ethiopian origin) called the Watutsi, or Tutsi, which by the 15th century had established its superiority.

They brought with them a more sophisticated political system based on a feudal overlordship, in which the Hutu became the peasant underlings, dependent for land ownership, protection and justice on the whim of their tall, arrogant and imperious masters.  Their ownership of cattle, which represented wealth, and their high ceremony, military structure and religious practices, gave the Tutsi a dominance which the unorganised and backward Hutu could not surpass. In the Rwanda area, the king figure or *mwami* exercised absolute power, authority over the life and death of every Hutu peasant. The latter, dependent on intensive agriculture, found himself without food once the land had been stripped of its vegetation, and in the competition over land use which ensued, the Tutsi cattle-owners inevitably and frequently visited famine upon their lower orders. But this first 900 years was not an entirely passive subjugation of the Hutu. They occasionally and locally rebelled, murdered and were themselves punished by violence, every step of the way.

Germany controlled the country from 1890 to 1916, when the garrison surrendered to Belgium. The League of Nations assigned Rwanda and Burundi to Belgium after the Great War and the two countries were administered together until independence in 1962, by which time the Belgians had surrendered any credibility they had as colonial administrators. They had used the Tutsi as their instrument of domination, degrading the position of the Hutu to the point at which immediate political reform had become essential. Amongst their more divisive tactics, the Belgians introduced an identity card system which categorised Twa, Hutu and Tutsi, principally by physical appearance. The Twa were short, the Hutu stocky and the Tutsi angular and tall. In proportion, they were roughly 5%, 80% and 15% of the population respectively. Noses and foreheads were measured to provide ease of definition. Realistically, the Rwandese were not so easy to characterise; they lived side-by-side, spoke the same language, had inter-married, shared the same culture. In a response to Hutu leanings towards power, a Tutsi clan murdered Hutu leaders in 1959, sparking off a bloodbath in which at least 100,000 Tutsis were murdered and many more fled into exile - the 1959-ers. From neighbouring Burundi and Uganda they mounted guerrilla raids which increased the cycle of violence against Tutsis, engendering yet more flights into exile, more smouldering hatred, more counter-attacks by night.

The massacre of tens of thousands of Hutus in neighbouring Tutsi-dominated Burundi in 1972 was the cause of another round of violence. From this carnage rose the new leader of Rwanda, General Juvenal Habyarimana, who successfully administered a decrepit, corrupt but reasonably stable Hutu-dominated government for over 15 years. This relative peace was shattered in 1990 by an attack mounted by the now well-organised Tutsi guerrilla army, the Rwanda Patriotic Front (RPF), trained in Uganda and latterly led by an exceptionally clever soldier-politician, Paul Kagame. Within days, Habyarimana had requested the assistance of military forces from Zaire, France and Belgium to help him defeat the rebels. Supported by these forces, the Rwandese Army was able to repulse the RPF and carried out a series of well-orchestrated reprisal attacks on Tutsis and moderate Hutus, causing tens of thousands of deaths, a forerunner of the genocide which was to come.

The RPF struck again in 1991 and, better organised and prepared, by early 1992 were close to the capital, Kigali. Quickly, Habyarimana sought peace and this was brokered in Arusha, in neighbouring Tanzania, leading to a stand-off in which the RPF was allowed some freedom of occupation and the prospect of military integration and the French were brought in again to support the Government. The role of France during this period and in the summer of 1994 bears some inspection, but will not be covered here.

By late 1993, the UN had assembled a weak force to oversee the peace. UNAMIR, the UN Assistance Mission in Rwanda, which crucially included a battalion from Belgium, was deployed without a clear mandate under the military command of a Canadian General, Romeo Dallaire, and overseen by the Special Representative of the UN Secretary General,

Ambassador Booh-Booh. The tension and hatred of the Tutsi were whipped up by the many armed Hutu militias, each one representing some political camp or other. The most notable was the Interahamwe, meaning 'those who attack together'.

President Habyarimana was weakening, unable to hold his many factions together. On 6 April 1994, his plane was shot down in the late evening, on its approach run into Kigali International Airport, killing him and several other political notables - on board too was the President of Burundi, Cyprien Ntaryamira. This act almost certainly served to be a signal for the genocide to commence, a reprisal for the murder contrived by the RPF. So claimed the Interahamwe and the Hutu extremists. The independent radio station *Milles Collines* directed the Hutu to crush the *inyenzi* (cockroaches), and pleaded for more killing - 'the graves are only half full'.

In the weeks and months of slaughter that followed, UNAMIR withdrew in disgrace, unable to intervene under its terms of reference. UN soldiers shredded their blue berets on departure, so disgusted were they to be associated with such cowardice. General Dallaire insisted on remaining, surrounded by a token force which could neither stop nor report the killings in any detail. The RPF, desperate to stop the murder of their ethnic brothers and sisters, swept through Rwanda, forcing the Government, the Army and a huge number of Hutu people towards Zaire and other neighbouring borders. France deployed a force which was ostensibly on a humanitarian mission - Operation TURQUOISE - but which served principally to protect the Hutu from the RPF. Behind this screen, the killings continued. As a former ally of Hutu Rwanda, France's intervention could only be interpreted as partisan.

In Zaire, the first real attention that the world had paid to Rwanda was beginning to focus. There had been pictures of bodies floating down the Akagera River and many tales of woe from New York. The USA had sent forces into Tanzania and

Uganda to clear up the lake-shores. But it was the plight of the Hutus, as they staggered on foot into Goma, which cried out for recognition. Typhoid, cholera and all the woes of an itinerant population, expelled by rebel invaders, arriving *en masse* at a barren, volcanic desert, hit the headlines far more than the killings. Little may have been known of the genocide at that stage, but somehow, nobody seemed to ask either.

Then in mid-1994, just as the savagery was beginning to peter out and the Hutus had been dispersed, the UN mandated a new force, UNAMIR II, to be deployed. What earthly purpose it could have served with its 6,500 personnel, when the original force had been withdrawn from the killing fields, was obviously not considered in detail. By August 1994, General Guy Claude Tousignant, another Canadian, and Ambassador Shaharyar Khan, the next SRSG, personally selected by Dr Boutros Boutros-Ghali, had taken up the reins. Every day, new troops arrived to preside over a complex, messy and clearly insoluble problem - the future of Rwanda.

# Chapter 1

Agathe Uwilingiyimana Uwilingiyimana was desperate. Since news of the plane crash had ricocheted across the city at around 9 p.m. the previous day, broadcast by *Radio Milles Collines*, she had known that her time was short. Her husband, Ignace, a university lecturer, was with her. So were her two guards. Outside were five UN soldiers acting as her security escort. Friends had spirited her children away; they were hidden close by. She was alive although she knew now that out on the street, many were dying. Her guards looked fearfully out of the window.

Hours earlier, another party of UN soldiers, ten Belgian paratroopers, had been readied and despatched to Agathe's house. Their mission was to escort her to *Radio Rwanda*, where she could make a plea for peace. Their progress was slow and a journey that should have taken 15 minutes took three hours, as they negotiated their way through countless barriers, manned by Rwandese soldiers and mobs of machete-wielding civilians. They arrived at her house at about 5.30 a.m., their officer making contact with the five Ghanaian UN soldiers already there.

A short distance away, 12 members of the Presidential Guard were also despatched. Their mission was to find Agathe. They had been ordered to ensure that she did not reach the radio station. They drove slowly through the tree-lined boulevards, yelling encouragement to those whose hatred had turned to violence, cheering as another machete blow was struck; there was blood running in the gutter.

Inside, Agathe was not ready to leave. She asked the UN officer to give her more time, as she tried unsuccessfully to contact senior government members on the telephone.

1

Reluctantly, on edge at the sound of gunfire and the sight of armed men on the rooftops around, he agreed. Suddenly, the air was rent with a massive explosion as one of his UN jeeps, parked by the gate, was hit by a tank round. Agathe had earlier telephoned her friend and next-door neighbour, the councillor at the US Embassy, who had agreed to let her in. On the other side of the wall, they were still desperately trying to organise the ladders to effect the escape. One of her guards had crawled across the garden and was now out of sight in the bushes, when she saw the ladder come over. He quickly steadied it. He had reached the top of the wall when shots rang out and he retreated swiftly to join her. It was too dangerous to go over the ladder; they would have to go out the back way.

Just seconds later, the group of Presidential Guard, despatched earlier, arrived. The Belgian officer and his men were surrounded.

He called UN Headquarters: In the confusion, Agathe had left without them. They were under attack. What should they do? He was told clearly: 'Stay where you are. Stay on the radio. Try to negotiate.'

A Rwandese Major stepped forward and demanded that he give himself up now and disarm and that he would personally guarantee their safety. They had his word.

The Belgian officer, 29 years old and with two years of peacekeeping experience, father of two children, received no advice from the Headquarters.

'What shall I do?' he persisted.

'It is your decision,' he was told by his Commanding Officer.

They gave up their weapons, were taken to a truck and driven to Camp Kigali, a few hundred metres away.

The sound of car horns blaring a block away and the noise of people screaming and people shouting on the main street 200 metres to the right, kept her senses jangling all the way to breaking point. Her face was wet with the sweat of her fear and her exertions  Blood from scratches had run down her chin and her throat, and had stained her dressing gown. There was no gunfire, no sudden shout from the main street, and she moved cautiously up to the corner, her husband and her guards slightly ahead.  A car was burning at the junction to her right, contributing its acrid stench to the heavy air. There were a few figures around the blaze and a shape lying in the street which could only be a corpse, perhaps the owner of the car. The main activity was further ahead, where they must go. She moved on, tempted to run all the way, but chiding herself for her stupidity. She must remain calm, alert. She could not outrun a crowd. Through slitted eyes she saw the railings of the compound. At the corner, she could cross and hope that somebody would help them. She knew that if there were nobody there to protect them, they would die. She closed her eyes briefly and said a prayer before running across to the UN Development Programme building. Where they might live.

At the barracks, the UN soldiers were made to stand together. The hatred and contempt which the Rwandese soldiers felt for Belgium, built up over many years, boiled over as a senior Rwandese officer shouted out that the President's plane had been shot down by the Belgians.  A group of Rwandese soldiers, including disabled war veterans, set upon the UN troops, battering four Belgians to death almost immediately, using the butts of their rifles, bayonets, stones and even crutches. Retreating in the confusion, the surviving troops defended themselves with their bare hands until they had managed to retreat to a nearby building, enabling a stand-off. One paratrooper, separated from his colleagues, was able to join them by crawling quickly under a nearby truck.

She hid in the compound, hearing the shouts of the Presidential Guard, as they searched frantically for her. They knew she could not have evaded the roadblocks.

The UN was now aware that its soldiers were in danger. The UN General, on his way to a crisis meeting with the Rwandese Army, tried to intervene, but he was rebuffed. At the end of the meeting, at around noon, he raised the subject, but was again put off. Close by, his men were still fighting for their lives.

They were very close now and she had nearly decided to come out from the bushes. But they spotted her and ran at her and, instinctively, she bolted, sprinting as hard as she could until she had reached the corner of a building. She leaned against the wall and gasping, turned to look around the corner to check the way ahead. She looked straight into the face of a small, stocky, grinning man. He was carrying a machete. '*Amahoro*,' he said quietly, the word for peace. Then he shouted, '*Amahoro, Amahoro, Amahoro*.' At the guest-house building, there was a group of white people, expatriates, sheltering on the veranda, unsure of what to do. But the crowd was upon her and her husband and her guards before there was any hope of a reaction. Now there were soldiers of the Presidential Guard. And it was the small man again. She moved away from him. He followed her, laughing. As she was about to reach out for support, he tripped her, and she fell heavily against the wall which surrounded the compound. Her whole face smashed up against this unyielding force, and the shock ran through her body. There were more figures running, she saw, as she felt the first kick, and then she felt someone pushing forward on her left, felt his presence.

One of the Belgians in the building was shot dead; the others tried to find cover beneath the beds in the room, even using his body as a shield, as they suffered a hail of bullets. There was a

4

pause as the Ghanaians were called out and allowed to leave; then the onslaught continued. The officer, who still had his pistol, shot one Rwandese soldier, trying to climb in through a window, and they took the rifle. Desperate now beyond their wildest experiences, exhausted, bloodied and short of ammunition, the UN soldiers knew it was only a matter of time.

She begged for her life, begged to be taken to the military camp. Her children were hiding close by and she needed to lead her attackers away. With her husband and the two guards, she was frog-marched back to her house. The people turned her around to face the crowd, a hundred laughing faces, more joining the outer edges all the time. They lifted her up, and held out her arms. Under orders of an Army Captain of the Presidential Guard, a police officer came forward, drawing his pistol. He shot her at point blank range, blowing away her face. And when she died, on 7 April 1994, an event of major significance took place. Until that moment, Agathe Uwilingiyimana Uwilingiyimana had been the Prime Minister of Rwanda. And later, when they left, in a final act of atrocity, a beer bottle was shoved into the woman they had called a whore.

The Belgians soldiers fought on until, after repeated tear-gas attacks, they were overwhelmed. Their mutilated bodies were piled up in the Kigali hospital where, visiting later, UN officers were initially unsure how many had been killed, such was the brutality of their dismemberment.

*

'And if you don't do as you're told, I'll have you court-martialled.' I felt the words echo around the room, the awful threat just hanging in the air. A week before, I had been personal staff officer to the Deputy Chief of Defence Staff, a strategic planning post of high trust, at the heart of the military-political machinery, and had been recommended for accelerated promotion. In career terms, I had been doing very well. But I had committed a terrible crime; I had decided to leave the Army. My punishment, now about to be meted out by this impossible bureaucrat, an officer from my own Regiment, was six months dreary imprisonment in the grey bowels of the Ministry of Defence, pushing paper. I had told him bluntly that I did not want to be there and that I resented his determination not to let me escape directly into a new career which awaited in a merchant bank in the City of London.

'With respect, Colonel,' I replied, feeling braver than I had felt since this awful interview had begun, 'I don't think you will have me court-martialled.' I watched his face as he got ready to explode again.

'And why not?' he demanded angrily, but becoming more wary, sensing my confidence.

'Because I wish to volunteer for operational duty.'

His boss, a wily Brigadier, also from my Regiment, was much more attuned to the human dimension. He knew how to turn a confrontation into an accommodation.

"Sounds like a bloody good idea,' he enthused. 'This place is desperate, a complete madhouse. I wish I could join you.'

\*

Within a few hours, the network which I had cultivated so carefully for two years had delivered. The news reverberated through the Ministry at SO1 (Lieutenant Colonel) and SO2 (Major) level. Practically every officer of my generation was thinking of leaving the Army. Some good mates, recognising my predicament and enjoying the drama and style of my rebellion, had pulled out all the stops. Of the options available, two stood proud. The first was to be Military Assistant to General Sir Michael Rose in Sarajevo; the second to be a

6

relatively lowly staff officer in Rwanda. Two years earlier, I would only have made the career decision. I had worked for an Air Marshall and then an Admiral, both distinguished officers, and could have completed the military flush with a General. Mike Rose was also a highly regarded soldier who would no doubt provide a brilliant education to his staff. But Bosnia seemed played out; there were too many crashing egos and too few political alternatives to make real progress and we had all watched with frustration as the efforts we had made to develop peace options in Whitehall had foundered on the rocks of international ambivalence. But Rwanda - on a continent which I had never visited - what was that all about?

\*

There was a pressure in the house, a sense of almost-bereavement. It seemed to penetrate the air, to hang heavy in the atmosphere. The two most boisterous children in Uxbridge were strangely quiet, content to watch a video, while in the sunny spare room, Sue and I worked quietly, the dust-motes from my kit reflecting in the sunlight, hanging in the air long after an item had been stowed. Funereal preparations for the departure of the living.

We drove to rural Oxfordshire in the late evening, to the RAF terminal at Brize Norton. Patrick, aged four, sobbed as we said our farewells, and although Rory, two years older, was more reserved, he was taking it hard too. And then there was the farewell to Sue. When our battered old Volvo pulled out, and her tear-stained face reflected in the headlights, to be followed by the frantic waving of the boys, I reached a total low. As the tail-lights disappeared down the country lane, I honestly wondered if I would ever see them again.

I handed in my warbag and battlebox. There was a brief argument while the RAF clerk tried to force me to dump half of my painfully packed kit.

'You're only entitled to 80 kilos, Sir,' he insisted. 'The scales show 160.'

'I have the kit list for Op GABRIEL, Corporal. It's all here.'

'Sir, you're only supposed to take 80 kilos.'

I waited long enough to develop a real edge on the atmosphere. I needed all my extra kit - dried food, emergency supplies, which the Army would not provide but which experience had taught me might soon become essential to survival, a problem which would not affect this young man in Brize Norton.

'How many people are there on the plane, Corporal?' A Tristar can carry about three hundred.

'Uhh, twenty-five, Sir.'

'Well be a good chap and find a spot for this lot.'

The foyer, dimly lit as a concession to those who were trying to sleep on the floor, was familiar. Surreal memories of a thousand such nights before, on long-forgotten exercises or in the early hours of a Belfast morning.

Takeoff was at 3 a.m., a cunning plan by the RAF to achieve its two main corporate objectives, at the same time. The first is to make sure that they arrive at their destination at the precise moment required to guarantee maximum 'crew rest' in the five-star hotel of their choice. The Kigali flight was probably worth 48 hours in Nairobi. The second is to ensure that their Pongo chums are screwed around. If people tell you that the RAF is the best air force in the world, it is because no competitor could achieve these dual objectives with such unerring excellence. There were flights to Canada and Cyprus departing at similar times, so the constant announcements at 140 decibels, and the movement of troops through the dark hall, as they stumbled over their comrades, was sure to begin the process of sleep deprivation, such an essential component of the second objective. While our crew remained tucked up in their nice warm beds, I resigned myself to another Service move.

8

At 2 a.m. the tannoy announced the departure of Flight KY 97 to Kigali, as casually as if we were off to Majorca for a week at the seaside. The lights came on, another concession to customer care. The officers gravitated together, eyed each other, introduced themselves, and formed a circle, a ritual which must be steeped in the mists of prehistoric military etiquette, but which serves the hugely useful purpose of sorting out who's who. The chaps looked on, as used to this ceremonial dance as we were. Amongst the officers were my companions for the next six months.

Short, rotund, dark and sporting the most amazing hairy eyebrows, Colonel Kieran O'Kelly, in his late forties, was to be the Deputy Chief of Staff (Support) of the UN Assistance Mission to Rwanda (UNAMIR) Headquarters. His charm and affability were undefeated by the early hour. The other officers were all destined for the British Contingent (BRITCON), save one handsome blonde Geordie Captain of Intelligence who stood out from the crowd. Captain Sean Moorhouse had been plucked from the anonymity of his Preston staff job, and pushed forward as a reluctant Military Information (i.e. Intelligence) staff officer at the Headquarters. While Kieran and I were volunteers, this 26-year old was a pressed man and that had to be both a waste and a mistake. Before we had even set out, he was as resigned to his posting as I was anticipating mine.

We stopped briefly at Nairobi, presumably so that the crew could order their wine for dinner, and standing on the tarmac under a blazing sun, on my first ever trip to Africa, the realisation of what was coming next really sank in. We were all subdued during the short hop to Kigali. Nobody spoke as the wheels touched down on the runway and the engines screamed into reverse, and even when the doors were finally flung open, there didn't seem to be much to say. The modern soldier can travel from home hearth to horror, in the space of half a day.

Amid the noise of jets and turbo props revving up for takeoff, the whine of our Tristar generators was vanquished. Great camouflaged transport planes, from all the world's air forces, were taxiing, waiting for others to come in, bringing with them the essentials of life. The tarmac was crowded with pallets covered in blue plastic which bore the logo of the UNHCR, and a plethora of other symbols - *Feed the Hungry, Médecins Sans Frontières, Save the Children*. Vehicles moved between these rows, being loaded by busy forklift trucks, internationally crewed. Shouts, languages, horns. High in the air, a few kilometres away, a large flock of birds circled lazily, wheeling over a central point, dark shapes contrasting with the bright blue afternoon sky. Their ominous presence caused a sense of foreboding as we waited for our transport. What catastrophe had caused so many scavengers to form up in this swirling vortex, we could not tell, but we hardly expected it to be anything pleasant.

Burnt-out vehicles littered every junction, many riddled with bullet holes. Every building showed signs of damage, some completely demolished, others peppered with machine-gun fire, or cracked open with an RPG-7. The roads were choked with African soldiers riding in camouflage-painted 4X4 vehicles, their legs hanging over the side, or clustered on street corners, in sombre, hostile groups, each man wearing a different coloured beret. This was the victorious Rwanda Patriotic Army (RPA), new rulers of Rwanda. And we were their guests.

At the Stadium, former home to ten thousand refugees before they had been shelled by the Presidential Guard, and now the base for BRITCON, I stowed my kit in a tiny room, which already contained eight Majors, including two chums from Staff College days. We met the energetic and switched-on Commanding Officer, Lieutenant Colonel Mike Wharmby. As he was bringing us up to date on the security situation, we were joined by another British officer who saluted smartly as he entered the room. Strongly built and radiating sun-tanned good health, he was wearing well-worn jungle boots and a battered but neat set of combats. Around his waist was a low-slung belt supporting pistol, water bottle and radio, and over his shoulder was a camouflaged daysack, which is a sure mark of the khaki-brained. Infantry or marines I decided instantly, based on years of exposure to all the 'types' the military spawns. In his late thirties, ruggedly handsome and full of professional bonhomie, he introduced himself around, flashing a boyish grin as shook our hands.

'Fraser Haddow,' he intoned in a civilised Scots burr.

Lieutenant Colonel Fraser Haddow was indeed a Royal Marine, working in the Headquarters as Military Assistant to the Force Commander (FC), Major General Tousignant. As he joined in our discussions, and brought us up to date on the day's events, his brightness and persuasive style were clearly evident. This, without doubt, was going to be a good bloke to work with.

*

After breakfast, Mike Wharmby took us all down to the UN Headquarters, in time for the 8 a.m. Morning Brief. The Headquarters was in the Amahoro Hotel, sister building to the Stadium, painted the same faded yellow and surrounded by the same barbed wire, sandbags and sentries in blue helmets. But these were Ghanaians, the first UN African troops I had seen, and their smart appearance and crisp British drill as we drove over the 'sleeping policeman,' created a positive first impression. The car park was choked with white UN vehicles, and a few camouflaged RPA 4X4s. As we entered the marble-effect foyer, the stench from the latrines in the hallway hit us. There had been no running water in the Amahoro Hotel since early April. The windows had all been shot or blown out but sandbags reached reassuringly above head height, limiting the light but increasing the sense of security. It was all pretty

11

makeshift and temporary-looking. Under operational conditions, with bullets flying, the finer points of presentation had obviously been overlooked.

The Ballroom had been converted into the Operations Centre. Plasterboard walls divided up the space into offices. The largest, the briefing room, was quickly filling with people, military and civilian, variously attired. While the civilians wore casual, bush-type jackets, interspersed with an occasional, oddly contrasting designer polo shirt, the military were dressed in the uniforms of at least a score of countries, including such unlikely contenders as Russia and Austria. Everyone seemed to find a seat in time for the arrival of the senior officers, preceded by their aides. First the Deputy Force Commander (DFC), Brigadier General Anyidoho, a huge and imposing Ghanaian, and when he had settled his bulk into a creaking folding chair, the Force Commander swept in.

'Gentlemen, the General,' announced Fraser, and we sprang to our feet. The DFC took a little longer. Major General Tousignant had been Force Commander in theatre since early August, and this was now a familiar routine. Tall, slim and neatly uniformed in summer dress, he waved us back to our seats and took the central position with a slight air of weary resignation. I had witnessed the very same routine in the MOD every morning for the past two years, beside my Admiral, and it all seemed so similar, a disjointed fusion of the two realities across 6,000 miles and across the wider gulf that separated the slick, hi-tech civilisation of Whitehall and the makeshift earthiness of the Ballroom in Kigali.

*

He was sitting behind his desk, poker-backed. His combats were well worn, so I quickly gave him some 'street cred' points, but the UN and Australian badges on his arms were brand new and as crisp as the rest of him. Beneath his

12

camouflaged Lieutenant Colonel rank slides, he was strapped into a black leather shoulder holster, which held his 9mm pistol.  When a staff officer carries his weapon ready for a quick draw, it is clear he means business.  His Irish-red hair was well-shorn, a perfect match for his tidy moustache.  Together, they framed a crinkled, leathery face, a few broken veins and patchy florid spots showing evidence of a man who likes to play hard and has recently done so.  His blue eyes stared intently as he sized me up, and they too, being rheumy and a little bloodshot, were testament to a recent 'night of shame'.  There was a hardness to him, a toughness which sits more easily in the US Army than it does in the British, but is not unwelcome in the Australian.  This man was not to be trifled with.  On the front of his desk, next to the neatly laid out files, and beside the overflowing ashtray, once a ration tin, was a piece of card boldly proclaiming: 'Lieutenant Colonel A D Brimelow - G3 Plans'.  As he rose from behind the desk to greet me, I saw that he was short and stocky, and he moved at a controlled, panther-like pace, which was at once intimidating and fascinating, his shoulders hunched forward into his holster, his arms held away from his sides in the mode of the body-builder.  But there was no macho squeeze in his firm handshake; it was a greeting of straight honesty, and I felt immediately his utter reliability.  He looked straight into my eyes for a few milliseconds longer than is entirely polite, before his battered face cracked into a broad grin.  'G'day mate,' he said.  'Welcome to Rwonda.'

Dusty, scruffy and as temporary-looking as the rest of the place, the office housed some basic wooden furniture, and on each of four desks, a computer.  Alan Brimelow introduced my companions of the next six months:  An Ethiopian Naval Commander, recently released after seven years as a civil war Prisoner of War and then recycled into this UN operation.  A Canadian Captain, awaiting a posting into the field as one of our three hundred unarmed Military Observers, but for the

13

present consigned to a desk job. A Ghanaian Warrant Officer, whose welcoming grin was accentuated by some ferocious tribal markings. And finally, the officer whom I was to replace, a Ghanaian Major.

He and I sat together. I was ready to absorb information quickly but to cover the events of the past five months, including a war, the withdrawal of the UNAMIR force and the deaths of so many people, in just 20 minutes, might reasonably have been considered a little slapdash. With a cheerful wave he was gone. I looked at my watch; it was just 10.35 a.m. on 8 September 1994 and I was the new SO2 G3 Plans in Headquarters UNAMIR.

*

In the early evening, we collected our kit from BRITCON and arranged transport to our new accommodation. Some rations had been scrounged from the Brits - the UN had been unable to give us food and water on arrival, due to 'administrative' problems. What happened, I wondered, to those who had no national contingent to scrounge from? After a short run on the main road, our 4-tonner pulled onto a dusty track beside the bullet-scarred shell of the Parliament building whose blackened walls described the recent battle for Kigali. We bumped along for another few hundred metres before turning down to the left, on a steeper, even rougher track, in the direction, according to the battered sieve of a bullet-riddled sign, of the Golf Course. A kilometre later a group of buildings appeared up the hill to our right, a splash of green vegetation in the brown and gritty landscape. We turned in at the gates, to be saluted by yet more blue-helmeted Ghanaian guards. Fraser joined us at the door to Building B-1, which was to be Britain House, and gestured us inside.

First impressions were very positive. The house was largely empty, with a few items of furniture pushed up against the

14

walls. The sloping roof topped a spacious living area on two levels, and on a third level above, the bedrooms led off from a balustraded corridor. Fraser had had the house cleaned up a bit for our arrival, with the help of BRITCON. The live grenade found in a smaller bedroom had been dealt with by the Royal Engineers Bomb Disposal Team. And the body of a Rwandan Government Forces soldier, discovered in another, had been taken away for burial some time before. The garage was filled with junk, detritus of the Belgian family who had lived there before - an unfinished model aeroplane, and some school books filled with the neat French writing of a young child, now hopefully safely home in Belgium. There was also a considerable amount of live ammunition, a battered helmet, perhaps the former property of our most recent predecessor, and a tatty rifle, which I decided would look very impressive on the wall. The kitchen was spacious, although the fly-screens had been ripped open, letting in some of the smaller wildlife, and the room was full of the clickings and dronings of a thousand insects. There was no running water in the Belgian Village and the cooker had been looted. A former visitor to the loo had opened the door with the contents of his automatic pistol.

The heavy, metal-grilled front door had also had its lock destroyed and even as we discussed how or whether we could get if fixed, in order to secure our possessions, a troop of African workmen filed in through it. They at once started to move through the house, armed with screwdrivers and pliers. Their white foreman, an employee of the UN contractor, *Brown & Root*, was more like an extra for *Easy Rider*. If the denims, cowboy boots and wide leather belt, clasped by an enormous cowhorn buckle, did not scream 'redneck', then the pony-tail, beard, dark glasses and chewing jaw should have clinched the typecast. We barraged him with the points we had so far noted on our brief survey of the house, in the hope of an easy triumph over bureaucracy, but he fixed Fraser with his blind, dark-eyed stare, and chewed mechanically, unflinchingly, as if in deep concentration, or overwhelmed with boredom.

'OK,' was all he said, before he disappeared into the garage. A few moments later, the lights came on and after a brief flutter, went off again. Fraser went to the garage to investigate and we could soon hear his voice raised in argument. The dude emerged, carrying the evident source of the disagreement, the circuit board and electrical switchery needed to power the house.

'Ah'm sorry, Suh,' he chewed apologetically, in the tones of the Deep South. 'Ah hayev instructions to move these atems to a higher priority facility.'

The other workmen, who we had assumed were here to fix our doors, finished their work with the screwdrivers, and left quickly by various exits, taking with them four of our doors, including the back door complete. And then the redneck left too.

Fraser explained grimly. The Special Representative of the Secretary General (SRSG) had now occupied a similar house, a little further up the hill, which also lacked some of the bare necessities; it too had been looted. All the UN staff officers' houses had been raided by *Brown & Root* to acquire the deficient items. In order for the SRSG to be comfortable, the British contribution would be that we would have to live without doors or electricity.

*

16

# Chapter 2

I was at my desk at 7.15 a.m., poring over the planning map. It showed few metalled roads, and these led mainly towards the international border crossings and the Prefecture seats. To get to the lower administrative levels of Sous-Prefecture and Commune, a cross-country journey over rough tracks would be required. While nobody knew how many people remained in Rwanda, the estimates for the refugee camps showed nearly 2.3 million in Zaire, most in the Goma region but some in the South at Bukavu, and nearly a million in Tanzania, with the camps in Burundi and Uganda housing numbers in merely tens or hundreds of thousands. In the South West of Rwanda, in the three Prefectures of Kibuye, Cyangugu and Gikongoro, up to half a million refugees were shown in a wide scattering of camps. These were Internally Displaced Persons (IDPs), a technical definition, since these people had not run abroad, but had been protected by the French, who had flown in to execute Operation TURQUOISE, the establishment of a line over which they had dared the RPA to cross. Just three weeks before, our Force, which now included a battalion from that French force, a mixture of small units from Senegal, Sierra Leone, Guinea, Guinea-Bissau and Chad, had taken over the TURQUOISE zone, and a few days later, under the glare of the international press, had allowed the RPA to cross, to take full possession of the sovereign country they had fought to possess.

Over the next few days, I read into the situation as much as I could, toured the Headquarters and tried to get my feet under the table. There were 150 civilian staff and about 40 military and these figures grew from day to day. The civilians were UN professionals, the multi-national cornucopia which the UN prides itself on. Their world was the same in Somalia, Bosnia or Rwanda - organise ration flights, demand stores from New York, send faxes to Geneva. Most seemed to use little initiative, defeated at once by their own burdensome

17

bureaucracy. How they had secured such critical operational posts, begged rather more cynical questions. Of the military staff, two-thirds were employed on logistics and support, now under Kieran's command. Rwanda was land-locked and had no easy access for materiel, except that which could be flown in through the international airport. Nearly everything of value had been removed or destroyed by the retreating Rwanda Government Forces, which meant that even to provide the necessary infrastructure for a 6,500-man UN security operation required a gargantuan procurement and delivery effort. The remainder of the military staff, outside the General's suite - about 18 - formed the Operations staff; of these 10 were watchkeepers, whose role was to answer the radio, and keep the maps up to date. Little action was taken over many of the radio calls, and some of the maps were weeks out of date. It came down to this: Of all the staff, probably fewer than 20 were really effective, only three or four of those involved in Operations. Most of the effectives were Western, with a sprinkling of talented Africans. You had to look at it one of two ways. Either there was no hope that anything would ever be moved forward, or, if you wanted to move things forward, nobody would be able to stop you.

For all its problems, the Operations staff was lead by an extremely competent and dedicated officer. Colonel Jan Arp, a Canadian Gunner, was the Deputy Chief of Staff (Operations), Kieran's opposite number. I had met him before in Canada and his youthful good humour and boyish enthusiasm had been as plain there as they were sorely needed in Kigali. Tall, blonde and fit, he radiated charm and common sense, although the burden of being responsible for such a sensitive and weak operational structure had clearly taken its toll over the three weeks he had been in Rwanda - he looked worn out. Alan Brimelow's opposite number under Jan Arp was an officer of presence and charm. An imposing, strongly built 40-year old, Lieutenant Colonel Austen Yella, another Ghanaian officer, had a smart, upright appearance which might have had some origin in his training at Sandhurst and Shrivenham. But he retained his African perspective, a toughness which did not conform to the more liberal ideas of the Western officer, and so had an even more important balancing role to play in the delivery of the security operation.

*

I wanted to know more about the humanitarians. Their world was apart from ours but its rhythm and its purpose echoed faintly throughout UNAMIR, occasionally rising to the surface where it could be more closely inspected. The UN Agencies (UN Rwanda Emergency Office - UNREO, UN Children's Fund - UNICEF, UN High Commissioner for Refugees - UNHCR etc) shared a deep suspicion of the military, which although it had to be expected - so many human rights violations had been committed by people in uniform - was particularly galling. Their ill-disguised hostility was evidenced in their body language, in their overt contempt for the UN soldiers at the gates and around the Headquarters. There was another, more physical problem which militated against our contact. The Amahoro Stadium and Hotel were located about 5 kilometres from the centre of Kigali, which was where most of the Agencies and Non-Government Organisations or NGOs (*Save the Children, Oxfam, Médecins Sans Frontières* etc) operated from. Traffic was mainly one way. They needed our maps, our information, since our reports were the most reliable in the country, and one most important requirement: Our people controlled the airlift and anyone who needed to get to Nairobi on leave or business had to come, cap in hand, to UNAMIR.

Our office was well placed to receive visitors. As the only source of maps in Rwanda, we were a major attraction. My first lengthy encounter was with a sixties throwback -

cheesecloth clothes, long hair and moustache, leather shoulder bag, a German citizen. He asked for maps from the *Parc des Volcans* area above Ruhengeri, home of the mountain gorillas. He was concerned that as the refugees and IDPs might return to their homes, they would move into the forest to collect firewood, and increase the pressure of land use. He had come to Rwanda to bring 'alternative' technology, and when I asked what that might involve, he admitted, rather sheepishly, that it involved kerosene. In the midst of all this human suffering, it seemed rather pointless to be worrying about the loss of a few trees to damage the gorillas' habitat, in a landscape which was in any case largely empty of human habitation.

*

The real vexation, which overshadowed all else, was our living conditions. At home, we had scrounged a few doors to provide some security, although the kitchen was still out of use. Fraser had liberated some simple, wooden slatted beds, and our friendly Australians next door, led by the indomitable Alan Brimelow, had helped to organise some other pieces of furniture. We were finally in receipt of some rations, both French and German, which were edible, if not palatable, and had received some bottled water to replace the original variety, now withdrawn because it contained too high a faecal content. One wondered how much the current, obviously lower-content version contained; zero seemed about the right amount to me. There was little choice, save the pumped water from BRITCON, which tasted like swimming pools and gave off chlorine fumes from the tea, strong enough to make your eyes water. Everything seemed to be a struggle; finding a bread source, organising transport for every drop of water, cooking on our stoves in one corner of the dining room. In the Headquarters, visiting the lavatory was such a ghastly experience that even the seasoned campaigners tried to fulfil that need before they left home in the morning. All these little tasks took up far more of our time than we would have liked, and added to a growing sense of frustration.

*

Saturday was a working day, but unexpectedly, Sunday was declared a half day, at about 11 a.m., a fact which the civilians must have known about in advance, since none of them had come in to work. Kieran had already been for a drive around Kigali, but Sean and I were desperate to see what conditions were like in the centre. Kigali was a town with a touch of class, but no glass. Many of the buildings were empty now and showed signs of the looting; a few had been burnt out. It was a hot dusty afternoon as we drove the long avenues of the outer city, the excellent roads marred only by the occasional mortar hole. Some unexploded bombs had the fins still protruding from the tarmac, and Kieran swerved to avoid them, with the help of loud directions from Sean and me. We parked at the swishest hotel in town, and scene of a major massacre, the *Hotel Milles Collines*. It was *Radio Milles Collines*, broadcasting from this building, which had exhorted the Hutu militias to do their work on and after 6 April, and had told the militias as they cut and chopped, that the graves were only half-full. But there seemed few reminders of those dark days, as we left the car under the nose of a youthful RPA guard, who saluted Kieran's red tabs with great gusto, and walked off down into the centre of town. At the market itself, there was little activity - at least 90% of the stalls were empty and closed, but of those remaining, one provided us with an aluminium kettle, for the exorbitant price of $6, while another yielded some small but reasonably fresh bananas, for $2. We were clearly being ripped off, victims of 'UN inflation' but on our few hours off each week, we could ill afford to be choosers. One unhappy stallholder took exception to my attempt to photograph the

21

wares on his stall, mainly 5-litre cans of cooking oil. On each can was boldly proclaimed: 'A Gift From The People Of The USA. Not To Be Sold or Traded.' We were wary. Sean and I kept our pistols close to hand and an eye open for trouble. As we walked along, we took particular care to avoid any ground not tarmacced. The place was alive with mines, we had been told, and we were not taking any chances.

Back at the *Hotel Milles Collines*, we arrived in the foyer at the exact time that the barman had decided to set up for the evening, a happy coincidence. While we sipped our first cold beer since leaving the UK, it was easy to forget the city outside. We were joined by Petra Campbell, an Australian UNESCO contract worker who we had met at the Amahoro Hotel during the week. She ordered a bottle of wine and proceeded to swig it in large gulps, much to the discomfort of the white-jacketed barman. Although she adhered to the convention of pouring it into a glass, that hardly seemed a worthwhile effort, as the bottle scarcely left her hand between refillings.

'You'd be drinking like this too,' she spluttered, 'if you'd seen what I have today.' She had decided to accompany a journalist friend to a church just south of Kigali at Nyamata. There, the corpses were lying three deep in the aisles, and were scattered throughout the churchyard. The entire population of the village had fled, or been butchered, the latter possibly by the former, and there was nobody left to bury the bodies.

'But why did you go?' I asked. 'What's the point?' She was unable to explain, drawn there by some unformed desire to witness for herself the evil of Rwanda's bloody lust. The reality of this suffering and death had proved far worse than the expectation, and for the moment at least, she had lost control. She talked non-stop, of women and children with their heads removed and piled up in the corner, of the dead being robbed by casual visitors, of the stench and of the awful desolation and loneliness of the place. We left her halfway into her second bottle, now joined by a friend to give more comfort, and it seemed that she had just taught us a very clear lesson. We already knew that there were many UN workers who set off on their Sundays to visit these places of death, and I had dubbed them the 'horror tourists'. Seeing the effect of the experience on this otherwise apparently well-balanced and sensible girl was evidence enough. I determined that unless I had to go to one of these sites for a very good reason, I would leave the dead to themselves, not to be picked over by the second wave of vultures that year, the Western voyeurs.

*

Three days later, Major Steve Govan from BRITCON and I left Kigali at 9 a.m. in a Land Rover driven by one of his soldiers. Steve and I had briefly been together in a Staff College syndicate and we got on well. After a week in the city, I was desperate to see what the hinterland had in store and this forward reconnaissance was the ideal excuse. We were to spend the night with 23 Parachute Field Ambulance (23 PFA), in Kitabi, the centre of their humanitarian operation.

Even after a week, I was struck by the numbers of people on the road through Kigali; it seemed as though normality crept closer and closer every day. But this was our illusion. Steve contrasted the situation with his experiences a few weeks earlier, and said how much things had improved since then. And everybody who arrived, right up to my departure six months later, remarked how they themselves had witnessed the place coming to life.

Outside Kigali, it was a different story. Once beyond the city limits, we drove for mile after mile, through the lush, hilly, terraced countryside, without seeing a soul. There were patches of habitation, perhaps groups of Tutsis who had survived and had now gathered together; perhaps Hutus who had returned from a camp in the safety of numbers. But the overall impression was one of empty desolation, the vacuum created by the loss of so many lives. In Gitarama, large buildings had been levelled, and as I was soon to find out was typical of Rwanda, there were many explanatory stories to fit each scenario: Demolished by departing Hutu businessmen; blown up by the advancing RPA; or razed by the RGF, in order to delay the advance of the RPA. Probably one of these stories was half-true. The difficulty with every story in Rwanda, I was beginning to realise, lay in deciding which one.

Our vehicle climbed up through glorious blue hills, carpeted with velvet tea plantations. The Commanding Officer of 23 PFA, Lieutenant Colonel Alan Hawley, was in excellent form. We had met before in the UK, and I had been greatly impressed by him then. Here, at 8000 feet on the edge of the Nyungwe Forest, he was in his element. Every morning, the troops headed off in small packets to the most remote IDP camps in the Gikongoro Prefecture. In the camps, they would quickly set up shop, provide immediate medical services to those who were in need, and then return by nightfall to Kitabi, where at least security was provided, and they could have a square hard-ration meal. It was exhausting work, but they were coping with great panache. Where the NGOs had first been scathing, they were now full of praise, and where the British medics went, so too went the goodwill of many thousands of Hutu refugees.

At dawn, Steve and I set off with a flying column to Kibeho Camp, the biggest in the country. From the metalled road, we travelled south for nearly two hours, at the rear of a convoy of ambulances. The roads were rutted and in places, culverts were starting to crumble under the weight of all this humanitarian traffic. And as we progressed, we encountered more and more little groups of refugee shelters or *blindées*. A hooped frame of sticks, stripped from the woods nearby, supported a skin of thin blue plastic, provided, as the logos showed, by the ubiquitous UNHCR. Each shelter was remarkable in its uniformity, about 3 X 2 metres, and by its orderly placement in relation to its neighbours. I wondered fleetingly if the NGOs employed

24

retired Regimental Sergeant Majors to arrange their IDPs so neatly on the terraces.

And then we came around a corner and saw Kibeho. I was not prepared for this. As far as the eye could see, mainly along the high ridges, there stretched an endless sea of blue. Thousands of shelters in every direction, and between and around them, a seething mass of dirty humanity, some people crouching around their little fires outside the huts, others walking in an endless stream down the road from Kibeho, with heavy loads of food on their heads. But most just staring at us as we passed by. A few children shouted for '*biscuit*', and some ululated, delivering that amazing sound unique to Africa. But most just looked at us, showing no feeling, no welcome. There was an edge to the place, all that hostility, and perhaps the guilt, at what some of them may have done.

The troops from 23 PFA set up quickly and efficiently by the school buildings. Already a long line of people had gathered, and was being marshalled by the infantry section accompanying us, from the Princess of Wales' Royal Regiment. I looked through the broken window of one of the schoolrooms. On a blackboard some words had been scrawled in a childish hand: 'There would be the greatest peace on earth when on every bad mouth a padlock is hung'.

Sergeant Major Stewart briefed us on what was happening, from a balcony above the queues. The infantry soldiers were becoming more skilled at sorting out the various cases, with the medics. Together, they divided up those with diarrhoea, those with other illnesses and those with injuries, siphoning them all off into the various treatment areas. Of the injuries, the majority were the result of violence, and many severe open wounds had been treated by this section, grim evidence of the machete attacks which frequently took place at night in the camps. There were interpreters at work, but the British soldiers had picked up one or two choice Kinyarwanda phrases too, and were able to use them to maintain some form of order. While the people outside may have seemed hostile, here they were just plain grateful. They were weary, resigned and beaten, but the kindness and the professionalism of the soldiers was as much a tonic as the medicine they dispensed. In the chaos of a refugee camp, such efficiency and purpose seemed to carry a moral weight far beyond its practical value.

In some schoolrooms, makeshift wards had been set up. In one, a young child about the same age as Rory, was lying in great pain. To compound the woes of kidney failure, from which he was recovering, he had slipped in the latrine and broken his femur. His leg was being tractioned using a tin can filled with stones as the weight. In another ward, we watched a child whose rectum had been turned inside out, how we could only guess, being given field surgery by one of the doctors. It was difficult to know whether we should have respected the child's privacy on the one hand, or at least recorded the experience on the other. We took our cue from everybody else, British and African, who watched proceedings with undisguised interest.

In the corner of the courtyard, away from the medical treatment area, an even sadder sight awaited. Here, in a low building, an orphanage had been set up, one of thousands appearing throughout Rwanda. As Steve and I entered, we were struck by an overwhelming stench, to make the camp outside smell positively sweet. Two hundred orphans were crammed into a small room. Between them, they had only half a dozen beds; the rest must have just slept on the floor. In the far corner, and working their ways towards us with brooms, two older children were sweeping up the night's accumulation of filth. It was inches deep on the floor, and they were moving it steadily, in its stinking soup of urine, vomit and diarrhoea, towards the door. Seemingly unconcerned, the children crowded round for photographs and for '*biscuit*', and I had no pangs of conscience as I unloaded pockets full of boiled sweets from the rations. They were so pleased and kept hugging my legs and pulling at my clothes. There was little I could do to stop myself hugging them in return, from gathering them up and kissing their smelly, sweaty foreheads. These wee vulnerable creatures were the saddest victims of that summer of slaughter. Whether they had been left on the roads because they were too slow, or wandered aimlessly about after the deaths of their parents, until they had been brought to Kibeho, it was these kids who now bore the brunt of Rwanda's pain. In the muck of that disgusting room, some small idea of the tragedy of the country began to take shape. For these were the lucky ones. These little ones had survived. And if we could do something useful with our time in Rwanda, it would be to see that the children might one day bring this country peace, where the adults had so clearly failed.

Before we left Kibeho, we stopped off at the International Committee of the Red Cross (ICRC) feeding station. It was ration day, the first for over a week, which explained the endless columns of people moving up and down the road, to receive their food. Nearly 200,000 Hutus lived in the hills around the camps of Kibeho and Ndago and in a dozen smaller blue plastic-tented outposts. I walked forward to the distribution area, to see it for myself at close quarters. The Ghanaian soldiers were keeping a very orderly queue, with a mixture of firmness, doled out by their sticks, and impassive eye contact, from beneath their blue helmets. The British troops had learned the technique from them well, but the level of control required and the cold ability to provide it was a vivid evocation of the need for African troops in an African setting. At the head of the queues, across a frontage of 200 metres, dozens of feeding points were doling out grain and oil, to a specification per person which must have been a nightmare to organise. They were using a registration card system, I was later to discover, but the awesome difficulty of keeping track of this highly mobile population, and ensuring that even the weak were fed, was a mystery beyond immediate comprehension, which I determined to unravel. And even more, the overwhelming experience of standing in the middle of that great mass of humanity, in the centre of Rwanda's largest camp, just a week out of England, made me say a quiet prayer of thanks, once again, to have been freed from the dreary shackles of the Ministry of Defence.

As we drove out of the camp, my mind was awhirl with the images of the visit. We pressed on through the crowds for a few kilometres before it became clear that we must have gone wrong. The people suddenly seemed to be more hostile than I had noticed even a few minutes before, and unconsciously I opened the flap on my holster. In the back of the Land Rover, Steve cradled his rifle, pointing down the main track. We turned around slowly, backing through the crowds, not wishing to be too pushy, feeling very vulnerable. A group of young men had quickly formed, staring, snarling. The tension was rising very fast. Suddenly a man thrust his head through the open window beside me, and shouted a loud 'Huuahh', so close that his hair brushed up against my ear. If the intention had been to scare, it succeeded, such was the shock of this unexpected invasion; had my pistol been in my hand, I might have lashed out. But this was not the time to be intimidated. As coolly as possible, I looked straight back at him and smiled my biggest smile and waved to the others. In the back, Steve was doing the same, our unconscious placatory gestures and feigned good humour were the lessons of more than a few scrapes survived in the past. As our driver, equally coolly, succeeded in turning the Land Rover around, I shouted my thanks and waved at the crowd, as they reluctantly parted to let us pass. Our friend, clearly the ringleader, stepped forward as we were about to pull away, and made a serious of slashing gestures across his throat, soon taken up by a score more, and then a hundred. As we pulled safely away, we laughed and joked, in the torrent of relief that always follows a near-miss, and I resolved to be more careful in future. But the event had a deeper significance than a brief encounter with danger. There was no doubt that we had just come face to face with extremists, Interahamwe, the Killers of Rwanda.

We threaded our way back through the network of tracks which ended at the main road to Gikongoro. After we passed Kibeho again, we stopped the vehicle at a vantage point which commanded the ground in all directions. I was fascinated by the way in which the camps had been set up on the tops of the hills, not in the valleys which contained the water supply. In Europe, so many population centres had arisen at crossing points, that the logic of choosing such a location had become entrenched. There was something very odd about this hilltop arrangement. I spent 20 minutes scanning the area with my binoculars, before it started to make sense. Even in the far distance, 15 kilometres away, it was possible to distinguish thin lines of colour in the brilliant sunshine, as the people moved to and from the feeding station at Kibeho. They were walking along the ridges, on thin paths, which covered the countryside in an arterial web of pedestrian communication. These were ridgeways, common throughout Stone Age Britain as safe routes, and leading, inevitably, to the security of the hill forts. What was laid out below us was not the African equivalent of a medieval social structure, which was how the guidebooks described Rwandese society. Much older forces were at work here; what we were examining was a pre-historical analogue of Rwanda. They had all walked to these places, and now it made great sense to believe that they would just as easily walk home over their ridgeway routes. Unless, of course, they were under threat. If they felt at risk, their pre-historical instinct might not be to flee at all. It might well be to stay on the high ground and defend their blue coloured hill forts to the last man, woman and child.

*

## Chapter 3

His henchman swivelled at me suspiciously as I was introduced. The SRSG had a sleek, urbane gloss to him, a healthy suppleness, testament to the value of his daily game of tennis. He did not look as though he carried the burdens of the world on his shoulders. Rather, he was relaxed and very much in control. A career diplomat, he had carried out previous ambassadorial roles for Pakistan until the Secretary General, Dr Boutros Boutros-Ghali, had appointed him to be his Special Representative. Shaharyar Khan was immediately impressive and warm, not remote and detached as one might expect; his humanity and openness bode well for our Mission. And as we shook hands and exchanged a few pleasantries, I hoped he was someone to trust.

But his bodyguard, who looked like a *Blues Brother*, clearly did not trust others as he tracked visitors with a robotic rotation of the head and locked on his black-glassed eyes with a minuscule clenching of the jaw.

*

Alan Brimelow was cracking me up. His mischievous sense of humour and deadpan expression made an unbeatable combination. The one-liners came in between the full-blown jokes at irregular intervals throughout the day. Despite his assiduous determination to do his job properly and to make sure we did too, he kept the office alive with his repartee.

'I phoned me wife yesterday and told her how horny I was,' he confided to me during the second week. I raised my eyebrows, feigning concern, but wondering what was coming next. He leaned closer. 'I told her that when she arrived at the airport to meet me in February, to make sure that she had a mattress strapped to her back.'

31

'And how did the Colonel's wife respond to that?' I inquired archly, to maintain the mock toffee-nosed mien of the British officer when dealing with Antipodeans.

'She said that was no problem, but to make sure that I was the first one off the plane,' he responded without twitching a muscle. Only when I had recovered sufficiently did he allow his face to crack into a grin.

He chain-smoked incessantly, frequently coughing like the cavalry trooper he was.

'You don't sound too good over there, Colonel,' I shouted across the room.

'You're right, mate,' he responded. 'If I'd known I was going to live this long, I'd have looked after meself better.'

And in a 14-hour day, with no pressures other than work, Alan Brimelow and I became firm friends.

I had completed my first major assignment, an 'appreciation' of the withdrawal and evacuation perspective of the UN. It seemed absolutely critical to place Kigali International Airport in the proper context of survival, and I eventually named it the 'vital ground', ground which if lost, would make our position untenable. This was a big decision. If there was to be widespread unrest, or another war, choosing to withdraw slowly and fight to retain a foothold, in order to continue our mission should the security situation improve, was a critical policy step. I based it on the humiliation which the UN had experienced in recent withdrawals, not just in Rwanda but elsewhere in the world, notably Somalia, and advanced a view that we should be tougher and stand longer. That I was able to lay out the alternatives and advance the most robust option as our proposed plan spoke volumes for the intellectual freedom which the uncoordinated, political-military thinking in Rwanda would allow. All the senior officers up the chain of command had scrutinised my logic but had advanced no real objections to the proposal of such a powerful political decision on behalf of the UN. From the limited information available, I postulated that the RGF, now principally based in Goma and the other camps in eastern Zaire, would not be able to launch an attack from Zaire onto the RPA in Rwanda for up to two years, but that the likelihood of an insurgency campaign against the Government would increase over time. The work of the UN should therefore be carried out as quickly as possible, while the current security situation obtained. I was sure that experienced military professionals would recognise the logic of the case, would increase patrolling, would establish border listening posts, would submit daily reports to the General. But perhaps this argument was lost in the detail, for there was no sudden galvanised action, no increase in tempo in our steady but erratic deployment of the troops and their logistics.

*

Sean was disappointed with his lot. UN 'intelligence' was emasculated and transparent – there were no secrets that the Ballroom cleaners could not have deciphered. He was a useful young man, funny and very bright – he had come up through the ranks at speed. But he was disillusioned too. Already, within a few weeks of his arrival, he had lost the incentive to work in a UN environment which placed so little value on the skills of information-gathering which he possessed. I watched him withdraw, becoming less enthusiastic, complaining more about the pleasant but inexperienced and unfocussed Malawian major he worked for. Sean had a lot of pent-up energy. It was surely going to end up somewhere.

*

A mass grave had been uncovered in the centre of Cyanika IDP camp in the Prefecture of Gikongoro. As the rains increased, BRITCON were concerned that the 20,000 bodies would wash into the drinking supply of the IDPs, a pond at the bottom of the

33

hill. The additional problems of cholera and typhoid, to add to the misery the IDPs were already facing, would hardly bear thinking about. The Brits wanted to bulldoze the site, lime the bodies and cover the whole thing over properly, and I was asked to help after days had gone by with no reply to the British request for support from UNAMIR. I promised to see what I could do. Over the next few days, I battered my way through the bureaucracy of UNAMIR, all the time conscious that an epidemic could break out at any time, and that the Brits were relying on me. The legal people did not want us to get involved. The genocide issue and the Human Rights forensic investigations were 'hot potatoes', overshadowed only by the emotional issue of burying murdered Tutsis in this way, in order to save the lives of Hutus, some of whom might even be the killers. Eventually, I approached the SRSG's Department, to enlist help at the highest Government level. The staff were offhand - I was disturbing their ordered world with my piffling problem. Persisting, I drafted a letter from the SRSG to the Minister of the Interior and presented it for signature. Incredibly, with no connection to their earlier dismissal of my arguments, the letter was signed immediately. I then passed it to the RPA Liaison Officer for personal delivery, thinking that the problem was near resolution, at last. Every day, I checked with the Liaison Officer to see how things were going, to be assured that the Government was about to make a decision. The whole thing was a revelation. The UN Headquarters was unwieldy and unable to respond to a simple request from one of its units. Problems on the ground were not translatable into Headquarters' problems, unless a staff officer took a personal interest. Advice was often conflicting, and there was nobody to knock heads together, to move things forward. But the most important concern, which persisted throughout the coming weeks until I realised that the Government was never going to give the authority for those bodies to be buried, was that in a minor country like Rwanda, with nothing going for it except

what the UN and the International Community could bring to
bear, a Government Minister could ignore a letter from the
SRSG, and it would not be questioned.

*

After my first morning, I had been banned from the Morning
Brief. Only Alan Brimelow could be allowed to represent the
Plans section. But the frustration of being removed from a
first-hand account of events in the field proved too much and I
slipped back in, after a few days. The DFC glowered at me and
I took a few barbed comments from one or two other senior
officers. But Brimelow understood my need to be involved at
the centre and turned a blind eye. The activities on the ground
were so hard to interpret already that any loss of capability in
the Headquarters would be significant. And I was hungry for
information, for detail, for the broader picture, and was
prepared to endure a little pain for the privilege.

*

It was Friday, the first Happy Hour. Complex logistic planning
had resulted in a C-130 Hercules transport plane from Nairobi
arriving the previous day, loaded to the gunwales with Tusker,
from Kenya. Tusker was the only beer, as Alan Brimelow
pointed out, which had a picture of the factory on the label.
But in the one international airport in the world where customs
regulations should have been unheard of, some minor official
had spotted the word 'beer' on the manifest and had impounded
the cargo. It was sitting out all night on the tarmac, and after
the sun came up the following day, it was starting to simmer in
its bottles as Happy Hour approached and as the freezers
brought in to chill it stood empty. This was no minor drama,
and the entire logistical focus of UNAMIR shifted to the airport
as negotiations continued. Finally, it was our Australian supply

doyen, Major Hilary Nicholson, who had a brainwave to compete with the heatwave. He bashed out an official letter on his PC, drove to the airport and flourished it in front of the bureaucrat. Beer, it said, was not a luxury; for UN troops, it was part of the rations. It was a close run thing, but when we climbed up the steps at 7.30 p.m. that night and pushed our dollars across the bar, we were rewarded with the coolest, sweetest drink imaginable to wash away the frustrations of the week. We thanked the elephants mightily as the first drops touched our parched throats.

Happy Hour was no ordinary party. The beer cost about 70 cents, so it had been decided, in order to simplify accounting, to charge $1 per bottle one week, and 50 cents the next. This first Happy Hour was a 50 center, and because there were no denominations lower than $1, you soon had your pockets clinking with 'spare' bottles. If you wanted to stop them getting warm, you had to drink fast. Everybody who was anybody was there. The SRSG, the General, UN workers, NGO civilians, and of course, the military component. It was an international bonanza, in great animation united in a common purpose - to drink the bar dry. By 8 p.m., the place was humming; by 9 p.m., it was leaping. By 10 p.m., the first BRITCON officer had already been thrown into the filthy swimming pool, and by 11 p.m., there was no turning back. The tiled floor was sticky with spilled beer, so that your boots stuck as you headed for the bar. This was our chance to make up for a week of hassle and grind. It had the release of a VE Day party and the urgency of a Klondike bash. It was the pressure valve of Kigali, switched full to 'open'.

I left the bar at midnight, and headed home, away from the wet grass where I might fall into a rhododendron bush or step on a mine, and via the car park. It was still packed with white vehicles, their drivers and passengers set to revel in the bar until the beer ran out. As I squeezed between the rows, a steady thumping became louder. One UN worker who had been flaunting her legs at Happy Hour was stretched out on the bonnet of a white UNHCR Toyota Land Cruiser, her short skirt rucked up around her waist. On top of her was a soldier, British or Australian, I could not tell in the dark, his buttocks and white legs framed in the moonlight by his combat jacket above, and by his trousers and boots below, as he pumped furiously into her. Quickly I moved away, embarrassed to find myself a spectator to what should have been a private act. I sat in the kitchen, suddenly sobered. It seemed a desecration, the culmination of a debauchery in which we had all been involved that night. While millions slept out on the hillsides, or in their mass-graves, we well-fed, prosperous hedonists were having a high old time. And on that symbolic white vehicle, the military and civilian components of the UN had demonstrated a union which they seemed unable to endure in broad daylight. And if it was symbolic, it spoke of our disdain for the seriousness of our mission, our contempt for the high morality which our supporters at home expected. It was an act of rape, the despoliation of our burnished image as makers of peace and givers of life.

*

The Under Secretary General for Peacekeeping, Mr Koffi Annan, was visiting the Mission in late September, when a human rights bombshell was dropped right into his lap. A UNHCR investigator named Gersony had written a comprehensive report detailing the systematic killing of Hutus in the south-eastern Prefecture of Kibungo. He claimed to have evidence that the RPA had been shooting alleged participants in the killing and burying the bodies in latrines at various stated locations. Passions were raised. The Government was devastated by the UN publicly proclaiming such atrocities, while it had yet to make any formal pronouncement on the genocide which began on 6 April. Even if the RPA were guilty, such a condemnation did not help the cause of progress; in the aftermath of such an appalling slaughter, some retribution should have been expected and UN moralising was not appropriate. In a fit of hand-wringing, we contributed a team of investigators, which included Jan Arp and Sean, to join with Human Righters and Government Ministers and go out on the ground to seek physical evidence of the RPA's atrocities. They collected no evidence one way or the other. The uncooperative nature of the people, themselves fearful of further reprisals, deprived the teams of potential witnesses. The physical evidence, even when tracked to specific sites, proved ethereal. And the fear of mines limited the enthusiasm of the team members from travelling far away from metalled roads. The nause, the mess and the inconclusiveness of the incident had all the hallmarks of an ill-judged and badly coordinated mistake. That it discredited the UN, imperilled the Government's fragile grip on the country and attacked the victims of the killing, by serving the extremist Hutu cause, showed how dangerously inept we really were.

*

On the humanitarian side, some progress was being made. We were all fearful of the effects of the rainy season, which was imminent, on the camps. Some, like Kibeho, depended on food delivered by heavy trucks on narrow, potholed tracks, never designed for this kind of traffic. When the rains came, we assumed, these would be washed away and the camps would go hungry. The need was to begin to move people to other camps closer to the road, and better, to move them home to begin the planting cycle. It was a Canadian logistician, Lieutenant Colonel Pierre Desnoyers, who stood up to be counted. His argument was simple. Full trucks delivering aid, now returning empty from the camps could be used to transport willing volunteers to their homes. This was the first evidence I had seen of real progress to try to do something more permanent than merely ensuring survival in the camps. Such was the speed of developing events that this work began on 16 September, eleven days after my arrival, and by 20 September, we had our first coordination meeting at the UNAMIR Tactical Headquarters, at Butare. This was a real opportunity to see the humanitarians in their home environment - about twenty-five had journeyed in from the field for the meeting. I inspected each one closely as Pierre laid out his concept for the plan.

By and large, they were young(ish), mainly Caucasian with a heavy European bias, they chain-smoked and they did not look as though they had just crawled out of a tent in the middle of an IDP camp. The men were bearded, or bespectacled; the women, seemingly in the majority, long-haired. Many wore T-shirts, shorts and sandals or trainers, simple, practical clothing ideal for travelling and working in hot climes. Some wore clumpy workboots, and where on the women, these were combined with cheap cotton skirts, it created an air of bohemianism which I had preconceived to be *de rigeur* for these benevolent distributors of aid. But this generalisation and the reinforcement of my prejudice could not detract from their individualism - they were also a bit of a handful. Pierre's idea had a number of easily recognisable holes, which they wasted no time in exposing. The difficulty of transporting people to their Communes, when there were no adequate reception arrangements and others, possibly Tutsis, had moved into their homes, could not be underestimated. And as the humanitarians advanced their arguments against Operation HOMEWARD, as it had been dubbed, the difficulties of dealing with them all in this way became evident. While I was frustrated and annoyed by their naiveté and unwillingness to cooperate, I was impressed by their spirit of independence and non-conformity. Their very diversity was what gave them their strength; an answer which satisfied the questioning of one would arouse the ire of another. To coordinate them properly required a very clear identification of common ground and unswerving insistence on keeping to it. Pierre did well. He was calm and persistent, and after some argument, they accepted what to me was starkly obvious. We had to give Op HOMEWARD a chance because it was a good thing to do and there was no alternative. The encounter was ultimately unsettling. While there was no doubt that all these people had the best interests of the IDPs at heart, their understanding of the complexities varied from sophisticated and experienced at one end of the scale to child-like simplicity at the other. There was just no professional benchmark with which to undertake such an operation. I also doubted that they all had the forbearance to push it through. And throughout UNAMIR and certainly, we had been told, in the Government, it was thought likely that many of the humanitarians just wanted to keep the people in the camps; providing disaster relief was what they had come for.

BRITCON would allocate many of the trucks for the Operation and a good deal of the coordination, while Tactical Headquarters would organise activity on the ground, holding nightly meetings at Butare to sort out the details of each day's move, three days in advance. The dynamo at Tac was a Canadian Major, Bob Lidstone, whose silver hair and thick cheroot created a punchy, Patton-like image. Bob was very bright, with a wicked sense of humour. His caustic wit and no-nonsense approach to the NGOs divided them firmly into two camps. They either loved him or hated him. During the meeting, his fiery clashes with the UNHCR representative, Masti Notz, herself a smouldering incendiary, caused a number of awkward silences to develop, which Pierre tried to smooth over. The UNHCR was the critical non-military player, owner of much of the transport. Without its co-operation, the plan would lie dead in the water. Bob was cranky and opinionated, but for me, he had one major redeeming quality that put him high up on the very short list I was compiling - he wanted to get the job done.

There was another presence in that meeting whose contribution was significant. Captain John Zegera gave every impression that he was just a young RPA officer, a local commander, until he started to speak. At 28, he was the Prefect of Butare, responsible for 20% of Rwanda; his intense concentration and deep understanding of the NGO arguments led him, simply and directly, to cut through the waffle.

'These camps must close,' he said, flashing his dark eyes at the assembly. 'There is no future for the camps. The people must go home.'

*

Anywhere else in this war zone, people acted sensibly and tried to avoid making a nuisance of themselves. The International Community tried to behave politely and with a sense of decorum. Minimal excitement, low-key businesslike behaviour. This was the code for getting on in a country which had just experienced such pain and was still in shock. But only the British Army could have produced such a simple answer to the knotty problem of how to celebrate Airborne Forces Day - the Kigali 10 Kilometre Road Race. The RPA and the few citizens of Kigali lined the route in open-mouthed amazement as 750 UNAMIR troops flogged their way over the hills of the city out past the airport, led by a couple of high-stepping Ethiopians. At 5,000 feet and with the early morning temperature in the 90s, I thought I was going to die. Avoiding the mortar holes in the road, and occasionally looking down at the chink created underfoot by running over spent 7.62mm cartridges, suggested that we had to be mad. Mike Wharmby's decision to stage the event, apart from sustaining the British reputation for eccentricity, a national-political goal all on its own, probably did much to rebuild confidence and restore some sense of normality. It was a touch of style in a town which badly needed it.

41

BRITCON had invited us to dinner in a stifling tent and the General was the guest of honour. He was so likeable and so pleasant. But there was a kind of weariness about him too, after two months in theatre. A week earlier, he had been standing out on his balcony at the Headquarters, enjoying a cigarette, when the BRITCON Royal Engineers team had detonated a mortar bomb, just a couple of hundred metres away, sending a huge plume of dirt into the air. He described his reaction with some panache. 'I was impressed,' he reported to the Morning Brief, 'but not favourably.'

He started off his speech well, in his charming French-Canadian accent: 'Did you 'ear about the traffic accident which took place outside UNAMIR Headquarters? A snail got run over by a tortoise. They asked the UN troops what had occurred? We don't know, they replied. It all 'appened so fast.'

\*

We drove out towards Ruhengeri, climbing steeply up the narrow ridge which led to the North-West, and the sun came up over Kigali, behind us. As it touched the top of the steep hills, it picked out, in sharp relief, the line of each terrace, casting long horizontal shadows, clean dark lines against the green. The contrast of yellow sky above and the green hills and elongated shadows below had a startling effect, especially on sleep-blurred eyes. Bend by bend, the view beneath unfolded, ever deeper depths of dark blue in the steep dip until we rounded one bend to find the ridge exposed on both sides. In the North, to our right, this fabulous living, changing sculpture. And on the left, to the South and West, a view to stun even the most seasoned traveller. Away to the West the blue ridges lay, rank on rank, as they marched up to the border with Zaire. We had arrived in time to view, in relief, the landform which had thrown these hills up, one on one, like rucked-up carpet. The sun illuminated each one in decreasing intensity and I counted 14 before they slipped down to Lake Kivu and away to foreign lands. But it was the sight in the valley between the ridges which made this vision of Rwanda at dawn complete. A thousand feet below, stretching as far as we could see and inundating those ridges, the valley had been flooded by the most perfect sea of pristine white cloud.

Sean, Andy Moore from Australia and I were on a mission. Accompanied by David Rawson, the US Ambassador, Bob Krueger, the Ambassador to Burundi, Tim Wirth, US Under Secretary of State for Global Affairs, and Wren, his wife, we were about to visit the 'Gorillas in the Mist'. With such an impressive range of companions, it was not long before the talk, in between hard-drawn breaths as we laboured up the rutted tracks, turned to the critical issues of Rwanda. Tim, Wren and Bob were well briefed at high level, while David's detailed knowledge of the war and the region was an education in itself. As we talked and debated, it occurred to me how much I had already learnt, in just a few weeks. The interchange was a major confidence booster, a realisation that some simple themes ran through any critical analysis. I filed them away, as yet unsure of where they might lead, but one was too starkly obvious to ignore: Unless progress was made quickly, things would deteriorate even further.

For the next five hours, we stumbled over the chaotic undergrowth as we followed the freshest gorilla trails. Occasionally, through the canopy, we could look down onto the lattice-squared countryside below, framed magnificently by the most exotic overhanging vegetation. We crawled underneath a fallen tree; the grass had been flattened - a nest! We moved uphill now and my boot squelched into something soft - fresh dung! We clambered over fallen logs and through deep, thorny ferns. We seemed to be going around in circles and were beginning to give up hope, when ahead, the column came to halt. Our guide motioned us down on our knees and then we were urged to crawl forward, through the deep undergrowth, until we were able to lie down and look over the lip of the slope. Forty metres away, in a thick tangle of undergrowth, I began to make out some dark shapes, hardly visible in the deep shadow. As our eyes became accustomed to the half-light, the individual shapes of the animals began to emerge. We had found what we were looking for. Beneath us was a whole family of gorillas.

We moved in, kneeled and then sat, not five metres from the nearest gorilla. The next twenty minutes were hugely memorable; they seemed to last forever. The gorillas showed little interest in us. We watched them chewing bamboo, grooming each other, the little ones playing. We sat still as a mother approached to inspect us closely; we could have reached out to touch her. As I gazed deep into her gentle eyes, it was hard to imagine that no intelligent life existed beyond them. The atmosphere was so convivial, our entrance into their society so intimate, that I could not help thinking of them as being anything less than human. Suddenly, the air was rent by a series of loud reports which were instantly recognisable from the wildlife programmes - chest beating. Our hearts were in our mouths as we watched a silverback come crashing through from the back of the group and charge towards us, veering off obliquely as he came nearer. The guides motioned us to stay still and avert our eyes. Across he came again, closer this time. At the end of his run, he stood up on his hind legs and beat his chest loudly, making those peculiar popping sounds as he beat the staccato rhythm out. 'This is mine,' he warned. 'Stay away.' His imposition on the group caused a smooth readjustment of position among the animals. I looked up to realise that the younger ones had gone - only the 'teenagers' and adults remained. The silverback ran across again, this time less aggressive in his demonstration of ownership. The others slowly melted away, one by one, and the protector carried out the rear-guard action, as he too faded noiselessly into the

44

jungle, turning back to look over his shoulder at us one last time before his evaporation was complete.

We moved quietly away, down the slope, to be stopped almost immediately by another amazing sight. The silverback we had seen was clearly only a youngster, for not thirty metres from our former position, Big Daddy had been keeping a watchful eye out. This massive male, with a coat of pure silver running off his back, was nonchalantly chewing bamboo as we halted in our tracks. Slowly, imperiously, he turned his head towards us. As it came full around, his chewing stopped, and he stared long and hard at our dishevelled group of travellers. It was a look which mixed casual interest, serious observation and half-feigned contempt. 'It's about time you lot cleared off,' was what it said to me. And so we did.

\*

The first major shooting incident took place in late September. Reports started to come into the Operations Centre in the late afternoon, and the details were initially sketchy. A UN convoy had been shot up. The RPA had fired on automatic. One of the vehicles had had its tyre shot out with seven rounds. I suppose that because this incident had taken place at the roadblock just outside Tac Headquarters at Butare, this could have provided us with a clue as to what had occurred, but when the message came into the Ballroom, confirming the sequence of events, the shock of the revelation caught us all by surprise. A UN vehicle had indeed been shot up, and the RPA had indeed joined in with their machine guns. But the cowboy slinging his gun down Butare way was not a guerrilla from Goma, or a bandit from Bukavu; it was actually one of our own UN officers. He had apparently shot the vehicle to stop it, fearing that it was about to run the roadblock. The incident, never fully explained, was as nothing to the ribaldry that followed it. Wicked jokes circulated the Headquarters faster than his bullets could have done. When he came in a few days later, sheepishly *en route* to the General for a 'short interview without coffee', he was ribbed mercilessly, on all sides. As he entered our office, the sight of Alan Brimelow wearing flak jacket and steel helmet must have been as disconcerting as the lack of supporting actors - we were all hiding under our desks.

His foible did not endear him to the hierarchy, but it brought relief and humour, in a bizarre way, to the rising intensity of our lives in Rwanda. The political situation was deteriorating, the security threat was increasing, but somehow this folly broke the tension for all of us. In a sneaking way, we would probably all have liked to empty a magazine into the nearest inanimate object; that this unfortunate officer actually did it was the tonic, the exorcism of all that stress, for the rest of us. But what the RPA thought of this example of temporary madness, nobody ever did say.

*

## Chapter 4

The French-Canadian Warrant Officer who ran the Canadian Logistic Base office stared at me wearily. Every UN officer in Kigali was trying to commandeer a vehicle and he was probably being approached five times a day.

'There's an old Chinese Jeep in the back of the compound, Warrant,' I mentioned nonchalantly. 'Looks like a write-off to me.'

'It's a piece a' junk, Sir,' he replied. 'You don't want to waste your time with 'er. And she 'as no roof. You will drown.'

'Well actually, there is another one in the BRITCON compound, completely shot through. Any objection if I get the two put together and see if I can make her a goer?'

'No problem, Sir,' replied the good Warrant. 'If you can get that vehicle goin', you're welcome to 'er.'

'What are you gong to do when it rains, Sir?' asked Craftsman Sommerscales, Chinese Jeep mechanic extraordinaire, when I presented him with a case of Tusker, one week later.

'Use this,' I laughed, pointing to my Gore-Tex jacket, stuffed under the seat. Then I roared off into Kigali. She was designed for a 5-foot 2-inch Chinese Jeep driver, not a 6-foot 1-inch British officer, and my nose was almost pressed up against the windscreen, but she was running. There were three forward gears and reverse was where you usually find first, which made for a few interesting departures from a standing start. If the hierarchy had known how much fun you can get out of a Chinese Jeep in Rwanda, it would have been instantly hijacked as the General's staff car.

*

Sean and I still had no door to our room at the end of the corridor. In an open plan house, every sound was magnified, only to be funnelled along to our room, which acted like an echo chamber. No such tympanic arrangement could survive the morning onslaught of a Royal Marine officer. When Fraser threw open the door to his room, bashing it against the wall, he probably thought he was on stealth mode, but Sean and I were immediately sitting upright in our beds, wondering whether the RGF had attacked. While Fraser crashed his way about the kitchen area, he probably thought how quietly considerate he was being, but to Sean and me, by now with sleeping bags pulled over our heads, it was merely the preparatory bombardment. When Fraser made it to the bathroom, noisily sluicing himself down from a jerrican of water, we could tell, from beneath the covers, that the cannonade had started in earnest but that he thought he was in the Marine version of silent approach. And when, as a finale, he finished with a flourish as he tapped his toothbrush against the side of the wash basin (three times every morning, no more, no less), we expected to hear the scream of the fast jets, the noise of the tanks and the shouts of the infantry at the charge, as our last attempt to hold the high ground of the night's rest, was blown away in the assault. Fraser went for an early run at 0545 hours, precisely. But Fraser was a Lieutenant Colonel, and we doorless junior chaps felt constrained to silence.

We were all up and about by 6.15 a.m. Half an hour later, we were in a position to gather for breakfast, individually prepared from a ration pack. Compo-rations contain thousands of calories and I was restricting my morning intake to jam and biscuits. But for Colonel Kieran O'Kelly, breakfast was a gastronomic experience. He would fuss about with the stoves for at least half an hour - a tin of bacon grill, some powdered egg and any other delicacy he could find. I watched him fight with his only garment, a towel around his middle, while he juggled with his pots and pans, and his beans and biscuits. In exasperation, no longer able to keep his apparel in place, he kicked it across the floor with his flip-flopped foot. There he was, our gallant leader, wandering naked throughout the house, as unconcerned as if he cooked breakfast like that every morning back in his quarters in Germany. A few moments later, he moved up to join me at the table. Unconsciously, I turned towards him, to be met, eye to eye, so to speak, with Kieran's corker.

'That reminds me, Colonel,' I said deadpan, slipping into the first banter of the day. 'We really must try to scrounge some fresh sausages.'

\*

He was standing in as the Head of UNREO, the Rwanda Emergency Office, the lynch-pin of the humanitarian effort, and as I listened to his serious but casual description of the issues of the day and heard him make, unerringly, three points at every Morning Brief, it became clear that he was a personality, a man with style. His bird-like head, skinny body and hunched shoulders did not betray his toughness, but when he revealed, under interrogation, that he had done his National Service in the French Parachute Regiment, it became more evident. Charles Petrie was in his mid-thirties. His academic background and most recent post as Special Adviser to Admiral Howe in Somalia gave some further insight. He was articulate, funny and immensely charming, and few who met him could escape his spell. He claimed ancestry which was 5% French, 95% British, except in the presence of a more partisan audience, for whom he would quickly reverse the proportions.

Once a week, Charles chaired the NGO meeting at the UNREO building. I slipped away from Alan Brimelow. By 5 p.m., the room was already filled with chain-smoking people of the wispy-bearded NGO variety, who continued to arrive in dribs and drabs throughout the following hour. After 15 minutes, Charles called the meeting to order, in both official languages but with sufficient emphasis on the French to prove that, in this company, he was only 5% English. With him was a tall blonde bespectacled Englishman, Barney Mayhew, who was the Operations Officer for UNREO, and the third person behind the table introduced himself as Lieutenant Cameron, the Liaison Officer to UNREO, a very tall, intelligent-looking, angular RPA officer wearing US Army fatigues and sporting a black beret.

As the introductions finished, a hush of expectation fell over the room. This was the forum where the 106 NGOs represented in Kigali, with the UN Agencies, would hammer out the crisis management of the coming week. I was hoping for action, for direction, which seemed to be so patently lacking at UNAMIR Headquarters. This would be from where the drive of the humanitarian operation would emanate, while the military provided a secure environment in which the NGOs and Agencies could carry out their humanitarian work. The first speaker was a Canadian officer from UNAMIR, who gave a review of security events in the clipped factual style of a British Bobby in court, occasionally referring to his notebook. It was well done in content but well wide of the mark in style, and the room bristled with irritation at the punchy, purposeful delivery. Sensing the flow, but misinterpreting its direction, the speaker became more strident, more direct. You could almost watch the gulf open up between the two, reinforcing each other's stereotypes, as the officer barked ever louder, and his civilian audience shrank ever further away. It was upsetting that such a critical relationship between UNAMIR and the civilians was being managed in this way. Perhaps the content did not lend itself to informal warmth - a catalogue of killings, shootings and reprisals throughout Rwanda over the past few days. As the list progressed, the RPA Liaison Officer was receiving its content less and less favourably and when the briefing was over, he jumped at the throat of the young UNAMIR officer.

50

'What do you mean the RPA carried out this killing, or that killing?' he demanded. 'You do not know what the RPA has done or not done. Where is your proof?'

The Canadian replied that this information had been gathered from troops in the field, NGOs and other sources, and that he had no reason to doubt it.

'But I have a reason,' said Lieutenant Cameron, raising his voice. 'You do not have any proof of this. And you should not say, 'The RPA did this, the RPA did that.' It is not Government policy for the RPA to kill civilians. You should say, 'It is alleged that the RPA did this or that.' And then you should say, 'An RPA soldier may have done this or that,' not make it sound as if throwing grenades into the *blindées* of the IDPs is the policy of the Government of Rwanda.' The Canadian defended his information stoutly, but his earlier rigidity had not endeared him to the audience and he soon had the sense to withdraw. Charles then went in to smooth over the damage created by this interchange, and as this required a translation into French, with Cameron repeating his points verbatim, I was not surprised to see that the first part of the meeting had already taken 45 minutes. This is going to last for hours, I thought.

I need not have been concerned. There were a number of points, purely routine, on local conditions in certain areas, given from the floor. The meeting ended with an administrative exhortation, which was fundamentally revealing. A large number of NGOs had not registered with UNREO, said Charles. These details were needed to compile a master list of contact numbers and Heads of NGOs operating in the country. Does this mean, I wondered, that the UN did not control the NGOs working in Rwanda? Did it mean that they could operate in some form of independent manner, that they were not directly responsible through UNREO for all their activities? The content of the meeting aside, it was the lack of content which was most unsettling. There were no urgent requests for

51

food or medicine - all those problems seemed to have been solved. There was no thirst for information, on what was happening in outlying areas. And most surprisingly, there was no mention at all of what the next moves were to be. I wandered out of the meeting hugely disappointed. I had arrived in Rwanda too late if, as clearly seemed to be the case, the emergency was already over.

I met Fraser at the house and we cut across the gardens to Happy Hour. As we clinked together our first cold bottles of the evening, taking in the glorious sunset over Kigali, I told him of my experience at UNREO. He was similarly disillusioned but was less convinced that the NGOs and Agencies had done the work they had come to do. Below us in the car-park, the white vehicles were arriving from the NGO meeting for the social event of the week. We started to add up the cost of all these runabouts and soon got into seven figures. Why, he asked, did an official from an NGO or Agency in Kigali require a brand-new 4X4 to waltz around the streets? I pointed out that UNAMIR was as much to blame; every officer above the rank of Major had his own 4X4. True, said Fraser, but the UN was inefficient and useless; everybody knew that. These people were taking cash directly from the public. Old grannies in Liverpool who were contributing their pensions to good causes would be horrified to see the money used in this way. Fraser had acquired an ancient Series I Land Rover from the scrapyard, the same source as the Chinese Jeep. Why, he asked, as 75% of all Land Rovers ever built were still on the road, did the NGOs need new ones? A brand new Range Rover probably cost as much as 20 second-hand, long wheelbase Land Rovers. More comfortable, perhaps, but the Land Rover was twice the workhorse. He was right. Many of these vehicles had expensive snorkel systems bolted on - and there were no rivers to ford. High frequency radios were fitted in abundance - were these of any use in such hilly terrain? We knew that some NGOs lived extremely well in walled villas complete with swimming pools and paid their staff phenomenal wages; one NGO was reported to be paying $135 per week for a cook, where even locally employed UN workers only received a highly inflated $20-25! Many NGOs had fresh food flown in from Nairobi; they were living in much better conditions than we were. It was all rather depressing and was nibbling away at the whiter-than-white image of the NGOs which was maintained at home. In the field, there had been no doubt that the people I saw were doing good work. But when you looked at their support organisations, you had to wonder how much more efficient they could be. We debated these issues long and hard over several weeks and I eventually reached a conclusion which I could live with. It would be easy to blow the whistle on these NGOs and to draw attention to those of them whose support infrastructures were clearly wasteful. But even if only a small percentage of the funds donated reached the people who needed it, that was better than the alternative. The answer lay more in ensuring public accountability and transparent cost bases for these charities than it did in righteous indignation. Disillusion the Western World with tales of waste in deepest darkest Africa, and millions would starve.

*

It was only the end of September and Op HOMEWARD was dying a silent death. The enthusiasm of the first few moves had been replaced by resignation and accepted defeat. Intimidation was a major factor. As IDPs had made their way to the truck loading areas to be registered by the UNHCR, they invariably been threatened by the extremist element in the camps, the Interahamwe. We had evidence that when, for one reason or another, the trucks had been delayed or cancelled, some aspiring Homewarders had been attacked and several may have died. The RPA had been unhelpful too; they had insisted on searching the IDPs several times on their way out of the camps, imposing logistical delays as well as causing fear among the people. One particular incident had caused a problem with BRITCON. There had been no accommodation for the British drivers, so they had been parking up the night before on waste ground in Butare, ready for the morning's deployment. That this had been next to an IDP encampment was bad enough, but the final straw was an incident which took place two weeks into the Operation. A soldier out on a midnight 'shovel patrol' had turned to fill in the hole to find that he had defecated into the rotting ribcage of a human corpse.

As I summarised the Operation at UNAMIR, in a deliberately positive and up-beat style, I was struck by several recurrent themes. Security had to be given a much higher profile for this type of operation to succeed at the camps, en route home and in the Home Communes. Only then would the IDPs be willing to move. And it was our information which let us down time and time again. We could not communicate to the people in the camps. The former government had its own 'bush telegraph' working out of Goma and Bukavu, which controlled the perceptions of the camp populations. One rumour that the UN was taking away IDPs to be shot by the RPA was enough to stop Op HOMEWARD in its tracks. Without some counter-propaganda, the UN had no chance of getting people to go home.

*

The Morning Brief included two incidents of note. In the first, a 58-year old woman resident in Ndago IDP camp was accused of being a witch. She was chased through the camp by the mob, had her clothes set on fire, was severely beaten and received a dozen serious machete wounds. Soldiers from GHANBATT intervened to save her life, but it was only a temporary reprieve. In the second, the unluckiest 12-year-old boy in Rwanda featured. At Kibeho camp, he had collapsed outside the church, victim of an epileptic fit. As a crowd assembled to watch, a passing dog saw his chance and moved in, to bite off the boy's penis and carry it away. The camps were nightmare places and these daily reminders in Kigali, delivered in the comparatively antiseptic cleanliness of the Amahoro Hotel, were the only real link we had with what was happening on the ground.

*

It was my third night without real sleep. I could survive throughout the day, developing my thoughts in the light of reality, clarifying questions, bouncing ideas off those with more detailed knowledge, until they were ready for incubation in the stillness of the night. In the Ministry of Defence, there had been all kinds of problems to expend this extra energy on and I had become used to self-inflicted sleep deprivation. Now the subject was Rwanda's future. Bit by bit, one possible solution was emerging.

I had been in-country long enough to make some broad judgements on what was going wrong. Two problems stood out clearly. The first was the lack of coordination, of 'unified command'. There was no single Agency in charge, no focus for the use of resources, ideas and energy in a concerted way. Beyond that, there was an even more fundamental problem. There was nothing to focus on, no direction, no plan to get us all out of this mess. We were just wallowing along, content to maintain the status quo, merely to achieve the routine aspirations of our deployment and this seemed to apply to the civilian element as much as it did to the military. This might have been an acceptable situation were it not for the addition of a third overlying problem. The political situation was not static; the UN may have had no plans but the Government had plans, the RPA had plans and the Former Government, with its

55

defeated army, had plans.  In the regional context, the dumping of three million refugees on the neighbouring countries had repercussions which many in Kigali seemed hardly to notice. Through the human weakness of concentrating on things we could do when faced with many we could not, and in the natural desire to shrink from problems of high complexity and interdependence because they seemed so apparently insoluble, we were losing touch.  We were trying to work a massive problem through with no strategy, in conditions of political vacuum.  And it just seemed obvious that it was bound to go wrong.

*

The evening drive home from the Amahoro Hotel was fraught with peril.  The RPA road blocks changed locations frequently and it was difficult to predict where the next might be, or what it might look like.  The placing of an empty beer crate in the middle of the road, or the stringing of a few rags between non-functioning lamp posts, might be the only clue, and if you came upon one by night, there was little enough warning to stop. Caught out in this way one evening, I screeched to a halt within inches of the broken crate which had emerged out of the gloom in the dim flickering lights of the Chinese Jeep.  Within seconds I was surrounded, one RPA soldier waving his rifle menacingly, and others moving behind me, causing more than a flutter of excitement.  'You are not showing respect,' he shouted.  'We are the RPA and you must show respect.'  I neglected to argue about the amount of respect due to a battered beer crate, but left it at that.  They had no right to stop us, and no right to search.

When Colonel Alan Brimelow had been caught out in this way, the RPA soldier, a mere teenager, had shoved his AK 74 into the cab, right into Alan's face and he had reacted in his own unique way.  Pushing aside the rifle, he had stuffed his own cocked pistol up the nose of the soldier and used some choice Australian phrases to express his wish to pass freely. I had no such desire to make my mark on the RPA and at night, in the open-topped Jeep, felt too vulnerable to attempt anything more than smiling ingratiation, which always seemed to do the trick.

Aside from the RPA, the night air was frequently rent with explosions, probably caused by hand grenades or mines. I had no desire to have one of these thrown into the Jeep and so kept my eyes peeled. The fact that we had not been attacked was no reason for complacency. The mine explosions were all too frequent and scarcely a day went by without some innocent being added to the casualty list, perhaps dumped unceremoniously outside the Australian Military Hospital. Sean was an inveterate collector of ordnance, and I frequently returned to find some lethal-looking piece of war machinery stacked up against his bed. I could handle the boxes of 9mm bullets - I had acquired a few of those myself and they might one day be needed. But I drew the line at the anti-personnel mines which he had collected and which lay scattered about. No matter that they had been disabled, their explosive and firing pin removed. There was something particularly evil about these nasty little lumps of plastic, their benign-looking rubber caps failing to betray their wicked purpose. Unceremoniously, I banned them from the room, and Sean was forced to find some other location from which to display his trophies. The laying of these terrible weapons, with so much malice of intent, was a serious impediment to the repopulation of Rwanda. In the empty fields, the number of hidden traps awaiting the unsuspecting refugees did not bear thinking about.

There were dog packs around too, gorged on human flesh during the summer, now hungry and vicious, their only easy meal one of their own number, perhaps hit by a truck. One night, en route to the Belgian Village, I came across a pack of about twenty dogs and drove through them as fast as I could.

Occasionally they got into UN compounds and the Canadians had been authorised to shoot them.

I was deeply asleep for the first time for several nights when the most unholy racket began outside. Emerging, I focused slowly on an enormous dog, standing a few feet away, and howling like a banshee. He was almost close enough to touch but for the security bars and mosquito netting which separated us through the open window. From Sean's side of the room, there came the click of a magazine being pressed home, before the familiar louder sound of the mechanism being cocked on a Browning 9mm pistol. From under his white mosquito net, Sean's hand emerged, pointing at the window, weapon at the ready.

'Sean, don't even think about it,' I said, loudly and clearly, for I wanted no risk of a mistake. Quite apart from the disciplinary implications, in that tiny room we would certainly have both been deafened. Slowly the hand withdrew, the magazine was removed and the action cocked again to eject the round. But Sean had not finished. From under his net, directed firmly at this loud intruder, still howling at the moon, Sean let out a barely audible 'Psst'. The dog stopped, stood up and trotted off into the moonlight, tail held high, as if he had just received some coded message from my room-mate.

'Aah,' I offered in pure *Blackadder*, as we both settled down again, 'Doctor Doolittle I presume?'

\*

I received an urgent call from BRITCON that I should ring Sue. She had called our 'emergency' number in Wilton, and so I knew there must be a real problem. There was nobody using the Operations Room phone to New York, so I punched the number through and then the International dialling code for the UK. It was against the rules, but I had no choice. Sue was distraught. Her father had been admitted into hospital a few

58

hours before and was now in intensive care, very seriously ill. I tried to give some words of comfort, whilst being watched impatiently by half a dozen Ops Room staff. It was incredibly difficult. The doctors didn't know what was wrong with him, she said, but the prognosis was not good; lung cancer was suspected. I rang off after 10 minutes, keen to avoid the abuse of a telephone system I would clearly need again. As the others filed out on their way to Happy Hour, I had no wish to join them. Gavin, Sue's father, had been a great friend and mentor for many years. I sat down to write him a letter, which even if it arrived on time, might be the last. What can you say to someone who has meant so much and who you might never see again? What words can you use to thank him, whilst maintaining some encouragement, not letting him know that you fear his end is near? I managed less than a page, each word a trial, then cleared my desk, half a world away from an ongoing family tragedy.

But the evening was not over. Heading through the corridors, I was nearly run over by the young Malawian Captain on duty. There was a tremendous racket coming from the Ops Room.

'Sir, there is a major security incident, what shall we do?' he gasped.

I walked in and put my kit down.

'Get me the latest report from GHANBATT. Write down every message in the log and make sure you record the time accurately. Get the General's MA on the radio. The General needs to get back in here now. Run and get the RPA Liaison Officer. Get UNREO Base on the other net.'

Dispassionately, I allocated work to the staff as the radio continued to blurt out garbled snippets of information. In the background of the Force Command Net, the shouting and yelling in the GHANBATT Ops Room in Gikongoro came over loud and clear during transmissions. They were in touch with the troops on the ground, and the odd snatches of animated

59

conversation we heard were the reports going in directly from the incident.

I gripped the situation, mechanically demanding calm, concentration and discipline. Not for the first time, I thanked the British Army for its excellent training. Slowly, the panic faded from the eyes of the staff and they started to behave professionally, barking out reports crisply, checking back to me as each message was sent and acknowledged. It was their first real test and, after weeks of inactivity, they had been caught by surprise. The RPA had attacked an IDP Camp in the Gikongoro Prefecture. Grenades had been thrown, automatic fire had been heard, *blindées* were burning. Thousands of people were reported fleeing. I was kicking myself as the incident unfolded. Why hadn't I acted sooner? What had prevented me from seeing this coming, now so obvious as a result of the rising tension? My personal woes, overwhelming though they had been half an hour before, faded into insignificance. A hundred kilometres away, the fragile peace of Rwanda had exploded on a bare hillside, and there was nothing we could do to stop it.

*

# Chapter 5

Sean was late. He had recently volunteered to escort the Human Rights investigators on their visits to the mass-grave sites of Rwanda, locating these charnel houses and recording in terrible detail, the nature of the deaths. He had not volunteered by accident. Most Human Righters seemed to be 25-35, female, nubile and single; one particular investigator from America, Lynne Goldberg, matched these criteria more precisely than others. Sean and his team had established the systematic and cold-blooded nature of the killings from the grim evidence of their finds. Each grave contained as many as 20,000 occupants, and the way that the corpses lay and the injuries from which they had died, was a chilling indictment of humanity. In some cases, the number of bodies, and the wounds, said more about the deaths than could any survivor. To be killed in this way, they would have had to be lined up, as lambs to the slaughter, so petrified that they went silently up the line until the last fatal blow, so paralysed that they could offer up no resistance save the skin of their necks, so forlorn of hope that they faced the inevitable without thought of escape or plea for mercy. As they fell, men, women and children were kicked into an ordered heap. As their line moved silently forward, so the killers moved relentlessly towards its end.

And when Sean came home that night, he brought those people with him. As the door opened, they crowded in around him, surrounding him and clinging to him. A thousand souls, disinterred from a Rwandese hillside, were with him as he crossed our threshold, as he walked over our floor. He was dog-tired and ready for bed.

'Sean,' I ventured, 'I think you should take your boots off before you go into the room, and you'd better have a sluice-down before you get into bed.'

Pre-empting his response, Kieran, thankfully, joined in. 'You could have anthrax on your boots, Sean,' he argued,

61

kindly. 'Best to take all your clothes off outside, and then go straight into the bathroom.'

One by one, we all ganged up on him. He was seriously outranked, and it was some relief to us all when he did as he was bid. We were all hugely sympathetic towards the victims of the Rwandese slaughter. But nothing in the world would persuade me that it was all right to spend the night with them.

*

Alan Brimelow was away on leave in Mombasa and Nairobi, with Fraser and Jan Arp - all very much in party mode. His last words, as he exhorted me to serve the UN well in his absence, were the ones that had galvanised me into action: 'That'll probably take up the rest of your time here mate!' I had no intention of spending my five remaining precious months in the Army writing Operation NIKE, the Security Alert Measures Plan, Operation JASON, the Contingent Reinforcement Plan, and Operation HECTOR, the Withdrawal and Evacuation Plan, and so gave myself a much more challenging target - 5 days. By working into the late nights, I had managed to release myself from a potentially horrendous burden, and I was counting on Brimelow being so impressed that he would let me free to pursue...something else. As he thumbed through the document, I watched his eyes narrow, as he picked up more details and cross-referenced the three plans, to make sure they showed no gaps. He walked over with the slab of paper in his hand, and dumped it on my desk. 'Tom, you have a problem.'

'Oh, er, right, Colonel,' I replied, trying not to look too disappointed. It seemed as though he had found some glaring error of logic, although I was sure that the thing was watertight. 'And what might that be?'

'You're an overachiever.'

*

The rains came as we lay in our beds one night, the weather too humid to permit even uneasy rest. At first, the opening cadences of the storm required some far-off definition. The rumble of thunder over the hills came faintly to us, no real indication of the turmoil to come; we had experienced rain before but it had been short and sharp, a watering of the city to brighten up the bougainvillaea, to wash the gritty dust from the banana leaves. The first drops fell at odd intervals on the roof of Britain House, then more frequently and, as the sound grew louder, so the intermittence dissolved until there was only one homogenous note, which grew and grew until the whole house seemed to shake under the impact. From beneath the mosquito net, I could see the water pouring off the roof of Australia House opposite and the plants and shrubs outside bend under the continuous pressure as though they would soon be pushed to the level of the ground. Sean reached out to close the window and we lay and listened to the storm as it found its natural noise level, there to remain for several hours until it once more returned to an unearthly silence, broken only by the faint, rushing sound of the storm-drains as they overflowed down the hill. They were late in the year, these rains of the 'short' season, but for those whose only protection was a thin membrane of UNHCR plastic, that could have been of little solace. Of greater concern than their comfort and health, however, was their very survival. If, as widely predicted, the roads to the camps became impassable, the food would not get through and so the people would starve.

During the daily drives in the Chinese Jeep, wearing my precious Gore-Tex jacket, I monitored the progress of the rains. The information from the camps was so infrequent and inaccurate that a much more accessible source of information was needed - the steep, rutted dirt-track to the Belgian Village became the control experiment. As the rains progressed, it deteriorated rapidly. Each morning the rivulets had carved great trenches through the stony clay, crossing the track obliquely before they fell off into the valley, occasionally taking chunks of road with them. Vehicular progress became slower, as trucks lurched from one canyon to the next, accelerating a few yards between each obstacle. Remarkably, the track still existed. It was slower and more precarious in places, a function of the heavy traffic which must have been mirrored on the lifelines to the camps. But it was still there, physical testimony to the explosion of another myth in the long stream of half-truths on which we based our meagre understanding of the country. Out in the south-western Prefectures, the massive Red Cross and World Food Programme trucks ground on with hardly an interruption. No IDP went hungry; no 23 PFA visit was cancelled. Where problems arose, they were dealt with by our own Engineers and the Government had a number of graders which were brought into use. As soon as it became clear that the short rainy season was going to have little effect on the sustenance of the camps, we heard rumours that the 'long' rainy season, beginning in January, would really put paid to the delivery of aid. But I had learnt another valuable lesson. From now on, I would ignore every snippet of information which lacked the country's most rare and precious commodity - a grain of truth.

\*

He was staring up at us from the filthy ditch, his eyeless sockets swivelled to the sky, in a last questioning gaze. The months since his death had taken away most of his flesh, but the sheer terror of his last moments would not be removed until time took the skull itself away. He looked benign, resigned even, but there was still something there, some shred of humanity which was deeply unsettling. His jaw had become detached and was lying beside him. Perhaps his head had rolled away and had been missed on an earlier clearout, and someone, finding him today, had thrown him into this ditch, so inured to death and misery now that such an act no longer carried any meaning. Sean broke the awful magic of the moment by turning the skull over. A large piece of bone was missing. During the war, we knew that there had been a night of desperate killing behind this row of shops beside the UN Headquarters. The screams had become so loud that the Headquarters had been forced to send out a patrol, since none inside could bear the noise. In the hundred metres or so the soldiers had moved behind these shops, they had counted 175 bodies, and had returned quickly, shaken and bringing tales of such appalling slaughter that none would dare to venture out again that night. Amidst the detritus of this latest clearout, one or two gruesome reminders might have been unearthed.

A small crowd had gathered as we two British officers started to dig a hole. When we had gone down a few feet, Sean scraped the bones in, and we covered this Rwandese citizen over for the last time. The sun was beating down. As I leant on my spade and looked about, the yellow, shell-pitted facade of the UN Headquarters came into focus through the barbed wire fence a few feet away. With the blue flag fluttering in the breeze, the comfort of that safe spot could not be at greater contrast to the last resting place of this person. We stood quietly for a moment, and I wished him a safe journey. Then we picked up our spades, cleaned them on the grass by the Headquarters entrance bunker, handed them back at the stores, and went off to our business, as if nothing had happened. But throughout the afternoon, I found myself mentally re-winding and playing back the last desperate moments of the first human being I had buried.

\*

The RAF had been bound to delay sending an officer to join the UNAMIR staff. They couldn't possibly spare someone for the six months we were all committed to - three months would have to do. The only chap available had been separated from his wife due to 'Service Reasons' for so long, that he had been promised Christmas back at home. He would have to be replaced on or about 14 December. Of course, we thought, who would want to spend Christmas away from home? We were all dreading it. Three months was the bare minimum theatre time needed to receive a UN Medal. In exceptional circumstances, it could be awarded after 80 days operational service. Today was 4 October, and today our Brylcreem Boy was arriving. Fourth of October to 14 December was.... 80 days. Funny thing that.

He appeared in the early afternoon. Tall and skinny, he was carrying enough mountaineering kit to scale up the South West Face of Annapurna, from a standing start in Kigali. Two enormous climbing rucksacks and a massive kit bag all looked a bit outdoor, rather than military, as he dumped them in the corner of the Air Shop. My eyes were immediately drawn to his feet, encased in brand new beige-coloured hiking boots; he looked like an advertisement for *Cotswold Camping*. His hands were stuffed deep into his casual, combat-kit pockets and he was chewing gum. Very unofficer-like. Dark, piercing eyes sat above a long, narrow nose on his thin, athletic face. By now, our new blue berets had become faded, neat and sharp looking. His was straight out of the plastic wrapper, as bright blue as the flag that fluttered on the General's staff car. It was monstrous, at least 12 inches across, and absolutely horizontal. 'Welcome to Rwanda,' I said, indicating his bonnet. 'Good of you to bring your helicopter landing pad with you.'

His name was Jan Janiurek (*pronounced and henceforth spelt Yan*) and he was a Puma helicopter pilot. He strolled into the house as if it were his own. 'Nice digs,' he mused. 'Could be quite comfortable here.'

'It hasn't always been like this,' we retorted. 'You should have seen it when we first arrived.' But he was off to check out the loo. 'Good,' I thought. 'A bit of discomfort won't do him any harm.'

He emerged a few minutes later, still looking dead casual and nonplussed. 'Water's not very hot,' he remarked, chewing slowly. 'Can't you chaps do something about it?'

Sean, Fraser and I looked at each other. Sean sped into the cloakroom and started yelling his head off. 'It's working, the water's working, and its hot!' We couldn't believe it. Four weeks sluicing out of jerricans and suddenly, the Crab turns up and.....

'Oh yes,' he said, chewing laconically. 'Aircrew never go anywhere without hot running water.'

\*

On the next Sunday, Yan dragged me away from the Headquarters for a helicopter trip to Kibuye. At the airport, we met up with Sean and Lynne, and Errol, a Scandinavian Human Righter, complete with stereotypical wispy-beard. Lynne and Errol, with Sean, would be investigating a massacre, I was disturbed to hear, but there was no need for us to get involved in any macabre visits - we could just wander around the town.

It was not my first flight over Rwanda. Each time I strapped into the Huey, however, the anticipation of the pleasure to come welled up inside. The country, stunning from the ground, was breathtaking from the air. The colour of the vegetation, much of it now riotous and overgrown in the empty fields, contrasted sharply with the darker brown of the eucalyptus clumps. All the land was criss-crossed with the lighter veins of the footpaths, running up along the ridges and down along the natural lie of the land. No pocket of productive acreage had been left untilled. From the thick thorny brush which bordered the river banks in the valleys, up the steeply terraced slopes of the smallholdings to the narrow thin edges of the ridgebacks, every plot showed evidence of former human activity. No wonder the population pressure on the land, an oft-quoted cause of ethnic strife, had been so intense. It was all spoken for, including the fast-growing eucalyptus which provided the firewood. One statistic was particularly telling. By the year 2015, it had been said, the entire country would have had to be planted in eucalyptus, just to maintain sufficient stocks of cooking fuel. My German friend of a few weeks before would have had an important role to play in these circumstances; but now the land below was empty. Except around the camps where the land was being denuded, a breathing space had been created in which the environment could recover from the population pressure.

We were met at the Headquarters of the French African Battalion (FRAFBATT) by a wiry, tough-looking Senegalese Captain whose tight, tailored uniform made his black boots look particularly huge at the end of his long thin legs. Conducting our negotiations in schoolboy French, we arranged a vehicle and guide to tour the town and the lake-shore.

After three miles on a rough road, we stopped at the main sports stadium, a football pitch of amateur-division proportions. The role of these places in the social fabric of Rwanda, it was becoming obvious, was significant. Venues not only for sports activities, these were the local foci of political information and collective entertainment. It was not surprising that so many people had fled to them during the killing, since they were associated with Government, the law and protection in numbers. That this reflex had been so cruelly exploited was indeed tragic. All over Rwanda, stadia, churches and municipal buildings had been where refuge was initially sought and subsequently denied. As we parked in the centre of the green pitch, surrounded by small children who had followed us up the road, the idea of a massacre seemed highly unlikely. There were thousands of bodies buried here, explained Sean and Lynne, according to the reports. But I was immediately sceptical; there seemed little enough evidence of dense human

68

population, much less the enormous mounds which bulldozed mass-graves were supposed to throw up. At the fringes of the stadium, under the shadow of a steep eucalyptus-clad hill, the Human Righters stopped to inspect the ground.

'Look, Yan and I are just going to drive around the town,' I shouted from the truck. 'You guys just carry on doing what you have to do.'

'Bones,' called out Errol. 'Look, everywhere there are bones.'

We climbed out and approached slowly. Along that edge of the stadium was the detritus of mass occupation. Old camp fires, rags, bits of burned wood. And in amongst this debris, contrasting sharply with the dark-red earth, were the unmistakable bleached-white, harder forms of bones, vertebrae, longer bones, and fragments of all shapes and sizes.

'Yes,' said Errol triumphantly. 'A very large massacre site.'

There was something immediately wrong with this speedy diagnosis. There were vertebrae and ribs all right, but they were enormous. I lifted my head, to focus almost unconsciously on the dark shapes grazing quietly on the lush green grass 300 metres away, at the other end of the stadium.

'These aren't human bones,' I intoned softly. 'Whoever left them here did so recently, and they obviously had a good meal.' I pointed over to the cattle.

You did not have to be a forensic pathologist to become a Human Righter, but a rudimentary understanding of human anatomy might have been a bit of a help; these people were as much amateurs as we were.

Sean had climbed over a low wall at the far end the stadium. 'I think you should see this,' he shouted back.

Inexorably, we were drawn in. Just over the wall, on a flat area of ground, a bare piece of earth had been largely cleared of vegetation. Errol was not willing to commit himself now. 'The records show over 20,000 bodies buried here by the French Foreign Legion.' We walked around. It seemed unlikely that so many bodies could be contained in such a small, flat space. Around the area, however, there was a strange flowering plant, a relative of the poppy, sprouting out from the freshly-tilled ground.

'Have you seen these before, Errol?' I inquired. 'They don't grow outside this area at all. Are they associated with graves?'

'Yes,' he replied more firmly. 'I have seen these flowers on other mass-graves near Kigali.'

I could not help myself from paraphrasing, 'In Kibuye's fields, the poppies blow.... If ye break faith with us who die, We shall not sleep, though poppies grow.' I tried hard not to imagine the sight underfoot, but it was the poppies and their symbolism which affected me as much as the idea of the people beneath, and I had to turn away.

Further up the hill, Sean was trailblazing. 'Skeletons,' was all he had to shout down to get us to follow. The realisation that we were slipping into the mode of the curious could not be prevented any more than the act itself - the ghastly chase was on, some primal need to satisfy our interest and to be seen to be unafraid, to confront death.

The first was in pieces, scattered over a wide area. There was no skull, just a concentration of unconnected bones. Human bones for sure. There was nothing to link these pieces to the life of a human being, no evidence of the complexity of even the simplest rural existence, no glimpse of personality, or strife or pleasure in life or pain in death. They were just bones. From up above, Sean called out again. As we scrambled up to him, a more complete skeleton lay down the slope, head pointing towards the stadium below. Only half the skull was there. We fanned out and continued to climb, each one calling out at the discovery of another former Rwandese. We paused by one as Sean, who had by now visited so many sites, provided two equally plausible theories - either these people had grouped together for safety at the top of the hill and had been chased down, being butchered on the way, or they had

70

fled the stadium during the massacre, to be hunted down and killed as they stumbled through the undergrowth on the sheer, wooded slope. The notion of escape, of breathless movement in terror was unmistakable in the way they lay. Most had been gnawed by the dogs, but here and there, some almost complete cadaver had a more arresting effect. One man lay propped against a tree, his clothes still attached at his wrists and waist and ankles, his head incongruously lying beside him as he looked back at himself in death. A few metres away, a woman's blouse still attached to the ribcage showed through the trees a startling red, to contrast with the white of her bones. At her side, lay the almost complete skeleton of a baby, spread out with legs akimbo and arms outstretched. On the tiny skull, the intact fur of a woolly scalp, the closely-knit cap of African hair, lost without its smiling little face below.

We had two more sites to visit. The first, down by the lake-shore, was at one of the most beautiful spots I had yet seen in Rwanda. Just off the road, two smallish areas looked recently cultivated. There was no sign of the 'Poppies of Death' but as we walked around, I looked down beside my boot, to see a human skull staring skywards from the dirt. Closer inspection revealed many more bones and we tiptoed away for fear of disturbing the site more - here was undoubtedly a mass grave. The second site was by a church. The people had apparently gathered there together for safety. If the story told us by our FRAFBATT escorting Corporal was true, the local clergy had herded the people in, had locked the doors, and then when the Interahamwe had arrived, had handed the keys over to the mob. There was little evidence of religion in the church on this steep hill overlooking the lake. The structure of the altar remained untouched, but the cross had been removed, leaving a lighter template on the wall above, and the pictures and ornaments were missing too. Whether they had been taken as part of the madness, or removed from this desecrated spot later, we could not tell. Just by the entrance of the church, there were further low piles of disturbed earth.

As the Huey pulled out of its steep climb over Kibuye that afternoon, I looked down across the lake and over towards Zaire. I remained strangely detached but confused. Although the skull in Kigali had had a powerful effect, out on the hillside, it was only the poppies and the clothing and the hair which broached the eternal wall of death. In the larger mass graves, the message was too overpowering to make sense; they were just piles of bones. Of course I felt sadness at what had befallen these ordinary people, already clutching the land for tenuous survival. In their simplicity and in their trust, they had been given up to the slaughter and that seemed especially poignant, bitterly cruel, to waste such frightened, blameless innocence with such uncaring, vicious force. But if any of these mixed emotions dominated as we turned towards Kigali, it was hard-jawed anger. In the far distance, on the other side of that hazy blue lake, the killers were alive. No hideous fear for them, no night-time scramble through the thick, scratching bushes, with the howl of the mob in their ears. No last-gasped entreaty, no desperate attempt to cover their darling, woolly-headed children with their own bodies, as the machetes sliced into their flesh. Seventy kilometres away, in the shadows of the Virunga volcanoes, the killers lay down in comfort, no poppy-clad grave for them. Beneath the blue plastic, protected by the UN logo, with our food in their bellies and our guarantee of certain safety, they lived.

*

72

## Chapter 6

I slept badly again that week. The trip to Kibuye had been unsettling; my time in the Army was nearly up and the opportunity to do something useful, which had catapulted me so quickly from the Ministry of Defence, was fading as the days went by. I needed the personal fulfilment of something as difficult and complex as anything I had done before, and now I was writing administrative instructions, instead of strategy. The weeks of detailed analysis and critical questioning had begun to solve the riddle of Rwanda. The people who should have been restoring the country after such a catastrophic human tragedy had not shown any signs of action. As the situation moved towards normality and the world's view of Rwanda became dimmer by the day, many NGOs were preparing to cut and run, in search of the next disaster, of the next adventure, without having done anything useful to prevent it from happening. If I had been the SRSG, my instinct would have been to get all the main players into one room and give them the bollocking of a lifetime. My anger was growing; and now it needed to be channelled. I started finally to put the pieces of the jigsaw together.

\*

I had been sent out by Brimelow to check the tracks on the GHANBATT Armoured Personnel Carriers, which the RPA claimed were chewing up the roads. I looked them over unobtrusively while chatting to the soldiers. The tracks were well maintained and no hazard - another attempt by the RPA to unnerve UNAMIR. Yan was driving. UN helicopters overhead, civil or military aircraft heading into Kigali International Airport, they were all picked out at great range, categorised and usually 'splashed' at the fantasy-manic hand of our combat pilot. The *Thunderbirds* impressions had me crying silently as we drove along, with Yan playing the part of Lady Penelope's driver, Parker. The face already fitted and the voice was perfect. He told me of an incident when dogfighting in Wales from his helicopter against a squadron of Tornadoes, he had tricked a Tornado pilot into flying right into an ambush position. As the plane came in low over the trees Yan had popped up right on his nose. The jet pilot had swerved to take evasive action, exposing his belly, but Yan could not resist the temptation to key the radio triumphantly, so that all involved in the exercise could hear Parker's nasal monotone: 'Too close for missiles, M' Lady. Switchin' to guns.'

At work, it wasn't long before he started. He was eyeing everything up and sorting out the Air Shop, which needed some modernising. The three helicopters were undertasked and being used with little control or imagination, by his standards. Reforming this system was not going to be easy. 'Customer' resistance to change was particularly strong. Senior officers had got used to taking the choppers because road journeys were inconveniently long. Their subordinates stopped tasking the aircraft then, seeing them as a taxi service for the bosses. Yan set out to change all that. He amended working hours, tasking types and turnaround times to optimise customer requests, at the same time as opening up a host of new ideas for helicopter use. Within a couple of weeks, he had had a major impact, a clear lesson to the Headquarters on the value of British officers. In fact Yan's reforms were, for him, quite easy. He was used to juggling far more resources under much tighter constraints.

*

A few mornings later, we took advantage of our new-found RAF tasking efficiency. From an information perspective, we decided it would be useful to monitor the routes into Rwanda from Zaire, since there were many reports of refugee movement overnight, which could not be substantiated. If we could fly out

74

at dawn, Yan suggested, we might just catch the last signs of overnight movement before the people dispersed into the countryside. That was the legitimate reason. Beyond that, we wanted to see the volcanoes at dawn. We flew up over the Ruhengeri ridge, scene of a glorious morning view a few weeks before. But now there was no mist in the valleys, just the clean, bright colours of morning, picked out by the rising sun as we flew along the border with Zaire, peering down to look for signs of human movement. Almost on cue, in the deep rural reaches of the mountains, well away from the beaten tracks, we surprised groups of refugees out on the hills, moving east into Rwanda. They stopped and looked up as we roared overhead, some even waving in relief, finding themselves so swiftly under UN observation. In order to cross the border, they would have had to sneak out of the camps in darkness. We knew that many had been killed by Interahamwe in their attempts to escape and begin their lives anew. Below us were people of courage and determination. And with a bit of a nudge and some good security in the camps, many more might be tempted to follow.

'Have you seen where they're walking?' shouted Yan from across the helicopter.

'What?' I shouted back, the noise too great to be sure what he had said.

'They're walking home on the ridges,' he shouted. 'Look at them, just walking high up out of harm's way.'

The tiny snakes of families or Commune groups were right on the ridgeways, just as I had thought they might be. With a rush, I felt another wave of certainty that some of the mechanisms in play over this frightened country could be understood. And my respect for Yan grew too. He had picked out the salient fact with his keen eyes, as we traversed the contours. The people wanted to walk, would risk their lives to walk home. But first, somebody would have to help them break the grip of the militias.

We flew on up the great Congo watershed, over the gorillas, whose rest our clattering blades must surely have disturbed, and along the line of the volcanoes, each one individually distinct, formed and broken uniquely and visible from many miles away. Yan spoke to the pilot into the headset.

'We're going over the big one,' he shouted.

Up and up we circled, still inside Rwanda, trying to gain the height we would need to peer inside the smouldering giant, Nyiragongo, which overshadowed the camps of Zaire. Below us in the fields of Rwanda, the perfect broken calderas of former volcanoes dotted the countryside. What looked like a conical hill capped with woodland revealed a hidden valley inside, a perfect bowl fringed with woods and dotted with the same white or brown homesteads and the regular lines of the field boundaries which lay outside. A hidden treasure of a place. A place to grow old in. And at 14,000 feet, with the bones of the Huey shaking with the strain of the ascent, we popped over the border, like a cork from a bottle, and circled the smoking crater at a very steep angle. I could not cross the helicopter to look outside, for fear of causing the machine to become unstable, but had to stand up and look directly down through the opposite window into the cauldron, to watch with horrible fascination the red lava clearly pulsating with an irregular beat, thousands of feet below in the crater. The heat rose quickly in the cockpit as we circled and the smell of sulphur came pungently to us, sucked in from the hot gases, by the helicopter's air intakes. It was an awesome sight, that sheer raw power of nature confronted in this unique way, a frightening reminder of our vulnerability in the flimsy machine above. One mistake by the pilot and we would have disappeared forever.

Beyond the volcanoes, there was another smoking mass, this time laid out across the plain below. From the foot of the wooded hills, and as far as we could see up the valleys in all directions, lay the smoke of a hundred thousand camp-fires. The people of Goma were rising to face their day. Of course, I had watched the news items with horrible fascination throughout the summer, as the cholera outbreak had struck, just as the survivors of the long march arrived in Zaire. Goma held a fascination for those of us confined to Rwanda which went far beyond its physical presence. It was the embodiment of despair and evil, the epitome of the depths of human misery and the lair of the most vicious malevolence ever to spread across the face of Africa. The people we had seen escaping on the ridges earlier were the lucky ones; they had survived the wicked onslaught of the Interahamwe and now had a chance to rebuild their lives. But for those with less courage, or the stain of guilt on their own hands, no such escape existed as a possibility. They were confined to this hell on earth below us. Looking down through the window of the circling helicopter, the view appeared first of the smoking cauldron, and then of the smoking camps, two hells placed side by side by some cynical trick of fate.

*

It was a Sunday lunchtime and another heavy downpour had just passed over the Headquarters. Outside in the car park, the Chinese Jeep was full of water, awaiting another excursion into the interior, to get to know Rwanda. I watched with relish while Yan carefully spread his RAF Gore-Tex camouflage rain-jacket over the soaking seat. It was a flimsy, thin version of my Army jacket, designed more for dashing between aircraft and hangar than for living in the field. Once in a while the Army gets it right, I thought, gleefully anticipating the next downpour, when on behalf of the Army, I would enjoy sweet revenge on the junior Service, for a thousand wrongs, real or imagined, which over the years had left us soldiers lying uncomfortably in the sodden undergrowth while the light blues flew away to their warm beds, with a cheery wave of their kid-gloved hands.

77

We drove out past the Amahoro Stadium towards the East and the road to Kibungo, which neither of us had travelled before. The fields were as empty as they were in every other direction, the occasional smoky fire the only evidence of human habitation in the overgrown landscape. The crops had been ready since the summer and now they grew either out of control, or to the point of rottenness. But the road was being used to carry some traffic; the occasional white 4X4, belting along at an inordinate speed and crewed by blue-bereted Military Observers, a few overladen trucks and pickups, moving every kind of item around the countryside, whether bought or looted, no-one could tell, and the usual pedestrians, kitted out in their Sunday best, looking frightened and hostile, lest the vehicular traffic spill out some evil upon them, unarmed, now living under constant threat. But as soon as we left the confines of Kigali, it always seemed to be the same. The people on the side of the road hunched in fear as we approached, but as we waved and shouted '*Muraho*' (Hello), they immediately broke into smiles and waved back frantically, the relief etched on their faces in contrast to their earlier apprehension. The Jeep was certainly an ice-breaker. Exposed and with our blue berets visible, we presented far less of a threat than a typical dark-windowed UN vehicle. And the Jeep too, with its smiley face, invited a smile in return. It was in search of a better understanding of all these social forces that we had come out, to visit an area where numerous security incidents had been reported in recent weeks, but no UN Military Observer patrols had deigned to investigate.

We drove on for over an hour, trying to judge our position from the country map. On a straight bit of road hedged in with banana plantations, a tiny sign to the left indeed announced our turning point  A hundred crunching, puddle-splashing metres later, we came to a fork in the track. Away to the right was scarcely more than a footpath; to the left, a cart-track opened up. I swung left and followed the track until it started to cut into a broad grassy area. Every now and again, some people stared blankly from behind the thorn fences which surrounded their mud abodes, unwilling to come out, too reticent even to reply to our enthusiastic *'Mwiriway'* (Good Afternoon). After a couple of kilometres, I pulled the Jeep to a halt and cut the engine. Inexorably, we had been drawn from our northerly course and started to head west. The track ahead was unpitted by vehicle tyres. It had been some time since anyone had ventured down here. 'Mines,' we both thought together. Over to the left, about 50 metres away, was a long low building, a former school perhaps, or a Commune building. The grass was growing up along the sides of the building. The windows were intact; no vandalism or wartime destruction here. But the brooding presence of what could not be seen within that building was clearly tangible. It was not the utter silence, the absence of the birds, the forlornness of the spot which described those hidden horrors. Above the clearing hung the sickly smell of violent death.

I reversed carefully until a muddy patch appeared, in which to execute the turn, praying that we did not run over a mine. Yan was up to the mark when *Blackadder Goes Forth* came forth to relieve the tension.

'Tell me, Squadron Leader,' I inquired artfully, 'what's the drill if we go over a mine?'

'It's very simple, Major,' he replied immediately. 'Throw yourself two hundred feet into the air and spread yourself over a wide area.'

\*

I was at the airport when I heard my callsign on the radio. It was Brimmers. The General was going on a visit and I was to accompany him, representing the Operations Department. I crossed the main runway in the Jeep, slipping in between the landing transport planes and arrived at the Presidential hangar, home of *Canadian Helicopters*, just as the chopper was warming up. The General's entourage swept in, riding their white staff cars, and with mechanical precision, the party mounted the helicopter. I squeezed into one of the centre seats - the others all had their pre-arranged spots, with the General sitting forward by the window on the pilot's side, in the best vantage position. Apart from an occasional chat and a short meeting when I had arrived, I had not seen much of him over the past six weeks. Today would be a good opportunity to learn a little more about what made him tick.

The General stared out of the window throughout the flight to Butare. Hunched over, his eyes moved quickly across the landscape below, showing no emotion. It was cold, steely stuff, the stuff that Generals do when the weight of the world is on their shoulders. While the rest of us were in combats, he was wearing a tight-fitting, Canadian tan summer uniform, complete with medal ribbons and shiny belt buckle. To complete this strange ensemble, around his slim waist he wore an elasticated black belt, of corset width, into which had been sewn pouches for his radio and spare battery - no weapon in evidence. With his flared tans tucked into shiny parade boots, it was all a bit too flash by austere British Army standards - more James T. Kirk than George S. Patton. Twenty minutes later, we landed on the car park of the Museum of Rwanda. At least eight white 4X4s, half the staff population of Tac Headquarters and most of the military commanders from the area were there to greet us. It was embarrassing. On my own, I would have walked up the grassy hill to the Headquarters, a straight hundred metres, but today it was pomp and circumstance all the way.

We were heading for a meeting with the Prefect of Butare and now, complete with RPA escort, we sped along the streets. We were led into a large meeting room to be told that the Prefect was not available, but his *Chef de Cabinet* was, with an entourage to match the General's. The General was nonplussed; such snubs in the disorganised telephone-less post-war country that was Rwanda were commonplace, and should not be considered as insults - there was much to be done by the officials. For 45 minutes, we listened to a monologue in French from this gentleman. My concentration started to waver after five brow-furrowed minutes. There was no talk of politics or civil-military relations - it was all to do with UNAMIR vehicles speeding or not 'showing respect' to RPA roadblocks. The General tried to explain that our right to move freely was agreed by the Government and backed by the UN Security Council. But the chap just droned on and on. I looked around the grimy room. Even at 11 a.m. in the morning, most of the non-French speakers were dozing quietly.

Before we departed in a cloud of dust, a change of plan was announced. A French-Canadian priest had been killed a few days before, in a remote Commune. The General was under pressure from Canada to make a visit, Fraser told me quietly.

Forty-five minutes north of Butare, we turned right at Kigoma and started to pick our way deeper into the countryside. It took nearly another half an hour to reach the Commune and we disgorged from the vehicles into the sunshine, at the top of a steep-sided hill, beside the church and school. Our guide was Captain Tim Isberg, a friend from my days in Canada, now a Military Observer. His Kinyarwanda was excellent, spurring me on to learn more. We were met by a former associate of the murdered priest and, in hushed tones, were escorted around the presbytery compound to be shown the priest's dining room, where it was thought he had been surprised over supper by a number of men who had asked for food. They had eventually overpowered him and taken him to his cell to search for valuables. As we crossed the courtyard of the building, the low earthen mound in the centre, covered in flowers, betrayed his resting place - it seemed an unlikely spot, so close to human habitation, but these people had clearly loved him. Fraser and I hung back at the door unwilling to carry out the final act of voyeurism, but the party moved on, and in

81

following them, we found ourselves in the tiny, simply-furnished room. As our guide described the killing, cutting through the air with his hand to indicate the machete blows, the awful reality of the loneliness of a good man's death came home to us. I tried to look away but the splashes of dark red on the whitewashed walls described the futility and anguish of Rwanda more clearly and succinctly than even the camp fires of Goma. For if there were no hope now, months after the killings began, would there ever be hope again?

Beside me in the helicopter, the serious, intense features of Captain Stefan Grenier, the UNAMIR Public Information Officer, were already focused on his laptop computer. Most professionally, his copy was being prepared for overnight transmission to the newspapers of Montreal, Quebec, Ottawa and Toronto. Tomorrow morning, the citizens of Canada would read of our visit, over their coffee and donuts. I peered over his shoulder. 'Canadian Major General Guy Claude Tousignant, Force Commander of the UN Assistance Mission in Rwanda, today visited the scene of a brutal murder, deep in the Rwandese countryside. Father...was killed late Tuesday night...motive unknown...General Tousignant expressed his sadness and condolences to the priest's family...' I looked across the helicopter at the General. For political reasons, he had wasted his day, a luxury even I could not really afford. I wondered how many more days he had already wasted, how many more he would be forced to waste in the coming months. As he sat hunched by the window, his grim countenance flicking over the unfolding countryside, I reflected on the loneliness of command, the essential barrier of discipline which separates those who may be asked to give their lives from those who may need to ask it of them. At least, I thought, I shall be spared that heavy burden.

*

82

# Chapter 7

The purpose of UNAMIR itself seemed slowly to be evaporating. The gargantuan effort to become established had fizzled out as the logistics problems had been mechanically solved, one by one. On the ground, the troops were too few and too unenterprising to be achieving much, with certain exceptions: The Ethiopians had laid aside their weapons in the South-West, where the population was still present, and were helping the people to cultivate the fields. This imported communism, when set next to the less proactive military operations, put them to shame. I had come to the conclusion, as others had before me, that UNAMIR's unwritten mission was to sustain itself. This it had already achieved, and so what was next?

On the NGO front, a split had already emerged, although it was difficult to draw the line evenly. Some NGOs were already packing up. They were only in Rwanda and the region for disaster relief and had no wish to go the long-haul. The prospect of feeding three million refugees in squalid camps for the next 40 years, a timeframe widely quoted in the press, did not appeal. In effect, this meant that the level of aid support was decreasing. In Tanzania, it was reported that some refugees were starving, a disgraceful reflection on the ability of the UN to coordinate resources. Unless there was a new, arresting dynamic, this trend was bound to continue, leading to further strife and perhaps another disaster. At the other end of the scale, the long-haulers were settling in for the duration. A 40-year operation would cause no problem to the large bureaucratic Agencies whose *raison d'être* was enshrined in such activities and who faithfully supplied refugees from Palestine to Somalia, with never a thought for an alternative. They seemed to be working away almost independently, and the ability of UNREO to draw them together was highly questionable. UNREO provided a forum for the exchange of

83

information and a location at which to discuss items of mutual interest. But it did not provide leadership to the Agencies or the NGOs. A new, vibrant initiative was required to force these people to work together and to achieve something constructive. UNREO's current stand-in leader, Charles Petrie, had been away for two weeks. One of his tasks was to join a British Army Staff College exercise at Camberley, wargaming a humanitarian crisis. The logic which took a key person away from a real operation, in which his own organisation was falling down badly, in order to attend an exercise, defied comprehension.

And the Government needed something fresh too. In any argument on the future of Rwanda, the sincerity of the Government was always a major factor. The role of the Vice President and Minister of Defence, Major General Paul Kagame, former leader of the RPA, was central. There was no doubt that he was the key player in the Government and that the RPA was fully backed. But there was more to the Government than that. The had established a Broad Based Government of National Unity, led by a Hutu President, which stood out as a powerful initiative for peace. In the aftermath of the killing of the Tutsis and of moderate Hutus, the construction of such a positive organisation to lead the country forward had the ring of statesmanship about it. The UN could have been faced with an extremist Tutsi regime and seemed unable to reward the initiative which had prevented one from springing up. All the signs were that the Government wanted peace and reconciliation, within the context of justice for the murderers. It got my vote.

But where was the help? There was plenty of evidence that Hutus were being fed and cared for in the camps, but no evidence that the Government was being put back on its feet. Communications were poor; they had few vehicles, a patchy electricity supply and little fresh water. In Kigali, the Ministries were meagrely equipped and had a desperate shortage of trained staff, since most of the civil service had fled. The SRSG had told us one morning that the Foreign Minister had been forced to come to UNAMIR to make telephone calls abroad, and outside the UN and NGOs, the number of computers stood at just a handful. Against this backdrop, we seemed to be asking the Government to perform miracles. If they had not the means of government, how could they govern anything, much less this smashed and damaged country, whose principal hope lay in speedy recovery?

The press was another factor. 'Donor fatigue' had seemingly already set in, which explained the withdrawal of those NGOs and the aid they brought with them. 'Rwanda fatigue' lay within this. Those harrowing pictures of Goma from the summer now worked against Rwanda, not for her. As the situation in the camps had improved, so had the frightfulness of the news reports diminished. With no disaster to monitor, no tragedy to thrust into the living rooms of the Western World, the press corps had departed for richer pickings. And less coverage in turn meant less aid and fewer consciences being twinged. For the Government, this was the worst possible situation. If aid was short, it was inevitably going to be focused on the camps, and restoration would become the lowest priority. What was needed now was renewed media interest, but centred on the Government and its humanitarian mission, rather than the camps. Apart from anything else, under such scrutiny, the motives of the Government would be more clearly exposed. If it was bent on restoration, as we all fervently hoped, this message could be carried strongly to the donors.

Information was also an important component of the crisis. From the Hutu strongholds of Zaire and Tanzania, it was said, a message could be carried overnight to every refugee and IDP in the region. No matter that it was a message of hatred, invariably founded on some isolated incident, which was then blown out of all proportion. The shooting of a person by the

RPA became a massacre; an arrest in a Home Commune quickly translated into a 'disappearance'. It was not surprising that the perpetrators of as many as a million deaths would seek to protect themselves by continuing the lie. And it was no use pretending that the Government or the RPA would ever be able to counter this rumour-mill. Amongst the camp populations, they had the confidence of neither the guilty minority nor the innocent majority. If a message of peace and reconciliation were to be transmitted to compete with the negative control of the Former Government, it would have to be carried by an organisation with credibility. To my mind, the UN could no longer stand on this sideline; it had to take an active part in the process of communicating the truth.

Abroad, there were already signs of impatience with the International Community over Rwanda. In Tanzania and Zaire, the vast refugee encampments were a security nightmare and, in Zaire particularly, intact units of the RGF sat complete with artillery and a huge arsenal of weapons. If these were not to be turned on the RPA soon, on whom would they be turned? The diplomatic efforts of the UN, led by the SRSG, had succeeded in retaining some level of status quo but the prevailing view was that this could only be tolerated in the short term. With no plan to restore order in these camps and to provide a structured way ahead for Rwanda, the risk of regional disturbance was growing daily. If things were relatively quiet in predominantly Tutsi Uganda, the same could not be said for Burundi. Aside from 400,000 mainly Hutu refugees, occupying camps in the North, the politics of Burundi were complicated by a Tutsi army supporting (or dominating) a Hutu government. Until 1976, the countries had been one and the ethnic divisions and a millennium of discontent were reflected equally in their bloody histories. Violence in Bujumbura, the capital, had increased in recent weeks as Hutu rebels had taken on elements of the army, who in turn had been reported as trying to 'cleanse' Bujumbura of Hutus. The links between these rebels and the refugee camps needed little further analysis. The situation in Burundi was deteriorating, almost in front of our eyes. The exodus of former Tutsi refugees from Burundi to the southern Communes in Rwanda was another dimension of this tension. As these returnees, many of whom had been away for 35 years, re-occupied the empty countryside, the potential for strife within Rwanda also increased, as did the chances that the more recent owners, now themselves refugees, would never willingly go home. Regionally, it was a mess. Some clear changes had to take place if more misery were to be averted, or if any chance of improvement were to occur. The clock was ticking. If progress was not made while the International Community was engaged in the region, it could hardly be expected when the inevitable UN withdrawal took place.

Of all the many factors at work in this complex situation, the role of the RPA was critical. There was a clearly defined character for this former guerrilla organisation. General Kagame's ascetic philosophy had sustained it at the latter part of a 35-year exclusion. Training had been carried out quietly in the background and it was rumoured that some RPF officers, posing as Ugandan troops, had been trained inadvertently by the British Army Training Team in Uganda. Their near-invasion of 1991-2 and the determination with which they had subdued the RGF earlier in the year spoke volumes for their professionalism and commitment. They had fought not just to liberate their country, as they saw it, but to save their kinsmen from slaughter at the hands of the Interahamwe and Presidential Guard, amongst other Hutu bands, and against the Hutu people themselves, so many of whom had their hands stained in blood. It was easy to criticise the RPA and the Western community, particularly the NGOs, were doing it all the time. But from a purely professional perspective, their restraint and discipline in the face of genocide received my respect and admiration. Their tolerance had also to be seen against the backdrop of another fundamentally important factor - they had not been paid for

87

months. Their ranks were now being swelled with new recruits, some of whom had, significantly, deserted the RGF in Goma. If they were prepared to consider inviting their former enemies into their ranks, in the cause of reconciliation, in my view, they should also be applauded. From the teenage gun-toting, surly individuals at the road blocks, sporting their many-coloured berets, dressed in East German combats, bought cheap as a job-lot, and with their feet thrust into oversized Wellington boots, right up to General Kagame himself, there was a cohesion to the RPA which was both impressive and ominous. Their disdain for UNAMIR was barely concealed - we had run away during the war, to save our own lives, while their families were being slaughtered. And if, as soldiers, we were to make any real progress in Rwanda, this yawning gap would have to be bridged.

\*

Bit by bit, I had skirted around these problems with the staff officers in the Headquarters, with the occupants of Britain House, with NGO and Agency people whenever we came into contact, and with myself, during the long sleepless nights. It was not just the complexity of the problem which was fascinating; it was its mobility, its speed of change, the tiny percentage of corroborated information on which any judgement had to be based. Rwanda was like a huge jigsaw puzzle, which nobody had yet tried to put together, although we all turned the pieces over every day. There had to be a key, a place to start and, quietly, I seemed to have chanced upon it. I now had this tiny treasure, this kernel of logic to which I kept returning every time a new fact was added, to test it against the theory.

The evenings at our little house had become more convivial since Yan's arrival. Our conversation was being revitalised in these nightly retreats from the chaos of UNAMIR

Headquarters. And the main topic of conversation was, of course, Rwanda. Yan was inquisitive, adversarial and persistent. 'What do the NGOs do? What is the Government role in reconstruction? Where's the money coming from? How is it all being coordinated? When are the people going to leave the camps? Who is driving the Hutu propaganda machine? Do the Tutsis want a Tutsi state?' It was all there, all the same questions that we had been tackling for a few weeks, and that had been keeping me awake at nights.

I had taken him to an NGO meeting. At the end, when it came to questions, one young rebel from *MSF* had shouted out: 'When are we going to start addressing the real problems in Rwanda.' His forthright challenge took the meeting by surprise. Charles, as UNREO chairman, had fumbled around a bit, but no Agency or NGO person had shown any interest in his question. They had shuffled out, looking sheepish, silent in their unwillingness to confront the issue.

I collared this firebrand before he left. 'So what do *you* think we should be doing?' I queried. He was hostile, defensive towards the uniform, but willing to talk; at least someone had showed an interest in his point. Yan and I quizzed to him for half an hour. Like us, he was reading the situation as one of decline leading to crisis, and the complacency of the UN was making him very angry. He said that many of the NGOs felt that way too, but UNREO was unable to articulate their concerns and they were getting desperate. They wanted to act but had no clear direction.

*

On 18 October, the RPA gathered the population of Ndaba IDP camp on the hillside and told them to leave. Trouble broke out, shooting started and four people were wounded. The camp population was expelled. Two days later, the RPA burnt down the empty huts. On 20 October, the RPA gave the population

89

of Birambo IDP camp until 25 October to vacate the camp. Some of the Ndaba IDPs, on returning home, found their houses occupied by others. Within hours, a rumour had circulated that the RPA was killing all IDPs who returned home from the camps.

\*

The information-gathering machine of UNAMIR and the Agencies was so poor that echoes of these events came only faintly to Kigali. But came they did, pressing ever harder on my conscience. My guts were knotted. It seemed as though, if we could act, it might be possible to stop this situation before it got out of hand. But I was wary. Here, there could be no risk of failure. I had come up with an idea, to be sure, but it seemed to be the only option. It had to be put forward in conditions created to assure success. Anything less could foretell misery, possibly for millions, over many years. This had to be handled perfectly.

Yan was not like most of my brother officers in the Army. He was irreverent and questioning, unconventional, relaxed and highly perceptive. He could sum up a situation quickly and would pronounce upon it just as quickly. If you asked him for his opinion of something with little substance, he would screw up his face and make a spitting gesture into the corner. 'Bollocks,' he would say, with no rancour, just plainly stated disdain. But with this unusual brain came another vital quality. Just like me, his passion and anger at the way in which Rwanda was being handled were major motivating factors. I did not have an idea which needed to be tested against mechanistic, procedural criteria; I was reasonably confident that it would stand up to pretty rigorous analysis. But this was something more. It was a thing of the spirit, and for that I needed to talk about it to someone who had a soul.

It was Sunday night, following one of our regular excursions into the countryside, and we were on our second gin. The other inmates were out. In between the banter, we were discussing Rwanda. 'I've been thinking a lot about all this,' I said quietly, 'and I reckon that the problem is that there's no strategy, no vision. Everybody is paralysed. Nobody is proactive. But time is running out. The RPA is getting tougher in the camps, and there is evidence that they have killed many people. If that gets worse, the place will go up like a bonfire again, but this time it will spill over into the neighbouring countries.'

'OK, but what's the plan? How are we going to pre-empt this? Who's going to make it happen?' He was off again, his persistent questioning now so near the mark that I could no longer resist. Bit by bit, I started to lay out the ideas that had been building up for the last few weeks. They were a bit raggy round the edges and there were still plenty of holes, which he was quick to point out, but the substance was there. I felt vulnerable and foolish to be suggesting that I knew what could be done to sort out Rwanda. Yan was the perfect recipient. He was sensitive, idealistic and determined. He didn't make me feel like a madman at all; he made me feel better than I had been feeling since this canker had started to work in my guts. If Fraser or Kieran had been there, I think there would have been less sympathy for some of the more radical ideas, but Yan was thinking along exactly the lines that I was pursuing, only I had a few weeks head start. I wanted him to catch up quickly and get on board.

'You have to do something about this,' he said. 'You have to get it going.'

'Why me?' I replied. 'Why don't I get someone else to do it?'

'No,' he batted back. 'This is your plan. You've worked with the big nobs in Government. You know how it all fits together. Nobody else in the entire country knows how to handle something like this better than you. If anyone can make it work, it'll be you, matey.'

He had stripped away my last defence, my inbuilt barrier to the pain, the huge responsibility, the fear of failure. Some things were sure. If I did not do this, probably nobody would, and Rwanda might fall apart. And if I did do it, and it worked, Rwanda would have a chance. And now that I had told him, it would be my failure of courage if I did not put the plan forward. The other major point was that the UN professionals had already proved themselves to be unworthy of the responsibility. If this was going to work, we had to keep it out of their hands long enough to get to their bosses, and from there, hand it down as an order, rather than push it up as a request. The SRSG was going to be key in all this. But if we could, I wanted us to take it all the way to the top.

*

I started writing on Monday morning, 24 October. Riding into work in the Chinese Jeep, the words had spun around my mind, waltzing with each other as I thought of punchy phrases to hit the main points home hard. In the office, I had turned my screen so that Alan Brimelow was unable to see what I was doing. I kept some Plans work up on another document, so I could switch screens if anyone came behind my desk. Brimelow was suspicious.

'Whadaya doing mate?' he asked several times on that first morning. He started interrogating me, and I obfuscated as much as I could. Eventually I told him that I was working up some ideas on Rwanda's restoration. My chain of command to the General and to the SRSG went to him first, and if he were not on-side, the game would be up. He was not impressed.

'Our job,' he explained very deliberately, 'is tactical and operational. So you can stop the strategic shit and get on with your work.' I was cut-up. I never thought he would have reacted in such a way. But he was under pressure; there was a lot going on, and I could understand his annoyance that I was taking time out to work on a personal project.

It was essential to conform. I could not risk his wrath. In the evening, I carried on writing. No notes, no research and a clear desk, a one-fingered manic typist jabbing away at the keyboard. 'One finger is all I need,' I always explained to passers-by, who laughed at my style. 'That's how fast my brain works!'

*

That next evening on Tuesday 25 October, the RPA closed Birambo IDP camp, fulfilling their ultimatum. Thirty thousand people were cast out into the night. A few went home. The majority headed south to the next camps, to blister themselves onto the sprawling blue villages.

*

By Wednesday morning, it was done. Sixteen pages of A4. It was not my best work - it was not properly polished. There was just no time.

Yan read it three times and had no comment.

'You must have something to say about it,' I railed. 'It's hardly perfect.'

'It's just the job,' he smiled.

I looked over it again critically. It seemed so powerful on the one hand, so weak on the other. It was hard to believe that a few pieces of paper could make any real difference here. The Headquarters churned through thousands of sheets every day, most of it complete rubbish. I had visions of this piece being consigned to that massive paper dump, being thrown out and nobody the wiser. Be calm, I thought. Be sensible. This was the most important thing I had ever done in my whole life.

There was no turning back now. I was really going to do this. The thought was overwhelming. I needed to get it going, to start this momentum rolling, not knowing when or how it would end. I remembered Robin Williams, quoting Horace: *Carpe Diem.*

I gave it to Brimmers at 12.30 p.m. He sat in complete silence for 45 minutes, turning the pages over slowly, again and again. At 1.15 p.m., he got up from behind his desk, lit another cigarette and started to pace the corridor. I was almost in pieces by now. He came back into the office and sat behind his desk.

'Tom, could you come over for a moment, please?' I went over and sat down. 'I want to discuss your paper.'

'Which one would that be, Colonel?' I quipped. 'Dress and Weapon Carriage Policy? Training Area Allocation?'

'The one about Rwonda,' he said quietly. My whole body was tingling. 'I've read it in some detail,' he said, formally, seriously, 'and there are some areas in which I cannot find myself in agreement.' I started to sag. 'But my overall impression, after some thought, is that it's brilliant.'

\*

On 26 October, the RPA was reported as being in pursuit of those IDPs from Ndaba and Kirambo, who were still on the move, in order to prevent them from establishing another camp.

\*

Fraser showed me in with a whispered 'Good luck'. General Tousignant came out from behind his desk, animated and full of bonhomie. He was on his best form.

'I've been waiting for this. Everybody's been waiting for this,' he exclaimed in his charming French Canadian accent. 'What took you so long?'

He confided his frustration at the way the Mission had developed and although he did not articulate it, he seemed to me to be talking about UNAMIR 'sustaining itself.' His previous appointment had been as Commandant of the Canadian National Defence College, the school for Generals. He was kind enough to remark that he thought my work compared well with that of his former students. We discussed how to present the plan to the SRSG, and I undertook to prepare a short presentation to follow a rewrite of the paper, focusing more on the diplomatic and less on the operational business.

'So, where did you get these ideas from?' he asked bluntly.

'Why from you, Sir,' I replied. The look on his face was a rare treat. And to some extent it was true. Over the past few weeks as I had been watching events unfold, his own views expressed at Morning Briefs had been an important component of my information-gathering. Many others had also contributed their ideas - the occupants of Britain House, the staff and the Agencies and NGOs, and Government officials. In finding the underlying theme and the common ground, it had been possible to mould them in such a way that the ideas of the contributors reflected back on themselves. If it was difficult to argue against someone else's well thought-out plan, it would be harder still to undermine one which contains your own reasoning. The idea I was putting forward was very simple. It involved the UN taking charge of a situation for the first time in its patchy history of success and failure, and changing the direction the country was taking, and I was sure he was up for it. But as clearly as I could, I explained my role to the General as that of facilitator, not originator.

I knew there was a long struggle ahead, and I had to find ways to spread ownership to those places where it really mattered. The last thing needed was a jumped-up Royal Artillery Major, pushing 'his' plan down everyone's throats. I wanted to be in support, to advise and to help the General and the SRSG to realise its objectives. I wanted to push and to guide the thing, but I needed the big wheels to do the table-thumping. The most important factor in the whole equation, as I knew from my experience at the Ministry of Defence, was how hard they would do that thumping.

Just before I left, he picked up the paper. 'I wonder if you might do me a big favour?' he asked. 'May I keep this original, for my records? And could you drop a copy in for the official file? I would like to retain this as a personal memento.' I was flattered - he had won me over completely. As I skipped down the stairs to report to Yan, Alan Brimelow and Jan Arp, I felt that the road to success was just opening up.

*

On the Jeep journey home that night, I spotted the General and SRSG on the tennis court as usual. But they were not playing. Instead, they were engaged in earnest conversation across the net.

*

I bounced down the stairs from the SRSG's briefing room, slowing down as I returned to the office. Jan Arp, Alan Brimelow and Yan were waiting, pacing up and down looking on edge and expectant, like fathers outside a maternity ward.

'How did it go? What happened? What did he say?' I absorbed this barrage of questions poker-faced. 'Sorry chaps, but we've been blown out of the water,' I said bravely, allowing the bottom lip to wobble, turning away, for fear of exploding in laughter. I waited until Alan Brimelow had started to curse and kick his desk and Yan Janiurek had looked as crestfallen as could be, before I burst out: 'Of course it worked; he loved it!' In fact, the presentation had been a breeze. The SRSG was well on-side; the General had spoken the right words. I was

96

tasked to rework the paper for delivery to General Kagame in a few days time. The pace was hotting up, in step with the nightly changes on the hills, created by the RPA. Next step, the Government!

We trooped off to Happy Hour. I felt hugely elated that the week had gone so well. With the General so bullish and supportive and with the SRSG now won over, things could not have looked rosier. Sean and Lynne were sitting quietly off to one side, glowing at each other. I had not seen Sean for days and he probably had little idea of what we had been doing.

'What's up with you two?' I queried. 'You look like you're in love or something!'

They glanced at each other knowingly, grinning away like idiots, before I cottoned on. 'Have you got something you would like to say to us?' I enquired of Sean. He got all formal, stood up, started grinning from ear to ear.

'I would just like to say that I have this evening asked Miss Lynne Goldberg if she would consent to becoming my wife, and she has said....'

'Yes!' shouted Lynne.

*

I sat at my desk on the Saturday morning, nursing the mother and father of all hangovers. I sat looking over at Brimmers for ten minutes, gathering my thoughts before I started the SRSG's draft for General Kagame. He was not gathering his thoughts; he was really suffering.

'This document describes a plan to restore...the UN seeks to provide assistance to the Government...We wish to state our intention to...we have developed a strategic concept to achieve this aim.... we now seek your agreement and assistance to bring it to fruition...I will be meeting the Secretary General on 7 November - it would help us both if I could put forward concrete proposals at that time...'

97

I was enjoying myself immensely, particularly as the hangover receded. Brimmers was in the same position I had seen him in two hours before.

'How much work have you done this morning, Colonel?' I shouted across. He studied his papers very carefully before turning two very rheumy eyes back.

'Nearly three words,' he replied, deadpan.

\*

That night the RPA expelled the 18,000 occupants of Rugabano IDP camp and burned their huts to the ground.

\*

Three days after my briefing to the SRSG, he called me into his office. 'I'm going to Geneva, Major,' he explained. 'I want to take the whole concept to the UN Council and the Secretary General.'

I knew this was coming, and Yan and Brimmers had been absolutely direct in telling me what they thought I should do next. I had shied away from being too pushy but the stark reality was that, without the advocacy of its author, the plan would not carry the weight that would be needed. I knew from experience that very high-level meetings often accomplish little if not properly focused. And in the face of the competition of all the other world-sized issues, I wanted this Operation to be their focus.

'I think it would be very helpful if I were to provide you with some briefing material, Sir,' I opened. He agreed. 'But it would be far more helpful if I were to come with you, as your military adviser.' He sat forward in his chair. 'And I think you would find it extremely useful to be able to get me to explain how the Operation will work on the ground, who would be involved, and what resources the UN should make available.'

98

He looked thoughtfully out of the window. The prospect of all those details was what did it for me.

'I think you are quite right, Major,' he said. 'Your presence would be most helpful. But first I want you to brief the Government here, in particular General Kagame, on our proposed plan, and then bring with you to Geneva the support of the Government. The Secretary General would be far more easily convinced, if we had that first.'

'Of course, Sir,' I replied, feeling giddier by the minute. He was off to London, Paris and Brussels, to gain donor support for the plan and would meet me in Geneva at the weekend. I would accompany General Tousignant on the visit to General Kagame, do the business there, and then hot-foot it to Geneva, hopefully with the Government's blessing in the bag. And if I wangled it just right, I might even get some time at home with Sue and the boys.

I left his office and headed for the Travel Section, to book a ticket from Nairobi to Geneva via London. Then I went so see Fraser.

'The SRSG has asked me to accompany him to Geneva, Colonel,' I lied glibly. 'And I have accepted.'

'Righto,' said Fraser, grinning broadly and shaking my hand enthusiastically. He was in on the scam. 'I'll let the General know.'

*

## Chapter 8

### The Plan in Outline:

**Op RETOUR - Strategic Plan for the Partial Restoration of Rwanda** (Partial because killers in Zaire and Tanzania would never come home voluntarily - an alternative solution was required for them.) [Note: the original name given to the Operation was RONDAVAL, which was shelved in late November 1994]

Identifies Strategic Imperative - **To Get the People Home**

Four Precursors:

- Provide the Government with the Means to Govern, particularly through the allocation of funds from international sources.

- Establish a positive security environment in the Camps and Home Communes, by improving UNAMIR's security focus and modifying the behaviour of the RPA.

- Develop a plan for fair land distribution using local methods supported by a high-tech Land Commission.

- Develop an information plan on three levels:

    ◊ Counter-Propaganda in the Camps.

◊ National Reconciliation - the political message.

◊ The Media - raise international awareness and the restoration funds needed by Rwanda through the delivery of the powerful image of the plan itself.

Principal advantages - the plan would:

- Restore Rwandese integrity, enabling the re-establishment of the nation state.

- Reconcile the majority moderates of both ethnic groups.

- Split the Former Government from its power base in Zaire and Tanzania without the prerequisite of a complex diplomatic solution.

- Undermine the growth of a culture of disaffected exile - 'The Palestinian Syndrome'.

- Limit regional overspill of the crisis and reduce immediate tensions.

- Restore the dignity of the Hutu population.

- Provide a structure for the future.

- Reduce growing dependency on the aid structure.

- Neutralise 'aid fade' and 'donor fatigue'.

- Minimise environmental damage already caused around the camps.

- Provide a feasible alternative to violence for the Government and RPA.

- Allow the UN to take the initiative and retain it.

Some features:

- Fully coordinated operation in a central Headquarters - first time ever.

- Military operational techniques to be provided by a core of UNAMIR personnel, particularly in the fields of logistic planning and project management.

- The Headquarters (later titled Integrated Operations Centre) to be based on functional Cells dealing with component areas of the Plan - food, orphans, medical, seeds and tools, security, water and sanitation etc. Leadership of each to lie with the talent e.g. Food with the World Food Programme and the Red Cross. All coordinated through a central operations room, and to a timetable and management plan determined by a Task Force.

- Aim to start small and build up - initial operations must be successful.

- Initially transport would be provided; as the scale of momentum increases, most will walk home.

- Aid to be redirected from camps to Home Communes.

- Timetable, based on complexities of planting seasons etc, as follows:

  ◊ Phase 1 - Preparation - November 94 until 1 March 95.

  ◊ Phase 2 - IDPs - 1 March until 1 September 95 - 350,000 people and some refugees.

  ◊ Phase 3 - Refugees - 1 September 95 until 1 June 96 - up to 2.5 million.

  ◊ Phase 4 - Consolidation - 1 June 96 until 1 August 97 - followed by withdrawal of the UN.

\*

Jan Arp was very serious.

'You'll have to decide soon,' he said, 'or I'll have to decide for you.'

It was some dilemma. We were trying to work out the RETOUR team and the subject had now come around to who was going to lead it. It was very simple really, I thought. I'll lead it. But it could not be as simple as that. Yan would naturally be my second in command; at least there was to be no question about that. I had earmarked much of the talent of UNAMIR. But there was clearly a major problem with this. They were all white.

'You'll have to give me some Africans,' I argued. 'We can't run this with Western officers only. We need a balanced perspective.'

I reeled off a list of names. They were all the best African officers. Naturally. We could hardly run RETOUR without the best people that UNAMIR had, I pleaded.

Reluctantly, he agreed to let me talk to one of his watchkeepers, a young Nigerian Captain called Adamu. But before I left, he reminded me of the real dilemma.

'The choice is pretty easy; there are only about four. It has to be a full Colonel, preferably an African. You can either pick a figurehead and hope that he lets you get on with it. Or you can find a tiger, to fight the cause for you. When you get back from Geneva, you can let me know who it's to be.'

There was something awesome about being given the chance to choose your boss. But it was bitterly disappointing to contemplate having to give up the chance to do it myself. Apart from the talent on offer, which did not seem particularly inspiring, no full Colonel, no matter how dedicated, would fight the cause with as much determination as I would. And adding another layer of bureaucracy was the last thing we needed in the early stages, when things could so easily go wrong. This was one decision I was prepared to put off for as long as possible.

*

Yan and I found Adamu a few minutes later.

'Come and talk to us,' Yan whispered conspiratorially.

He was young, very handsome, smartly dressed and alert. I had chatted to him several times before and knew him to be extremely bright.

'Right, Adam,' I opened. 'How long have you been in the army?'

He furrowed his brow. 'About 14 years, Sir.'

Yan and I looked at each other. 'How old are you?' Yan asked quickly, thinking that we had made a serious error.

'Twenty-seven, Sir,' Adam replied smartly.

We were perplexed. 'So you joined the Army at 13?' I enquired.

'That's right, Sir,' he beamed.

His record was impressive. From boy soldier he had worked his way up the ranks and eventually been commissioned. His last job had been as *aide-de-camp* to the Force Commander of MINURSO, the Western Sahara UN mission. My final question was answered unflinchingly.

'And what is your ambition?' I demanded.

'I want to be a Field Marshall, Sir,' he said proudly. After we had sworn him to secrecy and he had departed with a very crisp salute, Yan and I agreed that we thought he had every chance of achieving it.

*

Esperanza Duran was tall, middle-aged, slim and dark. She had all the flashing energy of her Mexican ancestors, encased in the smooth sophistication of high international society. Apart from being dramatically beautiful, she was also very sharp. We poured the drinks strong in Britain House but she quizzed me at length about Op RETOUR without missing a beat.

106

'How do you expect the Government will react to the plan?' she demanded just before her departure to the General's house for a supper party.

'I am sure they will welcome it completely, as soon as they realise its advantages,' I replied truthfully.

'Then we will have to see what we can do to help it along,' she smiled.

She departed in a flurry of gentility from the British officer corps, and I escorted her up the hill to the General's door.

'Well, thank you, Major Mullarkey, for your chivalry,' she smiled as I delivered her. 'And good luck with the Secretary General.'

'Thank you very much,' I returned her smile.

I jogged down the hill to be greeted by a chorus of cheers from my brother officers. They had obviously thought that it had gone well too. Esperanza was the representative of the World Bank. She had told us that $69 million were available for Rwanda now, with another $40 million on tap. If the Government could be engaged in the process of peaceful restoration, she had intimated, all that cash would be released.

*

The General's *aide-de-camp* swaggered about with an arrogance which most of us found hard to stomach. Not surprisingly, in honour of *Blackadder*, he had been nicknamed 'Captain Darling'. I went to sort out the details for the following day's trip to see General Kagame. I asked if I could squeeze in the staff car, between him and the General.

'No way, Sir,' he expostulated. 'The General never allows people in the back with us. No way. Positively never.' I was becoming irritated. I doubted the General would give two hoots about being a bit cramped over a short journey into Kigali, but this functionary was being over-zealous.

'Don't worry, I'll just tag along in my own vehicle.'

107

'No way, Sir. You cannot travel behind the General in that Chinese vehicle. He will not be impressed.'

'You've got that wrong too,' I thought. 'He will be impressed, but not favourably.' I resisted the temptation to respond to the slur he had cast on the Chinese Jeep. 'Don't worry, Captain,' I replied, smiling indulgently, using a formality never heard in the British Army. 'I'll make other arrangements.'

\*

My chauffeur was standing by the following morning, polishing his vehicle. In the busy schedule of the day before, I had found time to have another go at shrinking his beret but it still looked like a blue cowpat.

'And make sure you don't crash into the General's staff car,' I warned censoriously.

'Yes, M'Lady,' replied Yan, grinning.

\*

We were due to see General Kagame at 4 p.m. on Friday. The last UNAMIR flight left at 4.30 p.m. and the airport closed by 6.15 p.m. - there were no runway lights. Yan had fixed for the aircraft to wait until the last possible moment, with engines running. The other passengers would have to wait too, but that was just tough.

'Nothing too good for you, Major Mullarkey,' he lisped before switching into Hollywood epic, to take the mickey without mercy. 'The future of this whole country rests in your hands.' If the plan worked out, I could fly to London late on Friday night and have 36 hours at home. Fearing that I would not get home at all, I had still not told Sue to expect me.

It was Friday and it was 3.45 p.m. The white UN staff car was waiting outside the main entrance, all doors open,

Canadian driver and bodyguard standing by. With its darkened windows and crisp blue flag fluttering on the bonnet, it carried a surreal authority in a city where most of the running vehicles seemed to be held together with string and a coat of rust-streaked paint. Behind it, in Yan's Toyota Landcruiser, we sat quietly. My warbag was on the seat, ready for an immediate departure to the airport. In my pocket was my passport; in my hands the already well-used blue plastic folder, in which I had assembled the salient points of the briefing.

The General emerged precisely on time, ushered by Captain Darling, and the whole party climbed into the car in two swift movements, back doors closed first, then front doors. They purred out ahead of us and we followed, attracting a slightly less smart response from the guards than the vehicle in front. It was a beautiful, sunny afternoon.

'Are you nervous?' asked Yan quietly. 'I'm nervous and I'm only driving.'

I thought about when I first went to the Ministry of Defence, more than a little bewildered, an inexperienced staff officer, just out of the Indian Staff College, thrust from the tranquil tea-gardens of Tamil Nadu into the white heat of Whitehall. On the morning of my first day, I had met Malcolm Rifkind, the Secretary of State, in the lift. John Major, the Prime Minister had visited the office at lunchtime and I had spent the afternoon being briefed in the Cabinet Office. Two years working for Great Men had been an ordeal by fire at first. But now I could handle it. Without that exposure and training, I knew that I would not be following General Tousignant now, to our appointment with history.

General Kagame's Headquarters was a simple low, white building, at the far end of Kigali, next to the Australian-run military hospital. The approach road was full of RPA soldiers, lounging beside their vehicles, smoking, their multi-coloured Wellingtons and berets contrasting sharply with the sombreness of their attire and their camouflaged vehicles parked in the

109

shade. A barrier was raised and we drove into the compound and climbed out of the vehicles. Major Frank Kamanze, the UNAMIR RPA Liaison Officer, was there to greet us. He sauntered forward nonchalantly to the General and saluted slowly.

'I'm afraid General Kagame cannot see you now,' he explained, too casual and unconcerned for my liking. But the General did not flinch. 'He's in a cabinet meeting which should have finished by now, so he will be late.'

'How late?' queried the General, showing no anger.

'I will call the Headquarters on the radio,' said Kamanze.

More casual saluting and we were off, back to UNAMIR. What could the cabinet be discussing that would delay this meeting, I wondered. The letter had been delivered three days before and Frank Kamanze knew that I was going to Geneva. It must be Op RETOUR.

Yan was frantic. On the radio, he was organising the final airlift option to get me to both of these meetings. Soon the radio net was hopping, as more and more people got involved in the process. If he failed, I would have to make a straight choice - Kagame or Boutros-Ghali. It had to be the latter. But the General had me here. Would he let me go?

At 6 p.m., we got the call and repeated the whole tense exercise. On the second time around, the gloss had been taken away from it. As we pulled out of the Headquarters, the last flight swept away to Nairobi, over our heads, an Antonov whose passengers were going to reach their destinations. But would I reach mine? There was still a chance. Yan had arranged an extra flight tomorrow, just for me. If I managed to get on it, I would fly overnight to London and have just ten hours at home. Better than nothing.

Major Kamanze met us again. This time, the General and I were ushered into a waiting room. Kagame's staff were all very tall, angular Tutsi-types. The General knew them well and introduced me around. We waited for an hour, rarely being left

110

alone, so did not talk business. But at one point, when nobody else was there, I queried the General on the way they were making us wait.

'It 'appens every time,' he confided. 'They keep you waiting because they know that if you are prepared for a meeting, the longer you wait, the less prepared you will be.'

He was right. As I turned over the blue folder, I could feel the edge of my monologue blunting as we sat in the room and determined to keep it intact, to defy this tactic. At 8.30 p.m., an aide returned.

'I'm sorry General, but the cabinet meeting is still going on. I doubt that the Vice President will be able to see you today, or indeed until next week. What was it that you wanted to discuss?'

I watched the General's face as he absorbed the question. His Gallic temper seemed to rise to the surface before he pulled himself up. 'The restoration operation,' he intoned softly.

'I'm sorry,' said the aide smoothly. 'We know nothing about that.'

It was preposterous to suggest that they did not know why we were visiting.

'A letter was delivered to General Kagame from myself and the SRSG earlier this week,' he said softly, 'and you,' he turned to Kamanze, 'were tasked to deliver it.'

Frank Kamanze stared straight back at him. 'I know nothing of a letter,' he retorted defiantly.

We saluted the General as he drove away. I opened the back door of the Toyota Landcruiser, parked in the darkened shadows of the square and bundled Frank Kamanze in.

'What are you doing?' he exclaimed as the door closed. The guards outside could neither see nor hear what was going on in the vehicle. I opened my bag and scrabbled about by torchlight for a copy of the letter to Kagame.

'Give this to General Kagame tonight. Don't let him go to sleep without reading it, OK?' I snarled.

'And if you don't, we'll get you,' said Yan turning around from the front seat.

*

The post-mortem failed to establish whether the vital letter had been delivered or not, but the SRSG's secretary was nonetheless disciplined and was to be replaced. I gave another fair copy to one of Frank's RPA underlings, and he received it and a dictum to deliver it to Kagame, with typically insolent indifference. But on the positive side, the cargo plane from Nairobi would arrive at midday and I would be home tomorrow. I phoned Sue to let her know. 'Heathrow at dawn,' I promised.

*

We stopped the Chinese Jeep on the way to the airport. In a garden, a family of weavers was building spherical nests, hanging on the branches of an avocado tree.

'The male builds a few nests,' explained Yan, 'and then the female flies into each one, to check it out. She selects the one she wants and the others are left empty.' There must have been a dozen energetic yellow birds busying themselves in the tree, flying in and out, carrying the grass in their beaks. This image of colourful industry and vigour stayed with me until I reached the steps of the aircraft, as I shouted my good-byes to those kind souls from the Headquarters who had come to bid me godspeed.

Alan Brimelow was typically upbeat. 'You're gonna do it mate,' he said seriously. 'I know you are.' I could have hugged him.

Rattling down the runway, past the Presidential Hangar and up over the empty fields of Rwanda, the ageing Russian turboprop staggered into the air. I was the only passenger. It

112

scarcely seemed possible that I had arrived only eight weeks ago. And no crystal ball could possibly have predicted that I would be leaving under such circumstances. But the drama of the moment was soon dispelled as I dug out a sheaf of papers, to write up some notes. Attached to one was a yellow stick-on message, from the SRSG's secretary, dated the previous Tuesday. It was unambiguous:

'Major Mullarkey. Herewith your copy of the letter to General Kagame,' it read. 'Original delivered personally to RPA Liaison Officer, Major Kamanze, at 1610 hours. Many thanks.'

At least the secretary would now be saved, I consoled myself. But the duplicity of Kamanze's denial sounded warning bells. Who was lying to us now? The RPA? Kagame's staff? The Government? There was no point in speculating. Next week we could start the process again.

*

They were waiting just behind the barrier in Terminal 3, the little group of people who had never been far from my thoughts, despite the heady events of the past few weeks. The boys grabbed me at once, below the centre of gravity and I nearly went flying. Sue looked tired, more tired than even the early hour justified. Her father was a little better but still the strain of two months with all the constant worry had worn her out. We drove home to Uxbridge in the murky dawn of a British winter.

'Right lads,' I asked over my shoulder. 'Which videos do you really want to see?'

Those ten hours lasted ten minutes and ten days. As I pointed out the grey-haired distinguished gentleman just moving through passport control ahead, it scarcely seemed possible that I had enjoyed three meals, including a pub lunch, a walk in the English countryside, and the unexpected pleasure

113

of some time alone with Sue when our neighbours had asked if they could borrow the boys, while we carried out the 'household accounts.' Thank heavens for the Services, I thought.

But as we kissed goodbye again, and I followed the SRSG into the Departure area, it seemed that I was always asking too much of my family. Next year this will all stop, I promised.

*

I briefed the SRSG about events in his absence. He was not concerned about the letter. This was clearly a common delaying tactic as far as he was concerned. 'They will come round,' he promised. 'They just need to be coaxed a little.'

We parted at Geneva Airport and agreed to meet at 9 a.m. on the following morning, at the *Palais des Nations*. The hotel bed was luxurious after the string cot in Kigali but I was too wound-up to sleep.

*

It was a crisp bright November morning in Geneva. The taxi dropped me at the front door of the *Palais des Nations*, but I was about 30 minutes early, so I took a stroll in the manicured grounds, the hard frost lying in the shadows of the trees while the grass exposed to the sun shone a complementary brilliant green. In the distance, the sharp-edged peak of Mont Blanc, capped in crystal snow, provided an earthly link to the Virunga volcanoes, five thousand miles away. I walked along and tried to keep calm. I did not believe in fate, preordination, predestination. But from the moment I had delivered the paper to Brimmers, two weeks and a lifetime of chance away, there had been a certainty about this, an overwhelming feeling that it was all going to work out. No matter how often I doubted my

114

own ability to get it right, it always came back to the same thing: I just knew it was going to work.

We met in the ante-room to the Secretary General's office. The level of power in that room, the influence, the cash and the people to command, put this group amongst the most powerful, and the most intellectually sharp in the world. The Security Council might have a great deal to say on how the world's affairs were conducted, but this little group controlled, personally and despotically, the lives of millions and millions of people, and the fates of a dozen nations. They were all there. Madame Ogata, the UN High Commissioner for Refugees. Ayola Lasso, Commissioner for Human Rights, Dr Deng, Special Commissioner for Displaced Persons, Rolf Knutson, the *Chargé*, and Marrack Goulding. There was our own SRSG, Shaharyar Khan, the Regional Ambassador, Robert Dillon, the Head of Humanitarian Operations, Peter Hansen, and the Secretary-General's Special Military Advisor, General Maurice Baril. And there was Major Tom Mullarkey, the SO2 Plans from Headquarters UNAMIR.

We were called in precisely at 10 a.m. The security guards eyed me up suspiciously, as I tucked in behind Madame Ogata. We trooped into the Secretary General's office and he greeted us all formally at the door, one by one. I was the last.

'Welcome,' he said, shaking my hand firmly, 'I am Boutros-Ghali.' There were probably a hundred stunning replies to that statement of the obvious, but I couldn't think of any of them.

'Major Mullarkey, Sir, from Headquarters UNAMIR. I'm here to brief you on Operation RETOUR.'

He was utterly charming, warm and welcoming. 'Please come in,' he said, 'and find yourself a seat.'

He opened the meeting with a blast. Co-operation! He thumped the table. There is only one SRSG in each country. Cooperate with him! They squirmed under the weight of his attack. I would never have expected to see him like this; on the media, he came across so quietly. He let them speak in turn on

Rwanda. Very controlled. Very disciplined. They each expressed themselves clearly, not wasting a word. Superb quality. Pure intellect.

SRSG Khan held centre stage; it was his show. He spoke at length about the problems of the Government, the effort of rebuilding. I heard my own words a dozen times and felt proud to be there to hear them spoken and listened to.

'And now I would like to spend a few minutes discussing this new Operation,' the SRSG continued. I moved to the edge of my seat, the comforting blue folder sweaty in my hand. 'I think you will find that it is a very well-thought-out plan and we must do everything we can to make it work.'

They turned towards me and I prepared to deliver the best pitch of my life.

*

# Chapter 9

Kigali had not changed. But everything for me had changed about Kigali. My return from Geneva had included an overnight stay at home. I had rung to brief the General at the Belgian Village, had miraculously got through, and he had asked me what my plans were. When I said I would be back in Kigali in 24 hours, he had been expansive.

'I saw General Kagame today,' he explained, 'and I think the Government is willing to listen. The SRSG is not back until Friday. There is no probably no point in you returning until the weekend.'

Now, as I dashed across the airport apron in the pouring rain, the pleasure of that much-needed leave evaporated completely. The two worlds were so far apart, it was hard to understand how the transit through Kenya, even for a few hours, could change the focus so quickly. In England I had been detached from Africa, my little stories about Rwanda petering out as I tried to paint the picture for Sue. When I tried to articulate it, to let the worlds merge, the process somehow failed me, and I retreated into the solid domestic world of Uxbridge in November. I had drifted quietly for a few days. On the 11th, we sat in the darkening room, watching the cold wind blow the spindly bare trees outside. As visibility faded in the early afternoon, we switched on the lights and I read the War poets. The murky grey atmosphere outside gave the words a poignant atmosphere. And as I pulled out all my old favourites and let them float in the gloom of a winter's afternoon, we wept together for the boys who never came back.

I burst into the terminal building and ran straight into Yan.

'What happened - how did it go?' he was immediately into it.

'Brilliant hols, old chap. Restaurants, movies, legover and chips - couldn't have been better, thanks.' He sagged.

'It's OK, It's OK,' I soothed him eventually. 'It's a goer.'

It was a Sunday morning and a few people had gone to work. In the Headquarters, Brimelow was the first to congratulate me and thereafter, as the word spread, the staff came wandering in to say 'way to go', from the Canadians at one end of the scale, to the full embrace and kiss of the Ethiopians at the other. Back at Britain House, as I unloaded goodies from the warbag, folks wandered in to say hello. It was a real sense of homecoming, of occasion, and I was humbled at the expectation of fulfilling the aspirations of all these people. It was a huge responsibility and still I had no idea if I would even be involved in it.

*

Amidst the mail, there was a small brown *On Her Majesty's Service* envelope bearing the stamp of the Military Secretary's Department of the British Army. On one page, it summarised the decision by the Army Retirement Board to allow me to leave in April 1995. At last I had what I had wanted. And yet I had so little time left. It was wonderfully ironic to have received such a letter at the beginning of my toughest job ever. There was nothing to hold me back now. I was free.

*

It was going to be a busy week. First thing on Monday morning, I went for the meeting I had been dreading for over a week and therefore needed to be faced immediately - the Deputy Force Commander (DFC), the Ghanaian Brigadier General Anyidoho. He sat behind his desk on a huge chair, his bulk dominating the office. He was a very big man with some very strong opinions and I quailed under the assault of his questioning. I briefed him as clearly and succinctly as I could, maintaining a level of neutrality in my voice which I could not feel inside. He was not pleased at how events had developed

118

during his two-week absence in Tanzania, but there was nothing he could do about it. That he saw me as a young upstart, and a British one at that, was evident in every word, in every gesture. That I had succeeded in getting Op RETOUR right into the UN Secretary General's office in his absence was clearly a source of great irritation for him. Fate had intervened to make that possible for I was certain now that he would never have allowed it, had he been involved in the decision. But before I left, I had a point of my own to get across. Alan Brimelow had told me that senior RPA commanders were coming to the Headquarters the following day, to discuss how to quell militia activity out of the camps in Gikongoro. As cooperative operations between UNAMIR and the RPA were a part of the RETOUR plan, I pleaded leave to attend the meeting. Grudgingly, he concurred.

I presented myself to the General and then the SRSG and proposed a briefing schedule for the senior UN personnel in-country, the Heads of Agency, followed by the NGOs en masse. By Friday, I determined, we needed to get the humanitarian community together to discuss how we could make Op RETOUR work.

UNREO had a new head, the UN Humanitarian Coordinator for Rwanda, in the shape of Randolph Kent. His reputation had preceded him - he had analysed the Somalia debacle in a renowned piece, 'Anatomy of a Disaster', and he was known for his clear thinking and persistence. He had presented a paper to the General an hour before. With Jan Arp, I went over the details. It was not well thought through, a hasty improvised attempt to take ownership of RETOUR, certain to anger the General, since it required so much of UNAMIR's support. Its vagueness and lack of specific thinking was all the evidence which Jan and I needed to reinforce our view that the military would have to take a leading role. The General planned to discuss it with Kent on the Wednesday.

I had virtually lost my room-mate. His engagement to Lynne had heralded a gradual disengagement from Britain House. He would frequently be seen in civilian clothes and came back late, bringing news of which restaurant or bar he had been to. I didn't even know there were any functioning restaurants in Kigali. But there was an active social life among the NGOs and Agencies and Sean was now tapped into it, adding a dimension of incredulity to our bachelor lifestyles as we cooked up our rations or the dried or tinned contents of our food parcels from home.

*

*Brown & Root*, the contractors, had employed a number of house servants and the standards of cleanliness had increased considerably. My Kinyarwanda had continued to improve and I had developed a no-hesitation policy about trying it out on the locals. I arrived at the house that afternoon to find the girls, all survivors of the genocide, and a dozen of their female co-workers from other houses, lying out in the garden, soaking up some rays. After the usual pleasantries and two handed greetings all round, it was time to get more adventurous. But when the weather had been analysed and the excellent qualities of Chinese Jeeps extolled, I had run out of ready phrases. Groping in my memory for something to say, I settled on a few choice sentences, culled from the Canadian Forces Aide Memoire, which always seemed to help things along. 'I am a Canadian soldier serving with the United Nations. Please take me to your leader.' They loved that one. 'Please hand me your weapons,' caused a flurry of outstretched brooms, mops and dustpans, but 'Don't shoot' absolutely brought the house down.

120

'What did you say, Tom?' queried Antoinette, through racking sobs of laughter, big fat tears starting to course down her chubby cheeks.

'I said '*Nturase*', which means 'Don't shoot'.' I trailed off amid another explosion of hoots. They were starting to roll around in the grass. At least I've improved their morale, I thought to myself as I watched them in paroxysms.

'Say it again, please Tom,' pleaded Antoinette through her tears. 'We want to hear you say it.'

'*Nturase*,' I repeated seriously and they convulsed again, shrieking with mirth.

When they had calmed down enough, they revealed that they had thought I had said '*Muturase*,' which translates roughly into 'I want to sleep with you' (collectively).

While I was struggling with my Kinyarwanda, you have to see it from their perspective. About 15 nubile, young Rwandese girls, approached by a Western chap who exchanges some pleasantries, explores a few topical issues and then blurts out, 'Let's do it.'

*

At 10 a.m., Alan Brimelow and I went to the briefing room in expectation of the arrival of the RPA officers. As we pinned up the maps together, he explained what was in his mind. Over the past few weeks, the number of attacks carried out in the Communes around Butare had increased alarmingly. Brimmers had done some analysis, which had a powerful impact. Drawing circles out from the biggest IDP camps in Gikongoro, namely Kibeho and Ndago, he showed how easy it would be for Interahamwe extremists to infiltrate the rural Communes, kill and wound civilians and return to safety before daylight, causing fear to develop and rumours to return to the camps. Of course, by the time the rumours arrived, the perpetrators had become RPA, the victims innocent Hutus.

121

The DFC arrived in the room. He was even more bullish than I had imagined. As time went by and the RPA failed to arrive, he was able to get more and more into his stride. He wanted serious joint security operations, culminating in clearing out the 'bad' elements from the camps. As each point unfolded, as he described his concept for the operation, I felt the ground shift beneath my feet. The thought of UNAMIR troops shooting Interahamwe in concert with the RPA was too much to absorb. He had to be absolutely off his rocker. I looked to Alan Brimelow for support, but he stared neutrally, anxious not to up the ante. While I had been drafting the original RETOUR paper, it was he who had argued passionately that UNAMIR had to distance itself from direct RPA operations. I sympathised greatly with his awkward position, but I could not see the restoration of Rwanda fall apart, in order to satisfy the personal agenda of the DFC. I interrupted his flow to ask some precise questions about what exactly he had in mind. When he replied unambiguously that he expected our troops to operate side-by-side with the RPA against the militias, I felt I had to speak out. Slowly and as clearly as I could, using the most respectful language in my vocabulary, I laid out the penalties for failure - loss of neutrality, loss of confidence from the Hutus, as a minimum, and if it went wrong, departure in disgrace. To his credit, although he was very angry, he heard me out. Then he asked me to leave.

*

The Heads of Agency meeting had been called for 2 p.m. Yan and I arrived early, unloading the flipchart from the back of the Chinese Jeep. The SRSG spoke for 40 minutes. Then he left, giving me no chance to put the idea of RETOUR to the group.

As soon as they were gone, Yan exploded. 'And what the bloody hell was that?' He almost shouted, so that I had to put my fingers to my lips, for fear of our chagrin becoming public.

I could not account for the SRSG's behaviour. Perhaps he had forgotten that he had asked me to present the plan, or even that he had intended to introduce it. Perhaps he had veered away from a confrontation at the last minute, due to some unknown pressure. The net result was that an opportunity to bring the Heads on side had been lost, and with it valuable days of planning. Without them being briefed by the SRSG, we could not go to the NGOs. 'That,' I grimaced through clenched teeth, 'must be something called high politics.'

*

Major Bob Lidstone had done a good job. He had drafted an 'estimate', the military equivalent of a cost/benefit analysis on the methods required in practice to set up the machinery to get the people home. His conclusions, drawn on Op HOMEWARD experiences, were positive and optimistic. With UNAMIR providing high security, the RPA on board and all the Agencies and NGOs pulling together, it would be possible to get the people from the camps into Overnight Way Stations, from which they could be sorted into Commune groups, mounted onto buses and trucks in the morning and escorted under RPA and UNAMIR guard in convoy to their destinations. With more security and a strong reception committee, handing out seeds, tools, roofing materials and an initial ration, they could get home safely, immune to provocation from the Interahamwe extremists in the camps. There was a long way to go in the planning, but Bob's crisp summary of the Op HOMEWARD lessons gave us a good starting point. The pressure to put these methods into operation continued to mount.

123

There was a new kid on the block. Major Mark Cuthbert-Brown of the Royal Military Police had arrived, looking as bewildered as the rest of us had on our first days. Tall, dark and boyishly good-looking behind his glasses, he carried an air of determination which was set in his jaw. It was hard to look at him without grinning. Yan had been on a constant stream of 'copper' jokes since we heard Mark was due to take over as Force Provost Marshal. Whenever he spoke, Yan muttered something irrepressible like 'nick the bastard', or 'it's a fair cop', just under his breath so that Mark frequently turned to hear what was causing the laughter. It was cruel, typically cutting, Yan Janiurek humour, but it was still funny.

'Running water, a cooker, real beds,' Mark murmured before dumping his kit, 'a lot better than I had expected.'

'It hasn't always been like this,' Yan responded defensively. 'You should have seen it when we arrived.'

Yan had only been there for six weeks and we had borne his comments on our conditions, as much as he was now bearing Mark's.

*

The RPA had started to pressurise the population of Cyimbogo camp, near the Zaire border to be out by 1 December. In the week leading up to my departure, they had increased harassment in the Butare area, outside the mainstream encampments, forcing at least 2,000 Hutus to leave their homes and join Mbogo camp in the adjoining Gikongoro area. But their worst action took place on 10 November. While I was enjoying my domestic sojourn, Musange camp (estimated population 50,000) was forcibly evacuated and burnt down. At least 13 Hutus were killed, including a pregnant woman who was bayoneted a few minutes before Major Steve Moore, en route to Kibuye, arrived on the scene. He watched in disbelief as the people fled over the hills, in fear for their lives. In this ghastly incident, a ZAMBATT platoon was surrounded and threatened by RPA troops. Had they intervened, as they had surely wanted to do, the UN would have become involved in a shooting match with the RPA. Few scenarios caused more concern for the future of Rwanda than that one. And these were the people the DFC wanted to throw his lot in with.

*

Back at the Headquarters, I checked in with Alan Brimelow.

'Your name is mud, mate,' he confided. 'I wouldn't go out alone on a dark night if I were you. You might disappear forever.'

'But what could I do, Colonel?' I entreated. 'If the senior RPA bods had shown up, and he had agreed all this stuff, we would be in a bad way. Op RETOUR would just be dead in the water. How can we build credibility and neutrality with all the players, as part of our strategic plan, while at the tactical level we go and join forces with the RPA, who have enough blood on their own hands? It just doesn't make sense. And I had to stand up for this now. If I don't, who will?'

'I sympathise mate, I really do,' he replied. 'But you can't afford to have him as an enemy; RETOUR will never work if you do.'

Brimmers then told me that the DFC had questioned my loyalty and commitment. He had actually suggested that I was doing all this for reasons of self-advancement.

'Doesn't he know I'm leaving the Army?' I queried.

'I told him, mate, but he can't wrap his head around it. Perhaps doing the job for its own sake is not a concept familiar to him.'

I was extremely angry when I left the Headquarters that night. I was prepared to put up with virtually anything, but an attack on my loyalty was completely offside.

'What does it matter?' argued Fraser over a beer. 'You just stick to your guns, you'll be all right.'

'It matters,' I replied, 'because unless somebody shouts loud enough, he just might do this crazy thing.'

*

I had drafted the framework for the Op RETOUR organisation. A ministerial level Policy Cell, chaired jointly by General Kagame and the SRSG, a Task Force below this where senior officials could direct operations and advise the Policy Cell, and a Headquarters element, by far the largest, which Barney Mayhew had christened the Integrated Operations Centre or IOC. I floated this and the draft Terms of Reference through the Headquarters and to Charles Petrie and Barney on the quiet.

Charles had been very pragmatic. 'I think what you are doing is great and as far as I'm concerned, you military chaps can run the whole show,' he had exclaimed up front when I explained what was in our minds. No matter that Randolph Kent, his new boss, was now staking his claim; there was enough of a resonance of Somalia, and the military-civilian divide which had opened up there, to make us all very keen to avoid a repeat performance. Barney was equally helpful. These were two good guys and, with their support, I was certain we could build a strong bridge at the operational level

*

Before Geneva, I had tried to get the map store cleared out, next to Brimelow's office, where I could house the RETOUR team, until BRITCON left in a couple of weeks and we could take over the Amahoro Stadium. But nothing had been done.

The maps were still there, stacked untidily on their pallets; when I enquired, Jan Arp explained that this had been earmarked as a canteen area for the Canadian signallers and the General had given specific instructions to get it ready for them - the Operation would have to wait. I was incensed. Yan shrugged it off guiltily. He should have been on top of what was going on and stepped in to stake our claim. The computers which Major Andy Moore had ordered up were lost somewhere between New York and Nairobi. Without exception, all my hand-picked team members had still not been released. I manoeuvred around Jan Arp long enough for him to give me Yan. A pair of hands to add to the effort. I negotiated with the other bosses; even Kieran O'Kelly felt that some of the romance of RETOUR had been lost by confronting it with reality. Of course, he wanted to see it succeed, but naturally wanted to minimise the pain of losing the Majors Steve and Andy Moore, his key planners. So much for grand ideas.

*

On Wednesday, Randolph Kent met the General. Through the part-sandbagged window of the Ballroom, I watched Randolph leave the Headquarters and drive off in his white UN car with no shadow of self-doubt about him. I walked to another useful vantage point in Alan Brimelow's office. Looking up through the broken glass, I could see the General pacing up and down on his balcony, taking deep draws on a cigarette. It was clear who had won. I waited for the summons. He was very calm by then, and very frank.

'It was a good try,' he smiled thinly. 'But Kent has been sent here with the full authority of the Department of Humanitarian Affairs. It is his job to run the humanitarian mission. I have offered my advice and assistance. Of course he wants UNAMIR to help him and it is my duty to give him my support, which I will. But Operation RETOUR is now entirely

127

his baby.' He was magnanimous in defeat and I respected him even more then than I had before. But what had been a burning desire, what could have been the driving force behind our Operation was no longer there. The hunger to achieve something good had been driven out of him that afternoon. He was to be consigned to a support role. And the people he had a duty to support would certainly not have handled themselves so well.

To have the SRSG bottle out, the General neutralised and the Headquarters not stand up to help on the administrative side, in just a few days, were obstacles which I had just not seen coming all at once. The DFC's ideas with the RPA were another huge source of concern. Things were getting tough.

*

It was the weekly IDP Task Force meeting. The main point of discussion was on South Kigali, where Margaux van de Fliert, an UNREO coordinator from the Netherlands, had been carrying out a pilot version of what we had in mind on a larger scale. The area around Ngenda was a hot-spot, where thousands of 1959-ers had now returned to their former homes, displacing the remaining Hutus and surviving, established Tutsis. Margaux was not only determined and committed. She was also gorgeous. I hung on her every word.

Op RETOUR was still officially under wraps but there had to be some point at which we could go public. Now as the meeting ended, I suggested quietly that we could get a few like-minded NGO people together to talk a little about RETOUR, purely unofficially. Time was too short, I argued, to let the bureaucracy take its course. Charles gathered together a few UNREO and NGO people, and the RPA Liaison Officer, Lieutenant Cameron. Quickly, using the well-travelled blue briefing folder, I went over the tenets of RETOUR. They were stunned. There was something in it for everyone. It reflected all their views.  But most important, it drove ahead more quickly than anyone had been thinking so far.

'We have to act soon,' I proclaimed.  'We have to give the RPA a clear incentive not to close the camps.'  There was some tentative agreement on that.  For the first time, I felt we might be getting somewhere.  While the politics of Rwanda went on above, I wanted to be in a position to put some concrete proposals forward, driven by operational considerations. Would it be possible, I asked, for us to meet very informally again the following day, to start thinking about some details?  It would.

*

On Thursday morning, I was back in the General's office, discussing a number of operational support points.  We had hardly got going when the SRSG walked in  He was not a happy man.  This was not a good time to quiz him on the meeting with the Agency Heads!  I listened to a few seconds of his tirade against Randolph Kent before I tried to slip out, but he gestured me impatiently back to my seat.

'Why does he have to be so difficult?' he exploded.  'Why can't he see the advantages of forming alliances?'

It was clear already that Randolph had upset the General, but that he was having the same effect on the SRSG was an eye-opener - I saw him as the most calm of all of us, the moderator, the mediator.

When he had cooled down, I talked about command and control.  He had very clear ideas.  Grimly, he found a piece of paper on the General's desk and sketched in the components I had described in my paper.  Policy Cell, Task Force and an operational Headquarters.  He drew the main players in without pause for thought, until he came to Randolph Kent.  Slowly, grudgingly almost, he sketched him in as the interface between the Government level Policy Cell and the Task Force, where

129

the Heads of Agency would be represented. Kent had been given a position of immense power and privilege. No other UN Agency was represented in both bodies. I tucked the diagram into my folder. This was from the horse's mouth.

I re-emphasised that the camps were still being closed because we had not engaged the Government. There had to be this process in which they became involved. If we could present them with a solid plan, rather than just talk at the general level, supported by the Agencies and NGOs, I felt that we could move forward quickly. I thought there were two components, a set of principles for the Operation which we could all agree and would be the basis of any further discussions and a Concept of Operations, a military term to be sure, which spelled out how we intended to deliver the plan, on the ground.

The SRSG looked doubtful. 'Well, I will be amazed if you can get them all to agree this,' he responded. 'When could you have it ready?'

'On Monday morning,' I promised, crossing my fingers behind my back.

*

Charles Petrie and Barney Mayhew were there early, with a new UNREO manager, Mark Frohardt. Mark was a relief consultant, well experienced but brand new to Rwanda. Tall, blonde and about 40, he exuded an unusual authority for a humanitarian. The others arrived in dribs and drabs; being late for a meeting in Kigali was *de rigeur*, it seemed. Nobody ever arrived on time, a combination of the distance between venues, the traffic and the fact that every meeting overran - it was after all, crisis management.

Lieutenant Cameron was reasonably prompt. He might have been a lowly Lieutenant but his position belied his rank. He worked direct to Major Frank Osagara, who in turn reported to

General Kagame at the Ministry of Defence. Our words would not take long to arrive where they counted. Alain Sigg, a thin dark-haired, chain-smoking Swiss, represented Human Rights. Wilbert van Hovell from the Netherlands represented UNHCR. Tall, ginger-haired, with thick glasses and smartly dressed, in jacket and tie, he looked oddly out of place among the crumpled polo shirts. He was an experienced lawyer and we had already met. Kate Farnsworth was from DART, the US Government Response Team. She was probably not a key player now, but in time, when foreign aid would drive our Operation forward, she would become essential - it was important for her to be in at the beginning. There were two representatives from NGOs, both French. Pascale Lefort, a chain-smoking wispy-bearded type from *AICF*, which was running camps in Gikongoro and Vincent Cerssard from the legendary relief organisation *MSF*, based in Rwanda and the surrounding countries. Charles had not invited others; although the focus was probably too narrow, I did not want a large meeting either, for fear that we could be accused of going public. And moving quietly through the group, the source of constant banter and relaxed affability, was the arch-confidant - Yan Janiurek.

As soon as we sat down, Charles deferred to me. It was clearly an old trick of his. No sooner had I begun talking than Randolph Kent slipped in and joined us, without a word. I tried to summarise the background quickly, so that we could move on to the main business. My promise had been made and I had only four days to deliver. Arguments erupted every few minutes, questioning the fundamentals of RETOUR, and I treated them briskly. After a while, Randolph left, expressionless. Major Andy Moore joined us from UNAMIR. Another friendly face in a sea of neutrality, bordering on hostility, towards the military.

After an hour, I turned to Charles. 'I'm sorry Charles,' I murmured, 'I seem to be hogging your meeting.'

131

'Don't worry,' he replied charmingly, 'In fact you're doing so well you may as well carry on.'

I could not be defeated by Charles's smooth buck-passing.

'Why don't we move onto the principles then?' I started in immediately. 'These are the central ideas which will enable us to plan the Operation in some kind of context.'

I was cuffing wildly as I trotted out the first: 'Total Political Endorsement. All plans must have the support of the Government of Rwanda.' Cameron was the first to agree and I breathed a sigh of relief as the other principles I was grasping from the air started to be accepted. Soon there were contributions from the floor.

'The people must go home in safety,' offered Wilbert, a real UNHCR point.

'And dignity. They must go home in dignity,' joined in Alain.

I noted the principle: 'The people must be encouraged to go home in dignity and safety.'

After two hours, we had made great inroads. More, the process of making these highest of human ideals come alive, in preparation for moulding them into the fabric of this troubled country, had been uplifting and unifying for us all. We agreed to meet again the following day, Friday, cutting my deadline finer but moving ahead. Progress, sweet progress.

'How'd it go?' I asked Andy Moore bluntly, anxious for objective feedback.

'Not bad, mate,' he said quietly. 'You really held your own.'

'Actually, I thought you were rather boring,' quipped a *Blackadder* voice from behind. 'I'd heard it all before.'

\*

# Chapter 10

Word had spread, as we knew word would spread. Notwithstanding the official silence from the SRSG, the information net in Kigali had been humming all night. As we gathered at the UNREO building on the Friday morning, with a sinking feeling I realised that there was another struggle ahead.

As well as yesterday's participants, others arrived. More powerful officials. At least it was being up-gunned. Charles opened the meeting and this time I tried to keep him fairly and squarely in the chair. I did not want to become a one-man-band.

Almost immediately, the meeting exploded. Vincent, from *MSF*, set the room alight with his initial statement.

'As an organisation, *MSF* cannot participate in this process. There is a political agenda to this Operation and we have no mandate to become involved in it.'

I though this was a little rich. *MSF* had a highly political reputation; it was rumoured that the French Secret Services planted agents within it. Come to think of it, Vincent looked a little like an agent...

Pascale jumped in straight away. 'We agree with this position. *AICF* cannot get involved in this political process either.'

Clearly, the French political agenda in Rwanda was to support the Hutus. It was a clash of French interests versus the rest of the International Community.

Slowly we prevailed on them to contribute and eventually we got around to the agenda. I reviewed the principles so far and then got embroiled in another series of diversions, from those who had not been present yesterday and wanted clear explanations of what the Operation was all about. Nearly an hour was taken up, frustratingly, bringing us back to the point at which we had arrived the previous day.

133

The battering went on for another two hours until, at last, we had established a set of principles and a draft Concept of Operations which seemed likely to gain support from the many factions.

'What do we do now?' asked Charles.

'I'll type this up, distribute it tonight and we can meet again tomorrow to sign it off,' I replied. I was just grateful we had something tangible on paper at last, however fragile. Unless somebody else interfered, we might even have something to propose to the Government by Monday. Only then could the expulsions stop. Only then would we turn this idea into something practical, to benefit all of Rwanda's citizens.

*

We met again on Saturday afternoon. The words I had written summarised accurately the views given over the previous two days. But now they were on paper, to be turned, argued about and fought over. Like a pack of ferocious dogs, they picked every sentence apart, pummelling each other with their arguments, snarling over syntax. I was the butt of most of the criticism: 'We never said this,' they complained. 'You are misrepresenting our views.' For me, it was extremely painful in the detail, but immensely satisfying in the process. Each dispute, each point made, each word changed, created the sense of ownership which the document needed. After the paper had been ripped to shreds, I read them the new words they had created. Satisfied, they sat back in agreement.

'And what next?' Barney asked.

'I'll rewrite this little lot, distribute it tonight and send it to the SRSG, first thing on Monday morning, if that's OK with everybody?' It was. For the first time since 6 April, we actually had something positive and upbeat shared between the International Community. I could not have been more chuffed.

After a rainy drive in the Chinese Jeep, Yan and I were back in the Amahoro Hotel. Just as I was going to print, Wilbert van Hovell and Roman Urasa, Head of UNHCR, came drifting in.

'Could we just have a look at the final piece?' pleaded Wilbert. 'There is just some wording I would like to check?'

Grudgingly, I handed it over. Roman read the whole thing carefully, at least twice.

'There's just one thing I would like to change,' he stated firmly.

I sighed, certain that we would have to get them all together again, to debate it.

'Where it says 'safety and dignity', I would like to add the word 'peace'.'

Nobody could possibly argue the case on that one. Suddenly the idea of three weeks before looked like a reality.

*

The Document roughed out as follows:

**Aim**

To get the People of Rwanda home.

**Principles**

1. Total Political Endorsement.
2. No Enforced Camp Closures.
3. Initial Operations must be successful.
4. Conditions in the Home Communes to be established on the 'Pull' principle.
5. Confidence Building (particularly in security and information dimensions).
6. Impartial Information - the truth, delivered under close editorial scrutiny.

135

7. Return in safety, dignity and peace.

8. Co-operation - between all the players.

9. Flexibility - the plan must be flexible enough to allow modification.

## Concept of Operations

### Phases

1. Now. Plan for this new Operation. Intensify Op HOMEWARD. (This was a political position - nothing was happening on HOMEWARD any more.)

2. IDP populations (inside Rwanda) to return to their homes.

3. Refugee populations (those outside Rwanda) to return to their homes.

4. Consolidation. Completion of re-establishment of social, economic, legal and political infrastructures.

### Timing

My initial timings (as briefed to Boutros-Ghali) had Phase 2 commencing on 1 March 95, with Phase 4 not really happening for about two years. The resistance to this from the Government and the NGOs was immense; for political reasons Phase 2 was thus re-scheduled to start ASAP. In reality, even with a significant staff, planning the movement of 2-3 million refugees efficiently would take at least six months - a start date of May 95.

### Sequence

1. Initial Survey - to establish camp population structures and database.

2. Confidence Building.
  · Information on conditions on routes and in Home Communes.
  · Information on procedures for move.
  · Perception of the RPA as a guarantor of peace. (This to be achieved by modification of behaviour and limited cooperative operations with UNAMIR.)

3. Preparation of the Home Communes. (For each camp in order of move) Legal, aid, security enhancement etc.

4. Security in the Camps - to be increased.

5. Movement to Overnight Way Stations.

6. Movement to the Home Communes - initially by vehicle but later, as numbers increase, on foot.

7. Use of Open Relief Centres - a central source of security, legal, medical, aid, etc, set up in a Home Commune, run by an NGO with UNAMIR and RPA assistance, to which people can return as the need arises - but is not a permanent camp.

**Supporting Plans**

1. Information Plan.
2. Aid Plan.
3. Security Plan.
4. Transport Plan.
5. Human Rights Plan.
6. Land Commission Plan - if a Land Commission is to be established.

*

BRITCON were leaving. On the Sunday, I went to say farewell to Majors Steve Govan and Mike Russell, the two guys who had helped us administratively, made our lives bearable. There had been others too - Majors Ian Duncan and Ian James particularly. Formally, BRITCON had not been cooperative. But we would miss the regular mail, and could not help the irrational feeling of being abandoned.

*

I had prepared all the papers ready to go to the SRSG on the following morning, so Yan and I felt no guilt as we drove out for a Sunday afternoon's visit to the People of Rwanda. There were no fresh vehicle tracks as we turned off the tarmac and I gunned the engine to take the first incredibly steep hill. 'Perfect mine country, M'Lady,' remarked Yan. But there was evidence that people were using the track ahead - bare footprints in the mud. It must be OK. Just as we reached a very steep smooth rocky section of track, beyond some low houses, the Chinese Jeep died.

Yan was incensed. 'What the bloody hell's wrong with this piece of junk now,' he demanded.

'It's an old Chinese Jeep, of course,' I replied. 'It's just tired.'

In fact, one of the Jeep's petrol tanks was empty and I had to hand-prime the carburettor. Yan was becoming more and more impatient. A few weeks before, we would have had a good laugh about it as we sorted the problem out. Now it was a source of irritation to him. The pressure of the past week was evident in both of us as we argued.

Yan tried to hold out some sweets but the children sprinted for cover as we slowed down, their little brown feet slapping on the wet earth. We left some sweets in the middle of the track and drove off, keeping them in sight in the rear view mirror. It was not until we had gone 100 metres that a child emerged furtively from the undergrowth to inspect the gifts. I stopped the Jeep. But a woman called the child away, before moving up

138

to examine the sweets. Satisfied that they posed no threat and were not some booby-trap left by departing soldiers, she scooped them up and ran for cover. Nowhere else on our regular Sunday excursions had we come across such timidity. We had ventured far off the beaten track and it was clear that these people lived in some fear. Perhaps they were representative of a good percentage of the population - the only people the UN ever met lived close to the main roads. But these were the people to whom we had to bring peace and reconciliation. It would need a very gentle hand.

Somehow that afternoon, the shine had gone off the tour. Ahead, for me, lay three and a half months of extraordinary effort. It was what I had wanted but it was still sobering to see it come true. But for Yan, with only a month left in Rwanda, it was all too short to be real. For him, the tour was nearly over. And, despite this afternoon's short fuse, without his wit and good sense, his balance and detachment, where would I be when he left?

*

I needed to drop the paper off with the General on the way to work at dawn. He lived two houses up in the Belgian Village, with Captain Darling and the bodyguards. There was a chill in the air; the mist lay low. I had to stop 10 metres from the front door. The drive was guarded by birds – 50 or more tawny eagles and kites, settled in for their sentry duty, rigid and unmoving. I picked my way across the tarmac, barely causing a ripple in the phalanx of sentinels. They eyed me, moved reluctantly aside, flapped a few wings lazily. Captain Darling registering their presence, closed the door quickly, having taken the papers, and I repeated the exercise, this time striding forcefully and kicking out to see if I could dislodge them. There was more energy in them this time but the resentment was palpable. Every day the skies seemed more densely packed with wheeling, skirling swarms of raptors, their reproductive capability enhanced throughout the summer by gorging on the dead. They were slowly taking over.

*

On that Monday morning, I presented the Principles and Concept of Operations to the SRSG. By 9 a.m., I was in deep trouble. Isel Rivero, the SRSG's political adviser called me in.

'This is too much,' she opened strongly and loudly. 'The SRSG cannot take this to the top level of Government. It is far too direct, and too quick.'

I was flummoxed. For several days, I had been working with all the interested parties just so that he could take it to the Government. The first principle was Total Political Endorsement, after all. And I had promised it to the SRSG.

'But it has to go to them,' I retorted. 'We need to begin a very complicated planning process and unless they all agree the background ideas to it, we will end up doing it in a vacuum.' As far as I was concerned, the SRSG and his staff should have been ready to take this forward, not dispute the details of diplomacy or timing. We were up against the stops; the political situation continued to deteriorate. We needed to get them to stop closing the camps; we had to prove that here was an alternative. We were now in a position to open that dialogue. She was uncompromising and very angry that I should dispute this with her.

'The SRSG is your boss and you will do as he says,' she snapped.

'Of course,' I immediately climbed down. The situation was now absolutely clear. She had been wrong-footed; the SRSG had not briefed her. She was now taking control and I was just a piece of junior military low-life, a tiny bit-player in the big political game. By being too positive, too efficient and too demanding, I had fallen foul of the creaky UN machinery.

When she said the SRSG was my boss, she meant that he would do what she advised, that therefore *she* was my boss. I could have fought it out or gone over her head. But there was just no point. A disagreement with her, handled laterally, would have been my last disagreement. She would have wasted no time in despatching me for good.

I mended the fences with her as best as I could, becoming conciliatory, keen to patch up the relationship. I felt sick as I did it, hating myself. As I left her office, on reasonable terms, I reflected on the next much more tricky problem. After all our efforts, how would I tell the Task Force that our work was not being taken forward?

*

'What we need is a third party, someone else to come in on this one, in order to outflank Isel,' I suggested. 'What about Randolph Kent?'

Yan was aghast. 'He's so unpopular. If we throw in our lot with him, we will be tarred with the same brush. It's bad enough already, fighting through this mess,' he insisted.

'So we need a fourth party, to distance ourselves from the third,' I carried on.

We both looked at each other and said in the same breath: 'Charles!'

We drove across town to see him.

'Don't worry chaps, we civilians will sort it out for you,' he smirked, enjoying the moment hugely. I could not have cared less. Somehow, today, we had to put some pressure on the SRSG to go to the Government. Every minute spent wrangling was bringing us closer to a disaster, which perplexingly, so few could see coming.

*

At the Headquarters, life was getting more difficult. I was a marked man - very junior, and having an impact far beyond that which my rank and experience allowed. The fact that I had access to the SRSG, the General and just about anybody else, was not lost on my counterparts. Isel's reaction was just one of many. The veterans of the War were one of the factions, disgruntled that I had taken things forward, where they had had little success for months, and the DFC was certainly in that camp. But there was a pecking-order dimension too. A number of senior officers saw themselves as potential coordinators of the Operation and were pushing to thrust me aside; only Jan Arp's impassive resistance and the fact of my action were keeping them at bay. I knew that every meeting I attended was reported back in detail to the various lobbies. It was no fun having this lot sitting on your shoulder; I needed to go on the attack.

I persuaded Jan Arp to let me brief the military staff on the Operation, in order to go public and engage all these people in the process, rather than allow some of them to snipe from the sidelines. A few offered observations of insight and clarity which demonstrated the talent just waiting to be tapped. By the end of the morning, there was not just a hum of anticipation and energy in the Headquarters, but one by one, the staff officers I had selected had all been released by their bosses and had reported for duty.

'You are about to become involved in the most significant piece of humanitarian problem-solving ever undertaken by people in uniform,' I told them. 'We are going to apply our staff skills to the development of a unique plan. It's complex; it's critical for the future of Rwanda; it's bigger than D-Day.'

'God, you do rabbit on,' said Yan afterwards.

\*

We had agreed to tell the Task Force that while the delicate process of bringing our Principles and Concept of Operations to the Government continued, we should carry on the initial planning. There was no time to be lost. The first task was to lay out the planning guidelines for each supporting plan, the frame of reference for each component. None of us had ever done anything like this before; it just seemed like a logical sequence.

As we settled down to make some real progress, the meeting was interrupted by the arrival of another individual. Justin Murara was the *Sous-Minister* at the Ministry of Rehabilitation, the Ministry responsible for refugees and restoration. There was much shuffling of feet and shaking of hands as he settled himself down, now the centre of attention. At last, we had the Government involved in the process!

Charles explained the story so far, the business of the Principles and the Concept of Operations. M. Murara was not happy. He questioned everything, belittled our efforts, demanded a much better service from the International Community. With his thin, narrow, severe dark face and his slender, gold-wired designer spectacles, he was the stereotypical image of the imperious, haughty, intellectual Tutsi. As he became more dictatorial, so the UN Agency and NGO representatives became more entrenched. Where only a few days before, they had argued with me about the Operation and the impact it would have on Rwanda, so now they had taken on my role. Charles argued the case for the Operation; Pascale and Vincent were in the vanguard. When the Minister left, en route to another crisis meeting, it was as a subdued, mollified new member of the team. They had defeated him on every point of logic, on each objection, on all the issues. As we picked up our papers at the end, there was a buzz of expectation, a coherence to the group which had not been there before. They were exchanging jokes, and chatting as friends. And as we climbed in to the Jeep, to head back to UNAMIR,

143

the strangest thing of all, Yan and I agreed, is that none of them seemed conscious of this subtle transformation. And out of the blue, the Government had engaged at senior level! We really were on our way.

*

On Monday 21 November, Randolph and the SRSG discussed the way ahead at the weekly Heads of Agency meeting. The SRSG invited me; I sat in the background, watching the dynamics. On Tuesday, Randolph sent out a memo, inviting all Agency Heads to a discussion on the Internally Displaced Persons (IDP) problem on the following day, Wednesday 23 November. At last, a week late, were the formal opening bars of the diplomatic polka. It was extremely irritating to have done so much in the past week just to have to go back to the beginning - and the NGOs had still not been officially told of the Operation. I gritted my teeth. We had handed this to Randolph Kent on a plate. But at least it would start the momentum afresh. Consensus building was not, in my mind, necessary. Every Head of Agency knew what we were up to and was influencing the outcome through a lieutenant at the daily Task Force meetings. We were going full steam ahead with the planning anyway, regardless of formal approval. But now Randolph Kent would have his pound of flesh.

They were all there on time at the UNREO building, a remarkable result for Kigali. Alain Sigg from Human Rights and Wilbert van Hovell from UNHCR accompanied their bosses, Bill Clarence and Roman Urasa respectively, clear testament to the nugatory practicality of the meeting. We were all largely there for show. UNICEF, World Health Organisation, World Food Programme, UNESCO, UN Development Programme as well as a clutch of UNREO people and some minor players, were all there. Randolph talked without a break for half an hour, explaining what we were

144

proposing, hoping to achieve. The audience was restless. They had already got the message.

'Now what I have prepared here are some guidelines, some principles on which we base this Operation. Please read them now and then we can discuss them,' he intoned.

There was silence in the room apart from the rustle of paper. Yan and I glanced through our documents before making eye contact. Within seconds, it was apparent that our work had been retyped and reformatted onto UNREO paper, but verbatim; it was the piece we had already completed that weekend.

Alain Sigg was the first to point this out. 'We have already seen this. Why do we need to discuss it again?' he demanded.

Randolph smoothed over this minor obstacle in one easy movement. 'But now we just want to make sure we're all thinking along the same lines,' he smiled. 'Perhaps we can go through it and see if anyone has any points?' It was a masterful piece of *legerdemain*. Blatant, public theft. And he knew no one would denounce him. His own people would not dare and the rest of us all wanted it to be agreed. I had to admire him for his gall.

As they picked over it, someone came up with a minor amendment.

'We have already had many hours of discussion of that point,' Wilbert snapped. 'Please leave it as it is.' The rest went through without a hitch.

'Right then,' smoothed Randolph. 'If everyone is in agreement, I will have this re-typed and sent out to all concerned within the next 24 hours, and then onwards for Government endorsement.' The meeting broke up.

I could hardly contain Yan on the drive back to UNAMIR. If Randolph Kent had jaywalked across the road in front of us, Yan would certainly have reached across to turn the Jeep at him. Yan may have passionately believed in Rwanda and what we were doing, but he was the mildest of people normally. To see the incandescent Pole in him explode like this was a little disconcerting. He was shouting so loud that passers-by stopped to look at us, as we rattled through Kigali in the Jeep. 'And lastly,' he thundered, 'why don't you seem to care about this?'

I was not at all happy about the way it had been done, but at least it had been done. Randolph Kent now owned those Principles, that Concept. I had no doubt that his name would appear on them tomorrow. That meant that he had to realise them, he had to deliver. And the net was spreading wider. The Heads of Agency would have to accept ownership too. Their staff would demand explanations, their own bosses in Geneva and New York would have to be straightened out. Every argument mounted in defence of the document by them was a blow for the cause. We had lost time at the higher levels, but we were going well on the planning. The burden was shifting; the support would have to be forthcoming. With the NGOs about to be briefed and the Government about to be brought in formally, we were doing all right.

*

In the meantime, there was plenty to occupy us. Arrangements to occupy the Amahoro Stadium, now vacated by BRITCON, were underway. With my military assistants and the UNREO people, we were looking to begin occupation in a few days. The Integrated Operations Centre or IOC, the operational headquarters, was to be there. In a few weeks time, I hoped, hundreds of Government, UN and NGO personnel would be working together to bring about one of the most remarkable political and humanitarian turnarounds in history. And if I managed to avoid the slings and arrows, I might just get to play a major role in that.

*

146

There was no getting away from it. I now had to report to Randolph Kent as my new boss, with a parallel chain of command to the General. Jan Arp looked sheepish as he admitted as much. The General had been outflanked. Kent was now taking the initiative. Sooner or later, I would have to join forces with UNREO in order to continue the process. Our first meeting was scheduled for the afternoon. I wondered what it would bring.

Randolph was about 5 feet 10 inches in height. He sported the most amazing set of bushy eyebrows, beetling over intense dark eyes which looked a little bloodshot. He had only been in Rwanda for three weeks and already looked very tired. But we were all very tired. 'Are you sure you'll be all right M'Lady?' nasled Yan in his Parker voice, before I left. 'Mr Tracy can be a very difficult bastard.' As I sat in front of his desk, I marvelled at Yan's precise catching of the man. He really did look like a *Thunderbird* puppet.

He began slowly, his soft voice rolling over me as he turned on the charm. East Coast USA, Ivy League without doubt. Highly articulate, extremely clever. He talked and talked. I thought he would never stop. As soon as he paused, I prepared myself for a point, but he was off again, explaining, theorising, engaging me in his mental process. It would have been good fun had it not been so compelling, and so wrong.

'I want to use your work, this Operation, to build a model,' he intoned. The word model was long... mahddel. 'A model we can use again and again in every emergency.' I knew it had to be something like this he had in mind, something academic, something permanent, with two words signed at the bottom: 'Randolph Kent.' The fact that he was so brazenly prepared to use me was annoying. But what was really galling was that these humanitarian professionals had had countless emergencies to work all this out before, numerous opportunities to build 'mahddels', and they had done nothing about it. The world was littered with the debris of their endeavours –

147

Somalia, Ethiopia and all the rest. What was the point in all this intellectual genius if it couldn't deliver anything practical? I had no interest in the scholarly stuff. It was much more challenging to do the work on the ground, and let the bright boys fight over the academic laurels.

'No deal I'm afraid,' I replied. 'You can build models until you're blue in the face, when I'm gone. But there's no time for that stuff now. I have an agenda. We have a job to do. I will give you the momentum and the energy to make it happen if you use that fully and drive it home. There's no time for anything else. I need you to keep the politicians off my back so that I can deliver. If you don't, I can't.' I was leaving the Army. I had three-and-a-half months to get a clear run at the most significant challenge of my life, and I was not hanging around for anyone.

Randolph backed off. There was an unspoken truce. We discussed the big NGO meeting scheduled for the following day. Randolph was going to make a formal announcement on the Operation. 'Tell me, Tom,' he drawled as I was leaving, 'just how big is this operationally?'

'It's bigger than anything that's been tried before, Randolph,' I replied, remembering our comparison from before. 'It's bigger than D-Day.'

\*

Things were going reasonably well, I decided as I drove back down the hill from the city. I was doing better than surviving. I was taking major risks, but I could not afford to be the deferential British officer that conventional situations required. I was playing with the big boys and I had to be strong and tough, or they would gobble me up. And the military team had materialised. And we were going to make this Operation happen. So far, so good.

148

I was late for a Britain House rendezvous. Fraser had demanded my presence and I was annoyed at having to break my schedule for a social engagement. My compatriots were all there as I burst into the house - Yan, Kieran, Fraser, Mark and Sean - and in civilian clothes. Now I was really in the pooh. But they all seemed very nonchalant and evasive when I asked if I needed to get changed. 'Not just now,' replied Kieran, thrusting a precious glass of wine into my hand. 'There's plenty of time before we go.'

We chatted on for a while and then Kieran walked to the centre of the room.

'Gentlemen,' he announced, smiling and glancing down shyly in his formal, slightly serious way. 'I just thought you'd be pleased to hear a small piece of news I received today from the MOD. In recognition of his sterling efforts on the humanitarian front, the Powers That Be would like to extend a vote of confidence to one of our number. Will you please step forward, Lieutenant Colonel Mullarkey.'

I was stunned, completely speechless, as Fraser and Kieran moved forward to undo my epaulettes and slip on the brand new rank slides. And I kicked myself for my uncharitable thoughts at being called home so early. Kieran very kindly presented me with a bottle of vintage port which he had magicked into Rwanda, and then the party began.

Our first stop was Australia House.

'Good evening, Colonel,' I shouted as the stream of Brits entered.

'Hello mate,' replied Brimmers innocently. This was going to be fun.

'Anyone like a beer?' shouted out Steve Moore, already heading for the kitchen.

'I'll have one,' said Yan. 'What about you Colonel?' he threw mirthfully into the room.

'Yes, please,' said Colonel Kieran.

'Yes, please,' said Colonel Fraser.

'Yes, please,' said Colonel Tom.

Sean was right into it. 'Would you like to sit down, Colonel?' he asked.

'Oh yes, please,' we chorused.

'So tell me, Colonel,' I asked Alan Brimelow. 'How are you?'

Before he could reply, Kieran jumped in. 'No, Colonel,' he insisted, 'tell me how are *you*?'

It went on for a good 10 minutes; neither Brimmers nor Steve cottoned on. Eventually Yan moved a lamp across so that the light shone directly onto my shoulders. All the Brits started to stare at them.

And then Brimmers said: 'What's that on your shoulders, mate?'

The party lasted until 4 a.m. Just 10 days since I had received the final letter from the Military Secretary, I had been promoted. Just nine weeks since my escape from the Ministry and the threat of a court martial. And just as I was feeling the pain of exposure leading this Operation, under threat from more senior players - now neatly outflanked. Lieutenant Colonel was a rank senior enough to command Op RETOUR - just. I looked at Kieran who must have organised it, at Fraser who must have influenced the General, at Yan who then gleefully admitted that he might have had a hand in it, and at the rest of my friends, and I felt a great warm rush of feeling for them. In the most unlikely conditions and when things looked daunting, it was marvellous to feel supported and valued. And I had been promoted 'in the field', on live operations, the best possible promotion for a professional soldier.

*

## Chapter 11

Out on the hills, the RPA were continuing to do their work. Ruthlessly, mindlessly, they threatened and intimidated the IDPs, relentlessly moving through the rows of *blindées*, snarling, spitting. They were the victors in the war, their people the victims in the genocide. And these IDPs were associated with the killings, if not the actual murderers. There was no reason for the RPA to be gentle, to ease them out, to encourage them to go home. Instead there was every reason to close these camps, the sources of Interahamwe intimidation, the cauldrons of homicidal hatred, the objects of all that Western aid. There was every reason to clear the land for repopulation by the surviving Tutsis who lived in those areas and could not begin farming while the hillsides were alive with their enemies, were sown instead with the interred remains of their relatives. What might look to an outsider to be a brutal, harsh sweeping-clean, might appear instead to an RPA soldier to be an act of tolerance and persuasion.

*

If the weather was fine, standing out on the patio behind the back door at breakfast-time was a favourite part of the day. Breakfast cereals sent out from home in our food parcels and UHT milk from Kigali market; bread secured by Sean, burnt unevenly in the toaster I had brought from England. Above the back garden, a swirl of raptors rose and dived between the trees, a display of aerobatics which, Yan admitted, even the RAF could never emulate. He threw a piece of bread up and it was snatched before it reached the apex of its trajectory. There was nothing they would not go for – even a horizontal flick would bring them down to within inches of the ground. Then Sean, Yan, Kieran, Fraser and I all threw several pieces together and they vanished from the air in a blur of brown

151

feathers and talons.  As we trooped out to our vehicles, Fraser's routine refrain made us laugh as it always made us laugh: 'Another shitty day in paradise'.

*

It was to be named Op OVERTURE.  Over a period of several days, the RPA would surround the massive encampments of Kibeho and Ndago and thousands of UN troops would sweep through, searching every *blindée*, seeking out weapons and murderers.  This was beyond belief.  What if the RPA killed escaping Hutus without arrest or trial, driven onto their guns by the UN?  What if UN soldiers were killed by the Hutu extremists and the RPA used this as an excuse to open fire on a huge scale?  What if the RPA deliberately killed UN troops in order to develop that option?  The worst scenarios were unthinkable.  We were about to deliver an operation which would make the US debacle in Somalia look positively professional.  For me, this not just threatened the stability of Rwanda and the region, wiping out Op RETOUR at a stroke, it offered the potential to destroy the credibility and integrity of UN peacekeeping and humanitarian operations for many years to come.

While the concept lay with the DFC, I found the master-planner with the maps spread over his desk, quite clearly deeply into detailed analysis.  Alan Brimelow was in a determined mood.

'We have to do this mate,' he insisted.  'It will give us great credibility with the RPA.'

I launched into my objections, beginning with the practicalities.  'For a start,' I argued, 'this just can't be done.  It's too big and too difficult to control; the security dimension is a nightmare and cordon-and-search operations on this scale didn't work in Vietnam, don't work in Northern Ireland and aren't going to work here with less well-trained troops.  The

152

entire concept is fanciful.  The opposition just has too long to think through the alternatives.'

Then I started on the political risks.  He argued his case strongly at first.  The RPA needed to be brought in line; the 'criminal' elements in Kibeho and Ndago needed to be cleared out - didn't we have a duty to assist the Government in doing this?  Night time incursions into the Butare region would persist otherwise.  They were all good arguments, but they neglected to take into account that it was not our job to enforce the law in Rwanda and that we had a continuing obligation of neutrality which could not be put at risk.

Alan Brimelow's spirited defence of Op OVERTURE stalled under this attack.  'I'm sorry, mate,' he eventually acceded, 'you're right.  But I have my orders and I have to develop this plan to its best potential.'

Before I left, he gave me a further word of warning.

'The DFC is convinced that you'll tell the UN Agencies and the NGOs all about this,' he admitted ruefully, cringeing in anticipation of my response.  'I told him your integrity was a given, but he was very negative.'

I tried to be controlled.  This assessment of disloyalty was monstrous.  But it was clear that here was a problem I would have to solve on my own, in any case.  Somehow or other, I had to find a way to bring Op OVERTURE to a halt, without upsetting anyone.

I found Yan in his office.  His laconic exterior visibly cracked when I told him what our lords and masters in UNAMIR were about to execute, and what he would soon be helping to plan, but he still felt cool enough to cheer me up.

'Don't worry,' he opined, flipping into *Blackadder* mode. 'I'm sure that the British Army's newest Lieutenant Colonel will come up with a cunning plan.'

*

153

It was a Friday - NGO time. After our initial discussion, Randolph had agreed to bring all of the NGOs on side together. Tonight would be his chance - a public undertaking by the humanitarians to sort Rwanda out as part of a coordinated operation. He started slowly, his own newness in Rwanda showing through as he went over old ground. The audience was impatient. They knew what had to be done, knew what he was going to say, wanted to get on with it. Yan pinched my notepad (Yan did not require such things) and scrawled a message: 'Fundamental - 27 times.' I looked up just as Randolph said 'fundamental' for the 28th time, and received a sharp jab in the ribs from Yan.

'And now, I feel as though I've just given the Gettysburg Address,' said Randolph, 'but I just wanted to make one more fundamental point, in seeking your help.' Another jab. 'This thing is big. It's bigger than D-Day.'

My closing line would have been: 'Oh and we recognise that some of you will not wish to participate. Your exit visas will be issued on Tuesday.' But even in Rwanda, desperate, on her knees, with time ticking by, the politically correct niceties of open-toed liberal democracy had to be observed. And if the NGOs didn't help, or didn't want to help, there was nothing we could do about it.

*

'The Government is therefore proposing that a deadline be set for the return of the IDPs. The Government believes that with the active and full support of the International Community, it is possible to facilitate the accomplishment of such a goal before the end of the year.'

While I was trying to get a handful of people to plan something 'bigger than D-Day', the Government had issued a paper which showed that they expected us to achieve the same objective in less than six weeks' time. There was only one way

154

to move 350,000 people anywhere in that time - at the point of a bayonet. And if we did not do it, as we surely could not, did this mean that they would? Would the local action of the RPA on the hills become official Government policy?

*

At last the Stadium was ours for the Integrated Operations Centre. Barney, Yan and I were disconsolate as we wandered around. The place was in a shambles, little improved by the 12-week presence of our countrymen. The loos did not work, issuing an overpowering stench of urine; there was hardly a pane of glass in the numerous offices which we wanted to turn into the IOC. No electricity. No locks on the doors. The list was endless.

Captain Danny Gagnon organised some chairs and some good strong Canadian coffee. We scrounged up enough furniture to make one room look presentable. Tomorrow, when the NGO representatives arrived, we wanted to look operational.

A few came the following day. There were problems at the gate as the UNAMIR soldiers inspected the credentials of the civilians. There were problems because it was so far from the centre of town. But about thirty people turned up. Some of them were probably finding it difficult to contemplate sitting down in the same room as the military at all, much less finding a soldier playing a key part.

I ran through the operational concept, for the 40th time in 14 days. People were clearly surprised to see such a level of thought behind the Operation. With the support of the UN Secretary General, the moral force was with us. Now, God willing, we were on our way.

*

I needed to get out into the field. There were too few opportunities to see the people, talk to the troops and make contact with the RPA. That essential 'feel' for what was happening on the ground was just not there in Kigali. But while the NGOs and Agencies were happy for the two worlds to be split, with the field workers divorced from the policy makers in Kigali, my soldier's instinct was to get my boots muddy as often as possible.

'Stop, stop,' Yan shouted then lowered his voice into a whisper as the vehicle rolled to a halt at the roadside. Through the thick, untended overgrowth of the narrow field, disappearing up into a tight wooded valley, I could just make out the bright colours of two objects moving slowly and rhythmically but out of synch. They emerged onto a bare piece and strutted across – two heads, crowned beneath perfect white coronets, on slim necks, over enormous grey bodies and legs that went on forever. They were waist-tall. They picked their way across, not 20 metres away, planting each outstretched foot precisely, pointing their toes, like ballerinas.

'Crowned cranes,' he whispered as they disappeared into the trees. 'The finest birds in Africa.'

The *Bourgmestre's* office in Mugina was a small, low, reddish building, typical of the type found in every Commune. We arrived in time to witness a wedding ceremony. The bride and groom were in the *Bourgmestre*'s office; the friends and family outside, leaning casually through the windows. It was a picture of such simple informality and such optimism and hope that those in our party were all deeply touched and we cheered as the happy couple emerged, much to their pleasure.

The *Bourgmestre* was a Tutsi from Uganda, a lovely, caring man, transplanted into the Commune a few months before, to provide local government. He was the policeman, magistrate, jailer, cleric, administrator, land registrar, representative of the Government and all-round dogsbody. The colonial system of administration, so efficient in former years, had all but broken

156

down through lack of resources. The population was largely in Goma, he told us, but there were nearly ten thousand people in the Commune, representing 30% of the pre-war numbers, but not necessarily the former occupants. There were many incidents, caused by land disputes, rivalry and vendettas and many people did not feel safe, although things were much better than they were in neighbouring Communes. The RPA was feared by many of the people, he admitted, but we could not question him closely on the relevance of the ethnic split and its implications. It was just too sensitive a subject to air in public. Before we left, I asked him what he needed most to make his Commune work better.

'A car,' he smiled patiently, 'just like that one.' He pointed at Yan's Toyota. 'It would save me many hours every day on my bicycle; it would be my ambulance, my link to the people. Please can I have it?' It was tempting and I could see Yan weighing up the options, his thin face furrowed in concentration as he imagined all the lies he could get away with, back at UNAMIR. But the *Bourgmestre* was relaxed about our inability to help. Here was a man of compassion and great inner strength. It was impossible to imagine how the Hutu people in the Commune felt about him, but there was no doubt that he had all their best interests at heart.

After he had gone back to work, one of the Military Observers from that sector, who had been present at the meeting, approached us. 'This is a good man, Colonel, but there is no thinking going on in Kigali about his problems. The Government do not understand the way of the people, they do not understand the political message they must bring to the Communes, if they are to succeed.'

'And what do you know about these things?' I queried.

'I am Major Fidelis Mhonda, of the Zimbabwe Army,' he replied. 'I worked in Zimbabwe in this role. I was a political officer when we gained independence. I carried these messages myself to the people. I made it work.'

157

'That's very interesting, Fidelis,' I replied, forcing myself to remain cool, when I wanted to whoop with joy, at such a find. 'Would you be able to report to the IOC in Kigali on Monday morning?'

We returned to Kigali, refreshed and invigorated. Communes as good as this one might have been few and far between, but a patchwork of hope could soon be built up. The *Bourgmestres* needed support, to develop this fragile peace, to return to normality, albeit slowly. The people were well fed; there had been few acts of violence; they were living in peace. They actually seemed happy. If we could create similar conditions in Rwanda's other 172 Communes, we would have cracked it.

'Not too much to hope really,' agreed Yan as we pulled into the UNAMIR car park. 'Unless Op OVERTURE actually happens.'

\*

She was our ambassador, Her Majesty's Representative in Rwanda and her name was Dr Lillian Wong. She was tireless, forever getting about Kigali, gathering information, listening, supporting, advising. Despite the German, Belgian and French influences of Rwanda's chequered past, it was clear that now, largely thanks to her, Britain was a major player in the capital. Strictly, we believed, she had no strong mandate from Whitehall; Rwanda was still of peripheral interest. But in the Foreign Office, under the personal eye of Baroness Lynda Chalker, the Overseas Aid Minister, the role of representative in Kigali had more profile. Lynda Chalker fought the case for Rwanda every day and Lillian carried the torch. Beyond that there was Lillian herself. She was deeply involved in Rwanda; she loved the people; she had established excellent relationships with many of the Ministers. She wanted to help in every way she could.

158

I had kept her abreast of developments in the Operation right from the start. We needed Britain's help, just like we needed the support of the other Western donors. But with Lillian, it was possible to be more frank about my fears and concerns than I would be with any other diplomat. She was sincere and influential, qualities which could help us along greatly. I confided to her my worries about the lack of overt political endorsement of the Operation from the Government and the difficulties we were experiencing in engaging the SRSG on this track, as his highest priority. Immediately, she understood the difficulties. With the RPA still closing camps and the Government committed to a New Year deadline, the potential for disaster was as clear to her as it was to us. She would see what she could do, she promised. It was a source of hope and comfort in a situation which was increasingly fraught, becoming ever more complex. The right word, in the right ear, might be all we needed.

*

Six Indian Majors had been appointed to join the staff. We met as they arrived in Reception at the Amahoro Hotel. Four were my fellow graduates of the Staff College in Wellington, Tamil Nadu, three years before and, spontaneously, we embraced, comrades reunited by a fluke of a chance, thousands of miles from our last meeting. My connections with Canada from my posting there paid dividends every day, so now I could count on support from another major national contingent – INDBATT had arrived a few days before.

'But Tom Sir, you are a Lieutenant Colonel,' exclaimed one of them as they inspected my uniform. 'You are the first officer from our course to be promoted. How long have you been a Colonel?'

'A hell of a long time, chaps,' I replied, seriously. 'Just over six days actually.'

159

It seemed that we had no sooner begun to establish ourselves at the Stadium than Randolph had hatched a plan to get us out. It had been a hard enough struggle, by no means complete. Danny Gagnon had played a blinder, providing furniture, stationery, amenities, including a coffee room, as well as arranging works services for windows, doors, electricity and water. Bit by bit, it was becoming a more attractive environment. We were resisting pressure from the Ministry of Public Works, who were looking for a new Headquarters and from the Ministry of Sport, Youth and Culture, whose rehabilitation plan involved a heavy emphasis on reconciliation through sport. I had had to juggle a lot of balls to get us in and keep us in and now UNREO wanted us out.

Randolph wanted us to move to the Ministry of Rehabilitation, nearer the centre of Kigali, to send the right political message - we were working with the Government. I agreed with this in principle. But the accommodation at the Ministry was appalling and needed far more work than the Stadium ever had. It would mean disrupting the planning and there was not simply enough time to justify this.

Randolph was busily cutting himself off from UNAMIR, seemingly oblivious to the implications. He wanted independence and control, but the price to be paid, he did not seem to realise, was that we would be alone. Just 300 metres from the UNAMIR Headquarters, the Stadium was safe ground. It belonged to General Tousignant, who *de facto*, retained a great interest in the activities of the IOC. With him came 6,500 personnel including 300 Military Observers, hundreds of vehicles, and a nationwide communications system. No other organisation could compete with the scale and cohesion of UNAMIR. With UNAMIR's help, I felt that we had a chance to pull this

Operation off. If Randolph alienated UNAMIR, we would be in even more trouble.

*

I was leaving the Headquarters, just after the Morning Brief, in the usual rush to get to the first Op RETOUR planning meeting of the day. I picked up my rucksack and eyed Yan. 'Ready for the off?'

'I'll be there in a minute,' he mumbled.

I waited. He fussed about. 'I'll be right with you,' he promised, with that mischievous glint in his eye.

'Come on,' I started to get annoyed. 'Let's get going.'

'On my way, Guv,' he smirked.

At last I left in frustration. 'See you in the car park,' I fizzed.

Immediately, he dropped what he was doing and pulled in behind me, maintaining a distance of about five metres, as we walked through the Amahoro Hotel.

'Suspect is leaving the Ballroom, now,' I heard him intone into his radio, generating static by pressing the *Squelch* button.

'Suspect moving into the Reception area. Looks like he's about to make a break for it,' was all I could hear from behind.

A few bemused UN workers and the Canadian soldiers on the desk watched him trail me. To me, he was incorrigible. To them, he must have been unfathomable.

'Suspect in the car park now. Heading for a UN vehicle. Get ready to take him out.'

I threw my kit into the back of the Jeep and climbed in.

'He's taking the Jeep. He's taking the Jeep. All units, be on the lookout for a stolen 1957 Chinese Jeep, driven by a strange man with a dead rat under his nose.'

He jumped in beside me. I started the Jeep.

'Suspect is about to escape. All units open fire immediately,' he said into the radio, turning away as he spoke and then innocently back to me.

I turned to him, doing my damnedest not to burst out laughing.

'Have you quite finished?' I demanded neutrally.

'Let's not waste any more time, Colonel,' he replied. 'We really must be on our way.'

*

Time was flying and yet it stood still. In the strange surrealism of Rwanda, a day could be crammed with so many events of such enormous implications that looking back over it, as I lay silently under my mosquito net, I could only marvel at the pace and drama of progress. The activities of a week were a blur; I could scarcely remember how a Monday had led to a Sunday, and there was no longer the time to keep the daily jottings in my diary. In the frenetic pace of this Operation and our lives, there was no cohesion, no common thread; instead there was just action, fast thinking, heated debate, passionate argument, major victory, major setback, at every turn. I had never been so busy or so productive, never been more in my element, never happier in my work. But the halfway point of the tour was just around the corner. Now was the time to press on, to change up a gear and to deliver. In just over three months, my career as a soldier and the opportunity to provide something of lasting usefulness, in that capacity, would be over.

*

At Happy Hour, I sensed a change of heart. Yan and I drank beer with a few of the NGO people we had been working with all week. There were some pretty clear messages of support from unexpected quarters.

162

'You military are just like the NGOs, I am beginning to realise,' said one mature lady whose 12 major humanitarian missions were etched deeply into the lines of her face. 'We get things done; we don't let our time drip into the sand, in words.'

It was a stunning admission for her. She had objected, at one meeting, to UNAMIR soldiers being in the room at all. It occurred to me then, for the first time, that what we were doing was truly groundbreaking. I listened to her and others bemoan the fact that UNAMIR was not overtly running the Operation and heard her disparaging comments on the UN Agencies with growing disbelief. I had always assumed the Agencies and the NGOs were indivisible. Now, the latter were shrugging off the yoke of UN bureaucracy. They wanted action. They had come to Rwanda to save lives and they saw in us the means by which they could make it happen. Energy, power, determination. These were the forces we had to unleash.

*

In South Kigali, reports were coming in that returning IDPs were under threat. The number of Returnees (pre 1959-ers, all Tutsis) coming back to reclaim their former property was particularly high - well away from the camps, these areas were not under night-time threat. The upshot was that we knew, from Military Observer reports, that some IDPs had been killed or denounced as killers. With the RPA prepared to arrest anybody denounced by a Tutsi and with the pressure building on the homes and land in that area, we were going to be in trouble if we did not act soon. But if we concentrated on these Communes, we would lose our focus on the IDPs in Gikongoro Prefecture. Two opposing forces; too few resources, too easily dissipated.

*

And resources were now becoming a problem at the Stadium. Majors Steve and Andy Moore had both been holding down critical jobs in the Headquarters until they had started to work for us. Now, as the detailed planning for Op OVERTURE continued, they were being drawn back there daily, to take on work which their less-experienced successors could not cope with. I was incensed. The pressure on us was immense. And to add to it, key resources were being diverted to this appallingly high-risk Operation which should have been dismissed on conception. When Charles and Barney asked why neither of the Moores (and increasingly Yan, who was responsible for planning the helicopter support) was available, I had to be evasive. I was determined that if news on what UNAMIR was planning got out, it would not be from me. There was nothing I could do, except for one thing. Re-establish reason, focus UNAMIR on the main event - our Operation - and get everybody pulling in the same direction. In other words, somehow, on the inside, nobble Op OVERTURE.

*

It was late at Britain House. Mark Cuthbert-Brown, Yan and I were discussing the Number 1 topic - Rwanda. The activity in South Kigali was the problem. It was pulling us at least two ways. How should we react? What could we do? Slowly, I laid it out for them, empty beer bottles forming the salient features on the ground, the debris of ration packs strewn about the table to represent the towns and villages. We were planning an enormous event, with hardly any help, against a clock which we seemed powerless to stop. While the RPA were closing the camps, what was the point of planning deliberately, trying to get it right? We simply couldn't meet their timeframes. Next, in South Kigali and elsewhere, the needs of the Communes cried out to be met immediately. Could we afford to prioritise these requirements within our Operation, while they were needed elsewhere now? And the Agencies and NGOs were not engaged fully. They resented our methodical approach, wanted action and energy, shrank from our management rationale, could not cope with it, would not respond to it. So here's the idea: Accept that we cannot do everything, cannot even do something, well. Forget proper, rational planning and go for a reactive mode. Activate the NGOs. Brigade their vehicles, medics, food, water, seeds, tools etc in central locations and call them out, like a fire brigade, to the areas of immediate need. As we moved people, and problems were caused, react by despatching the Aid Brigade, supported by UNAMIR troops. Blitz the problem and return the units to their central area for re-tasking. In other words, gain a response by creating and managing a crisis.

I deflected the objections, argued the points. Finally, the extent of the problem was laid out for them both to see. 'What do you reckon?' I demanded.

Mark turned it over, pulling out what he found the most telling.

'I think you should go with the Aid Brigade,' he said.

Yan's eyes narrowed. It would mean risking everything we had fought so hard to deliver. A real strategy, delivered rationally, coordinated properly at the highest level.

'I think we should carry on as we are,' he said quietly.

*

Randolph visited the Stadium for the first time the following day. We laid out the details of the planning problem. Before we decided which camps to close down, we needed to establish which Communes had groups within them. From this, we could look at the Home Communes affected and decide what their immediate needs were - food, water, roofing etc. Without this, we could not dump a load of people in the Communes. Without this, we could not determine where to place Open

165

Relief Centres, to provide local support. But if the water supply was limited, how soon could we bring it up to standard? Who would do the work? Where were the resources? And from all this, we had to go back then to other camps, other Commune group combinations. Would these allow us to develop an earlier, more efficient movement of the people? The information requirements were enormous; the data highly inaccurate; as the RPA closed camps, the populations changed daily, with Commune groups moving off to other camps, splitting up, leaving the area. It was nothing short of a nightmare, but even when we explained it to Randolph, he seemed detached. At the rarefied levels of diplomacy and inter-Agency rivalry with which he dealt on a daily basis, this stuff was just not for him.

'You have a big decision coming up,' I told him straight. 'Carry on with this, or go reactive.' I could tell from his shifty response that this was one decision he was going to avoid for as long as possible.

*

We took a helicopter over the camps - Yan, Barney, Margaux, who had been driving the South Kigali operation for many weeks, and Mark Frohardt. I wanted to try to get us to some consensus on how we could defeat the planning merry-go-round. I kept pointing out likely options - Rukhondo, Kanyinya, Buhoro, but the shouts across the helicopter always raised some plausible objection. As we turned away from Gikongoro, frustrated and annoyed, I could not help but look down at Cyanika. There was something about that camp, which drew my eyes and held them until it disappeared behind us in the blue morning haze.

*

166

Two days later, we were in Randolph's office. Yan, Charles, Barney, Randolph and me. I wanted to bring this matter to a head, get some direction. It was not right that I should take the heat for this decision. Randolph wanted the power; he had to take the responsibility. I laid it out as I saw it, as I had described it to Mark and Yan a few nights before. The RPA was closing the camps. The people were being pushed west and south, from Kibuye and Cyangugu into Gikongoro. The way they moved was important. Few were going home. They were responding to the pressure of the RPA by pressing together into this southern enclave, moving closer for safety, coalescing into bigger camps, forming new camps, blistering onto established camps. As the RPA moved onwards, so the options for the people were shrinking. I thought there were three. They could scatter into the Nyungwe Forest. With no food and water, they would not last there long, so they would leave for Burundi and Zaire, or die. They could go home. If they were going to go home, they would have done so already. They feared the RPA, feared denunciation, felt exposed. We had not won their hearts and minds, had not even started our information campaign, could not guarantee their safety. They would not go home until we did provide guarantees. Or they could go south. Press across the border into Burundi, there to set up other camps, or drift into the huge encampments in Zaire. If they did this, I argued, we would have lost our chance. In Rwanda, they were within our grasp, we could change their perceptions, alter their mindsets. In Burundi or Zaire, they would be lost to us. In Burundi, their presence might blow the lid off the delicate ethnic cauldron. Our whole Operation hung critically in the balance. If we lost these people, we would not be able to encourage the refugees home next, as the subsequent phase. The 350,000 Hutus currently in Gikongoro Prefecture were our critical mass. Get them home, willingly, in conditions of peace and dignity, and the refugees would follow.

167

We talked and talked. As they toyed with the options and the room filled with Randolph's cigarette smoke, I listened to each problem being approached, turned over and put down again, without a decision being made. Yan kept glancing at me, his frustration evident. We had to lead or force the issue until we had a new plan. The old one was just not going to work.

My heart was in my mouth. For the past few days, I had been turning over an idea of pivotal relevance, something so radical that its opportunities were endless and its risks enormous. It was no good bouncing between the dilemmas of planning versus reaction. Both were implicitly doomed, the first because we had no time, the second because it meant anarchy, deliberately creating a situation which we could no longer control. Worse, Randolph would not choose. In such situations, bureaucrats carry out a third action - do nothing - and for our Operation, that had to be the worst option of all. I needed to offer something so novel and full of possibilities, that he would not be able to reject it.

It was my Mountbatten gamble: Damned if you do, damned if you don't. I really just wanted to sit there quietly and let someone else take the pressure. But as the arguments went round and round, there was no point in kidding myself. Knowing that I was walking on the thinnest ice imaginable, I decided to offer an alternative. I had been making the running up to now anyway, I reasoned. Whatever goes wrong, they will blame me. I might as well do something I believe in.

'It strikes me that there is another way to crack this problem,' I opened. In the stillness of the room, I went out on a limb, one more time.

*

After the 9 a.m. meeting in the Stadium, I got the team together.

'At a meeting at UNREO last night,' I began, 'we decided that it was going to be impossible to get the planning information together in time to activate this plan. So we are going to write the plan without the planning information. We are going to work out a camp closure schedule which meets our aspirations and the Government's timetable and we are bloody well going to expedite it. We are going to empty the camps peacefully, get the people home and sort the place out, and we are going to do it just as soon as the Government says we can start.'

It was an extraordinary atmosphere. The Government people could not believe, after weeks of meetings and prevarications and hand wringing and scrabbling about for non-existent statistics, that we were actually going to go ahead. As I watched their faces, it was a moment of sweet triumph. At last, we were taking the initiative. Now they would have to fall in with our plans, not the other way around.

I laid out several sheets of 'butcher' paper from the flip chart and, with Margaux's help, stuck them together. It was now 2 feet wide and 10 feet long. Barney and Andy Moore were on the map; the others had piles of camp statistics, populations, feeding figures, Commune groups – inaccurate, but what the hell?

'Where are we going to start?' asked Barney.

'Cyanika,' I replied. 'Close to the road. Thirty thousand people. Near to the UN base in Gikongoro.'

There was no dissent. After weeks of agonising, they accepted this unilateral decision with obvious relief. I could have gone for Kibeho/Ndago - that would have completely shut down Op OVERTURE, but it was too complex to undertake as a first objective and we had to show success, or the whole plan would fall down. Besides, I did not want our plan to get wrapped up in OVERTURE. We chanted out the figures, estimated time to empty each camp, truck capacities, Overnight Way Stations, Open Relief Centres, every fact and statistic, just being thrown into one pot. As we finished with each camp and moved onto another, I drew a line of progress against time

169

across the length of the paper, a massive project chart, on which we planned to change the lives of 350,000 Rwandese.

Within two hours, it was done - about 10 feet of paper with a mass of lines, dates, capacities, all highly impressive, all very flaky in the analysis.

Charles was impressed. 'I'm impressed,' he said.

'So you should be, ' I replied. 'How long would it take you to get political agreement, if we decided that we had to go?' I asked.

'About one day,' he replied, smiling. He had weighed it all up from the night before.

'And how long would it take your people to get ready from that point?' I demanded. UNREO were responsible for the humanitarian effort as I took every opportunity to remind them.

'Two weeks.'

I drew two lines backwards from D-Day. The plan was complete. The neatest piece of the whole idea was that we would present the plan to the Government and invite ministers to give the order to go into action. Once presented with the plan, they could hardly back off, or claim that we were not prepared to act quickly. But in giving the order to go, they would take ownership and be responsible with us, for the first time, for the collective outcome.

'Right everybody, from now on, we are at 15 days notice to begin this Operation. Let's get cracking.'

We were not ready. We were miles from being ready. But I was determined about one thing. On D-Day, however soon, the skies would be full of helicopters, the ground crawling with UNAMIR troops and NGO vehicles. The world's press would be there. The Operation would look fantastic and people would definitely go home. We would then have to work like dogs to hold it together, for what would happen on the day after that, was anybody's guess.

*

170

## Chapter 12

Yan was upset. 'So what have you done?' he demanded. I showed him the roll of butcher paper. The planning for Op OVERTURE was now taking him away at unpredictable times - there was no way I could have chased after him just to keep him in the loop. 'Doesn't look as though you needed me then,' he said quietly as he looked over the work.

'Well you should have come,' I answered a bit too harshly. I was angry that he was now adding to the pressure when I could have done without it, miserable that he had not shared in the excitement of taking the initiative. In just three weeks, he could go home, UN medal and all, and leave me to it.

\*

Just at the precise moment that we had taken the initiative, our capacity to deliver it was drained to the bottom of the pot. Fidelis Mhonda and Adam Adamu were working tirelessly to set up the operations room in the IOC, but virtually everyone else had disappeared. The other UNAMIR officers were taken away to work on Op OVERTURE. Our plan was still not approved and so, bored with the inaction, the NGOs felt no need to rush. At one 9 a.m. meeting, there was only the UNREO people, Fidelis, Adam and myself. The others were late or maybe they just weren't coming.

\*

We should have been out winning the hearts and minds of the Hutus we wanted to encourage to go home, by telling them what was going on, by informing them of the conditions we could provide for them in their Communes, by offering them hope of peaceful reconciliation. Chantale de Montigny, a volatile Quebecer from UNREO, whose task this was, had been

171

trying to get things moving for days, to no avail. In early December, she disappeared. She had scrounged up some rations from contacts in UNAMIR, borrowed a couple of vehicles and loudhailers from friendly NGOs, convinced some officials from the Ministry of Rehabilitation and the Ministry of Justice to join her for a few days, and they had gone. To Gikongoro. Just like that.

'So is this an official UNREO expedition?' I asked Barney.

'Well sort of,' he answered cautiously. Chantale had clearly not received formal UNREO sanction for it. It was brilliant, heroic, audacious leadership which gave us all a shot in the arm.

\*

I spoke to Sue, promising that I would be home for New Year. The RAF were flying a plane out of Nairobi on 29 December. The strain of my absence, the certainty of my leaving the Army, her father's illness, were all taking their toll. If anybody had to get home that New Year, it was me. And I would not be alone. Most of the humanitarians and many of the military staff officers would be going on leave too - the pressure of Rwanda could not be absorbed indefinitely and people might as well get away during the holiday period. We had to hope that the Government would not say 'go' to our plan until January.

\*

It was nicknamed the Gang of Five. Around the General, there were his advisers: The DFC, Brigadier Henry Anyidoho, Colonel Jan Arp, Colonel Kieran O'Kelly and Colonel Wayne Ramsey. Lieutenant Colonel Fraser Haddow was a powerful fringe player. I needed to cast doubt on Op OVERTURE, introduce fear that it was too dangerous for the UN to carry it out. Piecemeal, I decided, was the only way to do it.

172

Fraser was about to set off on a short biking trip round Kenya. He had brought his mountain bike on the cargo plane, blagged on board as I had done with my essentials. Now as he packed his kit and described his route, it seemed clear that nobody had ever done this before, or would ever dream of it. The chances of a lone white man cycling safely through crime-ridden Kenya intact were virtually nil. But Fraser was a Royal Marine, no mere mortal.

'Before you go,' I started one evening, just as his preparations were drawing to a close, 'I wonder if you might do something simple for me?'

'What's that?' he murmured under his breath, as he traced a route on his map of East Africa.

'Put the kybosh on Op OVERTURE.'

'Not that again,' he groaned. It had been the subject of countless disloyal discussions in Britain House, over the past few days.

We discussed it again, this time more forcefully, one on one. It did not take much to convince him. His clear mind was well focussed on the awful possibilities so I made it a moral thing for him to come to terms with.

'What do you want me to do?' he sighed eventually. It was clear that I would continue to harass him until he agreed to help.

'Talk to the General,' I begged. 'Quietly. Get him to work it out. Don't leave it to the Gang of Five - the DFC always browbeats everyone.'

'All right,' he promised. 'But this is the last time I save a country and the reputation of the world's only truly international military organisation for you. OK?'

Two days later, he grabbed me in the corridor of the Amahoro Hotel. 'Cracked it,' he assured me.

'You must be joking,' I exclaimed. 'You mean you've saved a whole country in just two days?'

173

Fraser was certain. 'I've talked to the General long and hard, and never mentioned your name. I went through the pooh-traps, in graphic detail and he's really bought in. He's going to put a stop to it at the next Gang of Five, on Thursday.'

I was overjoyed. I could never have believed it possible. It was too good to be true.

\*

And it was. On Thursday, a disconsolate Fraser found me again. 'All bets are off. He's changed his mind.'

'You mean the DFC's pushing him further,' I fumed.

'No comment,' said Fraser professionally. 'There's nothing we can do. They're dead set on it. Now it's a matter of losing credibility with the RPA and you know the DFC won't have that. He was here during the war and finds it difficult to look them in the eye.'

\*

Kieran knew what was coming when I ambushed him in the kitchen of Britain House.

'All right, I'll try,' he promised, resignedly.

This time it would be a full-frontal attack - at the next Gang of Five. Kieran was a man of principle and I knew he would not cave in without a robust defence. With Jan Arp away, the Gang would not be too flexible but with Brimelow (standing in for Jan Arp) also twitchy about what he was expected to do and Fraser in the room, I thought we had a fighting chance. Wayne Ramsey was bound to be on side, if his opinion was canvassed. He was a medic and had to vote for the humanitarian cause; in any case, his tactical voice was not loud, since he was not a combat soldier. I felt confident that Kieran's patient analysis would carve up the DFC.

Kieran returned defeated. He was not happy. 'Your arguments were heard, I promise you,' he said. 'But it's gone too far, too fast. There's no turning back and I just can't defeat the momentum with words. It's going to happen.'

In just 10 days time, Op OVERTURE would take place. I had little to lose personally - my discharge papers were through. I could be sent home in disgrace, but somehow I doubted that anybody could get away with that while Kieran still championed me and while Britain House was such a powerful voice in the Headquarters. Tempted many times, inevitably on some matter of principle, it was time, I now felt, to fall on my sword.

\*

The moment Jan Arp returned from leave, I was in his office. I told him the problem, spelled out my reservations, explained the disloyalty thing with the DFC. In Jan Arp, I had another champion. 'Get it on paper,' he agreed. 'That will make it very difficult to avoid the threat of an inquest, if it all goes wrong. I would be only too happy to receive your formal advice as the Officer In Command of Op RETOUR.'

In Britain House, they were not impressed that Saturday night. 'You've done enough,' sighed Yan. 'Can't you just see they're going to go through with this, whatever you say. You've tried everything. Now, if you carry on carping, they'll get you and that means us and that means the *real* Operation. Leave it now'.

Fraser and Kieran were even more direct. They had gone in to bat for me. Now it looked to them as though I was being disloyal to the General's wishes after all. 'The military decision is made,' Kieran insisted. 'You can't just dispute the General's ability to make this type of judgement.'

They left for an NGO party and I was conscious that I was pushing my friendships to the limit, as I settled in behind my

175

laptop for an evening's toil. By midnight, it was done. There was no ambiguity. The implications of Op OVERTURE were laid out for a blind man to see and it seemed impossible that the General could now avoid them. I had just 48 hours to turn this around. He had made his leave plans months before and he would be in South Africa when the Operation went in. There were immense leadership implications here and I hoped to prey on his guilt at being away at such a crucial time. The case was strong; the options clear. Critically, I did not ask him to stop the Operation - just involve the NGOs and Agencies so that their considerations could be addressed. *De facto* this would stop the madness, I hoped. Of all the stupidities of the Operation, the fact that it would take place without the prior knowledge of the UN Agencies and NGOs was central. Our trust, our relationship with them, depended on this openness. Without it, the future of the Mission was at stake.

\*

The paradoxes were not lost on me. The Deputy Chief of Staff (Operations), Colonel Jan Arp, was prepared to help me out - in theory he should have been completely supportive of the Operation. Kieran and Fraser, Alan Brimelow in his critical position as the author of the plan, and somewhere hidden from view, the General himself, were all prepared to put this lunacy aside, but somehow, it had not happened yet. Now, surely, the arguments would strike the mark.

It was two tense days before Jan Arp got back to me. The General had considered the points and had apparently consulted the SRSG but, eventually, he had delegated the decision to the DFC. Now, it was really over. There was nothing else I could do without actually being disloyal - and that was just not possible. As the most junior Lieutenant Colonel in UNAMIR, I had had a good run for my money. I had forced the issue far beyond the point of military etiquette and there was no point in pressing on. I could never go outside UNAMIR to gain further support - that was beyond the pale. From this point on, the only course of action was, quite literally, prayer.

*

We had been invited to a US Embassy party. The Heads of Agencies and the ambassadors were all there. Yan and I went out amongst them. We told them about Op RETOUR, how it matched the Government's plans, how it would take the heat out of the situation. General Kagame was on a tour of Western countries. One by one, we hit on the ambassadors whose countries he would visit. Pressurise him there, we begged. Stop him from coming back to Rwanda with anything less than a firm belief that the International Community meant business and we could deliver. David Rawson was an excellent host and the atmosphere was positive, even hopeful. I met Yan at the door on the way out. 'Everyone's promised to help,' he confided. 'I really think we've got somewhere.' There had been too many disappointments in the past few weeks to give me a huge feeling of comfort. But the fact that we were prepared to launch Op RETOUR had been a major surprise to most of these people. They were animated by the opportunity to take action. As we pulled out, Lillian Wong gave us the thumbs up. She would be talking to the British Foreign Office in the morning. General Kagame would walk straight into an especially warm British reception.

*

Kieran left us early in December. We all liked him and had valued his conviviality, and his tremendous support for me and Op RETOUR, so it was a major letdown to see him go. Yan was about to leave. Fraser had negotiated an early departure in January. That Kieran, as our senior officer, would be home for

Christmas was very depressing. We said farewell to him on a wet evening at the bar. The atmosphere was empty; there was no joy in the adventure any more.

We saw him off at the airport. He was a good man and had done much to enhance the reputation of the British Army. He turned and waved as he walked into Departures. And we drove slowly back to the Headquarters in the pouring rain.

*

During the Morning Brief, I noticed a 1:50,000 scale map stuck on the larger map on the wall. Even from the back row, I could make out the outline of the topography and the 'goose-eggs' which showed the locations of the companies during a phase of Op OVERTURE. This was a monstrous breach of security. With the room full of UN Agency civilians, it could not have shown up the inadequacies of the UN military more clearly. In the British Army, it would quite simply have been a sackable offence.

After the briefing, Charles Petrie and Kate Farnsworth breezed into the Plans office. 'That map,' said Kate, waving at the wall behind. 'The one showing the IDP camps. Can we have a copy?'

I felt numb as Brimmers went pale and started to mumble. Somehow, he managed to wriggle out of it. 'That's just a communications exercise,' he stumbled. 'Nothing very relevant.' They shot questioning looks at me as they went out. I remained impassive. Nobody was going to accuse me of breaking the tryst.

Major Steve Moore burst in a few minutes later. 'Have you seen what these dorks have done?' he demanded. 'Look at the distribution list for the Administration Order.' We looked over the last page of the document. Another hopeless blunder - *Brown & Root*, the civilian contractor had been included in the distribution. We thumbed through the pages to find a tiny

178

paragraph which described how *Brown & Root* were to set up a water bowser at Kibeho Church at 1000 hours on the first day of the Operation. A staff officer had sent them a copy of this secret document! With several hundred foreign and local staff working for *Brown & Root*, it seemed unlikely that Op OVERTURE would be a secret much beyond nightfall. The grim truth was despite these horrendous lapses of security, it would be me who the DFC would blame if word got out, assuming I had briefed the Agencies and NGOs.

'So are you chaps going to tell the DFC about this little development?' I asked cheerfully. 'Or would you like me to?'

\*

We were driving in the Chinese Jeep, out of the Belgian Village towards the Parliament building, when Yan grabbed my arm.

'Stop,' he shouted through gritted teeth. I pulled up and turned off the engine. 'Look,' he said quietly, as a large grey shape swooped in from across the valley, crossed the track 50 metres ahead of us and settled onto a sandy hillock to our left, about a hundred metres away.

'Tell me what you see. Tell me what he's doing.'

I focused Yan's binoculars on the large grey bird. As he came into relief, he looked enormous, but the hooked yellow beak made him look even more impressive.

'Some sort of eagle, I guess.'

The bird was walking around on the sand hills, his shoulders moving as he marched about, like those of a nightclub bouncer. But every now and again, he stooped to look into the burrows in the sides of the hills and then manoeuvred himself so that he could stick one talon in to scratch around, before moving on to the next. With this brilliant pair of binoculars in my hands, I was able to join him, to check out the burrows, to see what he saw. I described it all to Yan

179

'Here,' he said. 'Get a look at this.' I studied the page of his bird book briefly.

'Right then,' I said simply. 'It's a harrier hawk.'

As soon as I uttered his name, the bird took off. He glided over the Jeep and down into the valley. Effortlessly, he twitched the edges of his wings to catch a thermal, before beginning to circle silently up and up, until even through the binoculars, he became only a tiny black speck. Since take-off had been achieved, this whole manoeuvre had required not one wing beat.

'So what did you think of that?' demanded Yan triumphantly.

I quickly invented some clever retort but his fervour demanded honesty. 'I thought it was bloody marvellous,' I admitted.

*

Squadron Leader Carl Dixon had arrived, Yan's replacement, bringing nearer the moment of Yan's departure. He was tall and angular, with a very large nose. 'We call him 'Big Nose' in the RAF,' confided Yan. We all looked pointedly at Yan's enormous conk.

Carl inspected the house.

'Very comfortable,' he pronounced.

'It hasn't always been like this,' replied Mark Cuthbert-Brown. 'You should have seen it when we arrived.'

Carl was eccentric. He was the only person of UNAMIR's 6,500 personnel who did not wear a UN cap-badge. Instead, he had sown his RAF officer's badge onto his blue beret. This was slightly embarrassing for us in Britain House, especially Yan, mitigated wholly by the pleasure returned in-kind by the glare he received daily from the DFC, when he spotted Carl's headdress. Carl was sure to make his mark.

180

Randolph was caught out. The NGO meeting had started well on the Friday night. But it stalled as the startling news came in from Gikongoro, brought to the meeting at a rush: The RPA were going to close the camps of Kibeho and Ndago next week. And next week was Op OVERTURE. The RPA were finally showing their true colours and there was nothing UNAMIR could do to avoid the situation. At last, I sighed with relief in the smoke-filled room, reason will prevail.

'What shall we do?' he quizzed as soon as the meeting had broken up, abuzz with excitement and the fear of a major crisis.

'We must go to the SRSG' I argued. 'He must see the Government now and put a stop to this.'

'I will go to Gikongoro myself,' he promised. 'With the Minister of Rehabilitation. Together we can prevent this disaster.'

And disaster it would be. With 120,000 people in both camps, scattered before the bayonets of the RPA, it would be the crisis we had tried to prevent over so many weeks, delivered more swiftly and brutally than anyone could have envisaged.

Randolph could have no idea that this appalling plan was to be delivered in concert with UNAMIR. Now surely, UNAMIR had to slip away from OVERTURE. A cooperative operation was one thing; a joint camp closure was another entirely.

He drove me to the Belgian Village and we waited patiently on the white sofas while the SRSG finished his bath. The doors looked particularly fine, I thought. Britain House had not sacrificed them in vain.

The SRSG was shocked. He kept looking at me, trying I presumed to get some indication of whether Randolph knew anything of OVERTURE. I remained neutral. My understanding of the SRSG's knowledge and complicity in OVERTURE was purely third-hand. It even occurred to me that he had not been briefed on the risks. I had heard that I had

181

been reported to the SRSG as disloyal, and my paper on the risks had been repulsed, if he had ever seen it. But where before we had been warm and friendly, there was no mistaking the formality he had reintroduced into our relationship. I was no longer a valued adviser; now I was just another source of discord in the fractured UN camp.

The SRSG promised to bring pressure on the Government and that he would continue to press for the agreement to our 15-day plan.

As Randolph and I stood outside in the rain afterwards, there was one last opportunity to reintroduce another spin on the whole process.

'Ask UNAMIR to help you next week,' I suggested. 'Get the DFC to deploy UN troops to Kibeho to protect the IDPs. It would be a great help. But please don't mention my name.' Expose UNAMIR's hand now through Randolph, I reasoned, and a whole heap of new options might open up. But if the DFC caught wind that the suggestion was mine, I would be done for.

*

Randolph went to Gikongoro the following day, a Saturday. I was embarrassed not to join him but could hardly associate myself publicly with Randolph's attempts to stop the RPA from closing the camps. Randolph must have thought me weak but Yan and I discussed it at length and decided we could not be involved. Instead, we fixed a helicopter for him. He went off, disappointed, with a Rehabilitation Minister. It was a loss of face but there seemed to be no alternative.

In the evening, we were invited to a Human Rights party at a hotel in Kigali. There were waiters with white jackets; it was all very civilised. As soon as we arrived, Lillian Wong came forward.

'Have you met Dr Deng, the UN Secretary General's Special Ambassador on IDPs?'

'Yes, he was in the room when I went to the UN Council,' I exclaimed. I never knew he was in town.'

'Well he is and he wants to see you.' She introduced us and withdrew quietly.

He was one of those tall, ascetic Africans, very softly spoken, with such an immaculate command of the language that I felt like an East End barrow boy, mumbling incoherent answers to his cultured, incisive questions: What was the purpose of the new plan? Did we think it would work? What would be the consequences if it did not? How could he help?

I answered with an increasing sense of relief, Yan chipping in on cue. We were a great double act. Here, at last, was direct access back to Boutros-Ghali to tell him what was going wrong. Within days, I imagined, money would at last flow into Rwanda, the Government would start to listen and the plan would unfold, precisely, perfectly. Not this cheap version which now pointed a gun at our heads, but a proper, measured undertaking on a colossal scale with all the right components in place. Here, at last, was someone we could trust, at the highest level.

'I will do what I can,' he assured us. 'You can count on it.'

As we moved through the throng, ambushing the senior RPA officers to do some 'hearts and minds', a waiter pushed past with a tray piled high with fresh goat chunks-on-a-stick. I chewed through the almost-raw meat, delicious both because I had not eaten all day and because I had not eaten fresh meat for weeks. Yan looked disgusted. Gin in one hand, meat in the other, the Special Ambassador having left with our message, the looming crisis of Op OVERTURE, now only 48 hours away, seemed dim and distant. For the first time in days, I started to relax.

*

183

## Chapter 13

The cramps started in the late morning. Then I ran to the loo. By the afternoon, I was in bed, convinced I was going to die.

'I'm going to die,' I told Yan, as he looked in.

'You're right,' he agreed. 'Can I have your Gore-Tex jacket?'

The Australian medic Corporal who visited on the following morning was non-committal.

'What's wrong with you, Sir?' he enquired.

'I think I've got amoebic dysentery,' I groaned. 'What do you think?'

'I'll go along with that,' he agreed. A master of his trade, I decided gloomily. The world was about to be set on fire, and I was in my bed, dying.

Yan came in at lunchtime. 'The SRSG's told them,' he announced. 'He got the UN Agency Heads in and told them about OVERTURE, only they've changed the name - it's now Op HOPE.'

I laughed. Even the UN was able to do a bit of proactive PR, however crude. What a name for such a potential debacle!

'And what did they say?' I demanded. 'Did they go ballistic?'

'They said nothing,' he replied. 'They didn't even bleat.'

I could not believe they were so meek. Everything they were trying to achieve was about to be blown asunder and they were not even going to protest.

'Perhaps they just haven't been able to absorb it,' I guessed. 'Perhaps they're caught completely flat-footed.'

We argued the ins and outs, me rolling about trying to get comfortable as the pain of the cramps washed over me, Yan pacing the room.

'I'm going to tell Randolph,' he announced. 'I'm going to spell it out.'

He had six months more to run in the RAF than I had in the Army. It still had the potential to go very wrong for him. I didn't want to see him sacked over this.

'You don't need to do anything,' I pointed out gently. 'You've already done enough. And I've been nobbled, so why drop yourself in it?'

'Wish me luck,' he said wistfully, as he breezed out.

He was back two hours later, his eyes shining with the adrenaline of it, with the raw risk of it, with the sheer balls of it, going against his laid-back nature, at the height of a crisis. He had walked on ground that was virgin for him and I saw that now he realised how it had felt for me every day that I had gone into battle too.

He told me about it. How Randolph had been surprised to see him, how he had listened, the awfulness of the damage that was now only hours away sinking in as he got some realistic military advice. That this was not just a small scale security operation; it involved nearly three thousand UNAMIR troops, and that if it went wrong, it would be all over for the UN and for the ability of the Blue Berets to act in defiance of oppression ever again, regardless of how poorly they did it at the best of times. And that we were going to do what he had tried to prevent the RPA from doing.

'And what is he going to do now?' I eventually had to ask.

'He's going to phone Boutros-Ghali. As soon as he's awake.'

I checked my watch. It was four in the afternoon. In New York, the Secretary General would be ready for breakfast. Randolph should be on the phone now.

'How did you break the news to him at first?' I quizzed, desperate for more detail.

'Well,' said Yan. 'I looked at those *Thunderbirds* eyebrows and those lips, and I just said: 'Gee, Mr Tracy, we've only got 24 hours to save the world.''

186

*

Mark Cuthbert-Brown was on the ground for Op HOPE. He was able to fill in the details on his return from Kibeho, at the end of the following day. Contrary to all planning, the Operation had taken just one day, not three. Little wonder, I guessed. To do it properly would have taken weeks - an area 15 kilometres by 8 kilometres, with tens of thousands of *blindées*. Weapons would have been buried deep, if they were still in the camp - impossible to find in such a short time.

The Nigerian engineers had been given orders to erect holding cages for prisoners by dawn. They started work at 3 a.m. by vehicle headlight, right in the centre of Kibeho, next to the church. There could not have been a clearer indication of what was coming next. In all, nearly 800 weapons were 'discovered', an impressive figure until it became clear that no small arms were included in this. Apart from a few 'swords' and 'cudgels,' whatever they were, the vast majority were machetes. It was true that these weapons could have been used in the genocide. It was equally true that the machete was the standard farming tool of Rwanda - everybody needed one. In the Home Communes, NGOs were already handing out brand new machetes. It was hardly a triumph.

The press had been there with the NGOs and Agencies in force, and this had prevented an eviction. The RPA had no scruples about bayoneting and burning civilians out of the camps, but they were not stupid, and would not do so in front of the cameras. Forty-four men had been detained. Five of them had been picked out by the DFC personally. We asked Mark what evidence there was against them.

'They were men,' he replied. 'That was their only crime.' While we were building confidence with the IDPs, we could only imagine the effect of having people arrested and detained by the UN, on no evidence, with no trial. The majority had been singled out by young RPA soldiers and handed to our troops. When the genocide was being committed, these RPA soldiers were in Uganda, or fighting their way into Rwanda. They had no more idea of which IDPs might have committed genocide than we did. It was clear to all of us in Britain House that in an atmosphere of such poor security and control, the real criminals had long gone, taking their weapons with them. These poor fellows were the scapegoats of yet another political botch.

It was a typical UN solution. Neither a success nor a failure. Certainly we had lost much trust with the Hutus, but we had not killed any of them and we could rebuild what had been lost, if we worked at it. In the sense of anger that the Operation had gone ahead, there must also be thanks that it had not turned out to be a disaster. It was time to build bridges. As soon as I could, I congratulated the DFC on his success. He did not mince his words.

'I told you so,' he triumphed.

I smiled through clenched teeth. My own real test was coming; there was nothing to be gained from showing the frustration.

*

Randolph was badly bruised by the events of the past few days. His call to New York had resulted in a head-to-head with the SRSG, and Boutros-Ghali had been forced to choose. It was no contest. But he failed to realise what a positive thing that was. He had shown a determination to do the right thing, at the expense of his own career. He might look like a *Thunderbird* puppet, I told Yan, but from now on, he gets my support.

*

Operation RETOUR was on. I asked Randolph when we were going to get the go ahead and he looked surprised. 'But we already have,' he exclaimed.

'First I've heard about it,' I replied, aghast. Had the clock already been ticking, while I was suffering in bed? 'When do we start?'

'In 15 days,' he stumbled, clearly unsure of the exact terms of the agreement with the Government. We had promised and now we had to deliver. Amongst all the points, which I had been dreading in this scenario, one stood proud. The start date would now be 29 December. And unless I cancelled it, I would be flying home for my mid-tour leave on the 28th. Something was going to have to give.

*

If I thought life was busy before, it became manic now. I started working 18-hour days as we pressed on with the plan. The NGOs were coming back to the Stadium, still convinced by all my tenuous alliances, still willing to take on a major challenge. We prioritised Home Communes and some NGOs came forward immediately to build Open Relief Centres. Of the first 12, nine were agreed, a triumph by the normal standards of Rwanda. But there was a great deal to do, to meet the deadline of the 29th, even though I knew it would initially be largely a cosmetic exercise. There was just not time enough to do it properly.

*

Yan had only 'days to do' and would be in Blighty for Christmas, just a week away. He was not the only one. One by one, I had canvassed my UNAMIR officers and then the UNREO staff. Rather sheepishly, they admitted that they would nearly all be away for the New Year. Only Mark

189

Frohardt from UNREO would be around for the 29th. I could hardly complain; my own carefully laid leave plans were equally precious. I was not going to cancel anybody's leave before cancelling my own first. Every time I thought about this leadership dilemma, I felt sick.

We were now trying to get dozens of individual plans together from the NGOs and Agencies, covering food, seeds and tools, water, unaccompanied minors and so on, whilst I was pretending all the while that the standards to be achieved were those which the military provided. In the background, unbeknown to anyone, I was also now holding up UNAMIR's end, continuing the lie that all at the Amahoro Hotel was under control. Because so many had already gone away, including Alan Brimelow, the Operations area had ground to a halt, having barely lurched through Op HOPE. I visited Lieutenant Colonel Austen Yella every day to pressurise him into producing the Security Plan for Op RETOUR. It was clear that he really needed some help and guidance. Reluctantly, I got involved. As I tried to help Austen, so I got drawn further in. I started by giving him some headings, then another level of detail until eventually, I was writing the plan. He had it typed onto a PC and asked me to go through it with him, on the screen. As I made some amendments, he then pointed out numerous minor 'staff duties' changes which needed to be made. As I was more adept on the machine than he was, so eventually, I ended up doing the typing, night after night, once my day job was over. In fulsome irony, I was strategist and typist in the same breath. There was just nobody to delegate to.

*

Barney came to say goodbye. Of all the sheepish people, there was none more sheepish than Barney. Barney's positive optimism, his integrity and his constancy in the face of all our setbacks, were some of our major strengths as a team. He was

190

hugely guilty as he wished us a Happy Christmas. He would not be back until 7 January.

Yan was next. In the usual way in which he lucked in, he had cadged a lift on the SRSG's Lear Jet, returning to Nairobi in soft-spoken comfort - no wooden-seated Antonov for him. On his last day, 23 December, we rode out at dawn in the Chinese Jeep, up on to the Ruhengeri Ridge at Tare. I turned the Jeep at the hill and we bumped and bashed through the puddles for a magnificent view of the volcanoes. We had bought a bottle of champagne in a shop in Kigali, unsure of our maths and our French and had ended up spending $55, where we thought it was $25. But as the sun came up over Rwanda and I popped the cork, it could not have been better value. The intensity of our relationship and its lurching decline under the pressures of Op RETOUR were evened out under the influence. And we put it all behind us.

I drove him to the airport in the afternoon, the Jeep piled high with his rucksacks and mountain-man paraphernalia.

He climbed out of the Jeep and walked around to clamber back into my seat. 'Is it alright if I park it?' he asked pleasantly. He was up to something. He parked it expertly.

'That's a neat bit of parking,' I congratulated him.

He had started to lay this ambush months before. 'They don't call me Parker for nothing, M'Lady,' he grinned. 'Gotcha.'

The traditions of Britain House dictated that we would all be there. And I was certain, despite his bravado and his jibes about the excellent Christmas that he was going to have, that he knew that he would never have another 80 days like these. And we watched him stride into Departures, with his cowpat blue beret still on the side of his head and his tan walking boots still so incongruous under his camouflaged uniform. As he turned to wave, the light flashed briefly on his eye. It was definitely wet. 'Gotcha too,' I thought.

191

*

It was the last Happy Hour before Christmas. Most of the NGOs were not involved in Op RETOUR. They were winding down. I was approached by a pretty young American girl, Tara King, whom I had met before. She worked for *Friends in the West*, a North American NGO which was well respected.

'I'm delivering some presents to an orphanage in Ruhengeri on Christmas Day,' she explained. 'Is there any chance I can borrow a UNAMIR truck?'

'A truck,' I expostulated. 'On Christmas Day? Have you any idea how difficult it is to get a truck on Christmas Day?'

She looked crestfallen. 'Let me introduce you to a colleague of mine,' I said. 'Just don't stare at his nose.'

*

It was a very tough meeting. Mark Frohardt and I were uncompromising, even though it was Christmas Eve. Pascale Lefort from *AICF* was absorbing the blows. If the NGOs do not stop feeding the people in the camps we are about to close, we argued, the RPA will close them by force. Pascale squirmed. Cyanika, our first camp, just 5 days away, was about to be fed by *AICF*. It was to be for the last time, we demanded. Under the huge pressure which we brought to bear on him, he acceded, but his resistance had been noted by a steely-eyed Lieutenant Cameron at the end of the table, who had said nothing at all throughout our discussion on the potential behaviour of his soldiers. Pascale did not know it then but his organisation was about to be taught a very sharp lesson by the Government. On 28 December, hours after they had distributed the last rations to the 30,000 population of Cyanika, they were to be expelled from Rwanda.

*

Carl and I drove to the airport, to be met by Tara. She had never flown in a helicopter before.

'It's your Christmas present,' Carl told her gruffly, obviously pleased to have made her day.

We flew up the Ridge, looking down on Rwanda's breathtaking scenery. At Ruhengeri, the Tunisian Battalion had prepared the Landing Zone in a Stadium by the orphanage. We off-loaded the presents and made our way up the road to the former school that now housed 50 'unaccompanied minors'.

They waited patiently as we unloaded the presents which Tara sorted into piles by age-bracket and sex. There were spares for the orphanage workers. Each child received a Christmas package in a shoebox. In each box was a letter from the Christian North American family who had given it, with a photograph. Carefully packed beneath was treasure. About $20 worth of toys, sweets, small items of clothing. For children who had never before received a toy or a gift, they were in instant heaven. Silently, they inspected the boxes. Then they pulled away the Christmas wrapping paper and burrowed inside. The noise started slowly. At first, you could only hear the tentative tear of the paper, then the involuntary cries of surprise and delight, then the squeals of pleasure. Then the room was filled by the biggest sound of all sounds as they began to ululate. Spontaneously, the older girls started to dance and sing, their hands clapping as they leapt about in perfect rhythm, melodious, their voices intertwined.

'They are saying thank you,' said one of the workers. 'They have never been loved so much before.'

Outside, each of the four of us Western blokes found a corner of the courtyard from which to study the hills of Rwanda. As I blinked away my tears, Carl who appeared so hardened, brushed away his. Bogden and Jim, the two *Canadian Helicopters* pilots, were in the same condition.

193

In Uxbridge, I knew, two Western boys would already be bored with their toys. Here in Ruhengeri, this day would be remembered forever.

We took off and made a low pass over the orphanage, the little people grouped outside in a bunch, their white-patched hands waving wildly as we screamed overhead. I felt like a boy scout for the rest of Christmas Day 1994.

*

The General came back from leave, looking refreshed and healthy. I briefed him up on events on Op RETOUR in his absence.

'And what will you be doing on the 29th?'

'I'll be on leave, General,' I answered.

'How can you go on leave when your Operation is about to begin?' he asked sharply. He had been in South Africa with his own family when Op HOPE had gone in. Pot, kettle and black.

'I've weighed it up, sir,' I explained. 'If I don't go on leave now, I will not get another chance until March. By mid January, Op RETOUR will just be starting to move. I have to give my family some consideration.'

'Of course it's up to you,' he said dismissively.

*

Commanding Officers and their staff had been helicoptered in over the past few hours. For the first time in UNAMIR, we were all going to embark on a single military operation to move things in Rwanda forward. This was not like Op HOPE, where only those directly involved had been briefed. This was the whole package - over 6,500 personnel and all their resources. Although I had tried to avoid the star turn for so long, I was now going to take the lead. I had authored the military plan as well, but now it was time for me to ask UNAMIR formally and publicly for its support and assistance, in my capacity as Officer in Command of Op RETOUR.

The General arrived and we all came to attention. When we had settled, he said a few, distracted, noncommittal words, which seemed barely focused on our undertaking. There was something about a defining moment in Rwanda's history, but it did not articulate clearly. And then he left. We all jumped up again. If I was surprised, I was not the only one. Even the DFC looked shocked. If there was a better way to give a loud vote of no-confidence to Op RETOUR, Major General Guy Claude Tousignant could not have found it.

I looked out at their upturned faces, multi-ethnic, multi-coloured, some grim and questioning, others plainly supportive and positive. This was my moment to influence them, for better or for worse.

It went well. There was the right blend of hard information, honest appeal and oratorical theatre. I finished with a very simple message:

'As Charles Petrie departed on leave a few days ago, I stopped him outside the airport. Charles has seen many humanitarian disasters unfold and many political plans emerge to solve them. I asked him what was the most important thing we could do. He said simply: 'Make sure the security plan works and the rest will follow.' Gentlemen, it's in your hands. Good luck.'

The Commanding Officers had their say next. After a string of whingers who complained that they did not have enough radios or vehicles to do the job properly and were using the opportunity to moan to the Headquarters, Lieutenant Colonel Dan Luyie from Zambia stood up. He waited, eyes down, until you could have heard a pin drop. Then he spoke out clearly.

'I have received my orders,' he said simply. 'I know what has to be done. My Battalion is ready to go.' As he sat down, the audience shocked into stunned silence, I nearly spoilt the moment by cheering.

195

*

I flew out on a grey day, D minus 1, the rain beating down on the airport roof as I waited for the Antonov to Nairobi. It is not fair, I thought, that anyone should have to live with guilt like this.

*

# Chapter 14

Sue and I made up for the weeks of separation. Her father was improving but the strain had been too much. She needed me to be at home. And despite the guilt, I could say with certainty, once I had absorbed how difficult things had been for her, that I had not come home a day too early.

I had to keep in touch with Op RETOUR. For hours every day, I tried to get through on the phone. Once in a while I would reach Fraser, or Mark Cuthbert-Brown, or Carl Dixon. They would tell me what they knew, at once removed from the action on the ground. It was going slowly, but it was going. There had been no trouble. Many of the people were very nervous; some may have been using the transport to go home in order to determine whether it was safe and then were slipping back to Cyanika in the evening, to get their families.

I phoned and then wrote to the BBC, to Channel 4. Did they realise, I asked, that in Rwanda right now, something extraordinary and unique was happening in the history of the UN? An integrated plan, including the Government, the RPA, the UN, the Agencies and NGOs was bringing the IDPs home in conditions of peace, safety and dignity. They were bored with Rwanda was the message I got back. People were sick of seeing the piles of bodies on the shores of Lake Victoria. As the bodies had disappeared from the screens, so the problem had disappeared from the minds of the viewers.

On Radio 4, I heard that the RPA had killed people in Busanze camp. It took another day before I got anyone sensible in Kigali to talk to. Carl had flown to Busanze. Mark had visited the following day. It was bad, he had said over the crackly line, his voice still betraying the shock he must have felt. The UN soldiers had found the bodies in the latrines, and had pulled them out to confront the RPA. It was a local commander, the soldiers had insisted. He had thought the small contingent of RPA was under threat, he then claimed, and had opened fire in the night. Then why, asked the UN, had they thrown the bodies into the latrine?

The following morning, I was relieved to hear the updated report from Rwanda on the radio. General Kagame had ordered the RPA commander and five of his troops to be arrested, pending trial. It was the first time that they had admitted that they were wrong.

*

Sue and I met Yan and Jane Janiurek for dinner at a halfway point in the Chilterns, on the crest of a bare hilltop ridge. It was a strange experience, the wives not too sure how to handle the close banter between us. As we parted in the car park, the wind whistling over the eaves of the English pub on a cold starry January night, I put the big question to him.

'So will you come back?' I demanded.

'Just say the word and I'll be there,' he promised. In perspective, it was clear that there was nothing else for him or me, just then. Rwanda had taken over our lives.

*

As the turbo props stopped turning in Kigali on Sunday morning, it was as if I had not been away. Once again, I had been transported across several thousand miles and simultaneously across a huge cultural divide. Mark Cuthbert-Brown met me.

'How was your leave?' he asked politely.

'Great. How's it going? How many people have we moved? What does the Government think?' The questions just tumbled out. I wanted to get up to speed immediately. I interrogated him all the way back to Britain House.

'And what about the new boss?' I enquired. Kieran's replacement had arrived. His support was critical.

Mark was evasive. 'The jury's out,' he murmured. Perhaps the next few months were going to be tough, I thought resignedly. All we needed was an officious new Senior British Officer.

I was pretty exhausted as we stopped at the first RPA checkpoint, but somehow the Kinyarwanda greetings just rolled off the tongue as if I had never been away. The Tutsi head-nod, a slight upthrust of the chin, administered laconically as the soldier pulled away the string barrier, confirmed it. I was really home. Not home, back, I reminded myself.

Colonel Kelvin Tutt was well groomed. On the dapper side of smooth, evinced by his sharp creases and clean chukkah boots, he cut an unaccustomed dash in Britain House. We were scruffily operational - a pretty slovenly lot. He was in his late forties, well spoken and well practised at speaking. He started talking before I had reached him to shake his hand and then just carried on as we sat down and eyed each other up.

'He'll talk the hind leg off a donkey,' Mark had promised. 'You won't be able to get a word in edgeways.'

From the corner of my eye, I watched Mark and Carl, sitting on the other side of the room, making 'yak yak yak' gestures, behind Kelvin's back. I sat back, shattered from the journey, listening to Kelvin's monologue and only one question sprang to my mind: 'What's this cuckoo doing in my nest?'

*

It was raining on the Monday morning as I pulled the Jeep into the parking slot at the Amahoro Hotel. Morale was low. I had been unable to get any detailed sense on how the Operation was progressing until later the previous evening. The results were very poor. Since the incident in Busanze, very few IDPs had decided to go home. The infrastructure was weak. The Stadium had been closed in my absence. I had only been gone a few days before Randolph had ordered everybody in the

199

Integrated Operations Centre we had so painfully set up to be moved into the Ministry of Rehabilitation, on the steep hill which led into Kigali from the western routes. That was bad enough, to know that if you were not there personally to advocate a course of action, the decision would be taken anyway. But Kelvin had really brought me down. He did not accept that I needed the Moores in the IOC. I would have to justify their contribution by Wednesday, or he wanted them back. It was the sort of thing the British Army does very well in peacetime - write justifications. But it was about the bottom of my list of priorities.

I protested to Jan Arp: 'Can't you get him to leave me alone?' I begged. 'At least until I take up the reins again?' But he was caught out too. The General was not happy about the use of military manpower in the IOC either, he warned. 'Don't get into a fight on your first day back!'

The Morning Brief was full of doom and gloom. The Operation was failing. Hardly anybody was moving. There was no information campaign. There were big questions about food resupply and whether we should carry on feeding the IDPs. It was a shambles, was the message, hammered home with some glee, by one or two of UNAMIR's staff officers. I watched the DFC's eyes as this information was imparted. Uncharitably, I decided he was enjoying it.

The IOC really was a shambles. We had taken over a floor of the Ministry of Rehabilitation, one of Kigali's largest buildings, but with no power and no water, hardly one to settle into easily. To make matters worse, or better, an NGO team led by an energetic Aussie, Simon Fallon, was constructing the IOC fabric, the offices and meeting rooms around us. It was hard not to be grateful and impressed, but it was impossible to talk in a normal voice, anywhere in the building, the noise of hammering and sawing was so great. I pulled Barney out and we found a relatively quiet spot, while he gave me a very thorough briefing. Despite the setbacks and the current state of

200

play, he was typically upbeat and positive. He was keeping the IOC going through his combination of good humour and hard work. Fidelis and Adam were both pretty unhappy, he warned, but there was nothing anybody could do. The Operation was quiet. The IOC was struggling as an organisation. I cursed the political decision Randolph had taken. The timing was appalling. If the IOC were ready for occupation, it would have been a different story. But it would be weeks before you could hear yourself think, much less do any serious work in peace.

Mark Frohardt was now in charge from UNREO, having taken the place of Charles Petrie. Within hours, I had picked up the vibes from Margaux and the others. Mark was very unpopular. I could immediately see why. They were just not used to a manager of his calibre. He was tough, and he took no prisoners.

Steve and Andy Moore were trying hard to work in conditions of discomfort and chaos, as everybody was. Apart from the noise and the dust, there was no clear idea of what was going to happen next and how it would come about. Mark was not at fault. Nobody was. It was just one of those awful situations in which command had deteriorated in so many ways that nobody was able to control the decline any more. There was so much to do, so few hands to do it, so little time. No feedback from the Government. No contact with the Minister in whose building we were set up. No communications equipment, except that which I had scrounged from UNAMIR, grudgingly given. No information from the ground. No idea whether the water was working at an Open Relief Centre. No response to an alleged RPA murder which now had the people in that Commune sleeping in the fields, just as they had done when the killing was happening. I had just walked in on operational mayhem.

There was only one place to start. I tried to look after my own first. I gave the Moores the task of writing their justification for Colonel Kelvin Tutt. I knew they would do a good job; they did not want to go back to the Headquarters, they promised, even though the IOC was shambolic. This was where the action was. I felt sorry for Fidelis. He was stoical and rugged and I had pulled him out of the field to do this. But he was clearly very cheesed off. So was Adam. I took them aside and told them what a great job they were doing, how Barney was impressed with their professionalism. It was what they needed to hear. I watched them pick up speed, as if they had just been woken up and realised they had a lot to do. They were both men of immense character and I was suddenly very proud to be working with them.

Mark was less easy to please. He had been banging his head against a brick wall for two weeks, which must have seemed like a lifetime. In that period, he had launched the Operation, from the humanitarian perspective, moved the IOC, fought off the immense political pressures and survived the result of Busanze. As I questioned him and pummelled him with my own views, made so much sharper by two weeks away from the heat of Kigali, he started to realise that something good was happening to him too. Every time he laid out another point of despair, I just replied, 'Look what you've achieved. Look at the progress.' Mark was suspicious at first but began to come around. I only had to be honest. When I looked at the conditions and the results, I was just damned impressed. And every time I told someone how well they were doing, it had that simple effect - the road ahead looked brighter. I didn't manage to do any real work on that first day back. I just ended up doing a turn as cheerleader.

*

The summons came that evening. I was to brief the Gang of Five on the following morning. I had a tense evening deciding what to say, but there was no going back on this now. We were committed to Op RETOUR, and so it had to be successful.

They kept me waiting. Even a few weeks before, I could have breezed in to anyone's office in UNAMIR, sat down and had a chat. Now, the message was clear: The Operation wasn't working, *ergo* I had failed, *ergo* I was no longer to be treated equitably. The door opened and Fraser ushered me inside. There was nowhere for me to sit and nobody offered to have a chair brought in. They were all sitting around the table, surrounded by advisors. I stood formally at one end. I was the accused and this was the jury.

I looked them over. There were only a few friendly faces - Fraser, Jan Arp, Kelvin Tutt. The others were distinctly unfriendly. The DFC, glowering at one end of the table, was hostile.

'Please give your report, Colonel Mullarkey.'

I set off slowly, building the case. That the Operation had had four prerequisite criteria before delivery and that, for political reasons, none had been met. We had not given the Government the means to Govern. We had not provided a high security environment. We had not prepared the Home Communes and we had not won the information battle. But still we were doing well. We had moved four thousand people and the numbers were increasing again following the incident at Busanze.

As I was about to get into the meat of it, the DFC interrupted.

'Please hurry up, we do not have all day,' he said, showing his irritation.

They might not have had all day but there was nothing else of real significance that they had heard for months. There was nothing more critical to the future of Rwanda than Op RETOUR. I remained calm, inside hugely depressed. It was not a good scene.

'In conclusion,' I announced immediately, 'the Government is willing to listen and we have demonstrated a capability to deliver our promises which they could not have imagined. We

203

must now capitalise on this initiative, all the while building momentum in the movement of IDPs. All the experts, Charles Petrie and Mark Frohardt included, think it is only a matter of time before we break through the crust, the numbers increase significantly and we develop the critical mass in the Communes to the point at which the innocent refugees will slip away from Goma and Bukavu. We're not there yet; we need UNAMIR to keep up the pressure, the commitment. If we don't, the NGOs and Agencies will falter.'

There was a stony silence as I finished. Nobody had any questions, any interest. 'I'm going to be finished off now,' I thought.

The DFC spoke slowly.

'You must not forget that you need an African perspective on this. A Western understanding is not enough.' I thought I had assimilated a reasonably balanced perspective, with the assistance of many others, including Africans, but now was not the time to make the point.

'Thank you Sir,' I replied evenly. 'That is very good advice.'

The atmosphere in the room had lightened a shade in my few minutes of concentrated effort, but there was still silence as I saluted and marched out. Fraser winked at me as he held the door open. It may not have been a hand-slapping success but in the DFC's largely irrelevant point came an important message, which could not be lost on the others: This bloke is talking sense. All we can do is pick nits.

*

Brimelow was in his office, nursing a hangover. His face was particularly wrinkled and puckered - the Brimelow Corduroy Pillow Effect, Fraser called it. I had not had a chance to talk to him since before Christmas, when he had gone on leave. He was very cheesed off.

204

He had been on holiday with his wife in Mombasa. She had flown in from Australia. One day, sauntering along the beach together, they had watched a middle-aged white man surfing, doing quite well. When he had come to shore, Brimmers had recognised him as his best friend and arch surfing buddy from his schooldays, 25 years before. They had got talking, then drinking, and then Brimmers had entered the Mombasa Veterans surfing competition, to be held in three days time. Three days of drinking and surfing later, he noticed that his wife was packing her bags. He had blown it. It was typical Brimelow - wild coincidences, high adventure, casual gambling with the chips of life.

'Will she come around, do you think?' I asked him.

'I hope so mate, I hope so,' he said ruefully.

We were joined by Fraser.

'Well, did I survive?' I begged him for some feedback.

'You did survive,' he admitted, 'but it's close. Sacking the Operation is top of the pops for the General right now.'

'But why?' I questioned. 'What else have they got to do?'

'I know,' agreed Fraser. 'This really is the only role for UNAMIR. But it's the fear of failure. Most of these people don't give a stuff whether the Operation succeeds or not, but they don't want anything to do with it if it fails.'

'Well, it might fail,' I retorted. 'It's a series of enormous risks laid one on one. If they don't support it, it surely will fail.'

'Tom, me ol' mate,' said Brimelow, gently. 'If you want to get this Headquarters to work for you and with you, rather than against you, there's a critical new technique you're going to have to learn.'

I listened with interest. Brimmers picked up his cylindrical ashtray and made some obscene licking movements with his tongue.

'No guys,' I entreated. 'I can't do that. It's the old integrity thing.'

'You'll just have to learn,' grinned Brimelow evilly.

*

As the hours and days went by, I never betrayed my inner despair. Everything we had worked for hung in the balance. The arrangements were crude and largely ineffective. Every attempt to improve them was a circular argument: We could not improve the Communes because we could not get NGO support. The NGOs would not support because they could not see the Operation as a success. The people would not go home because the conditions were not right and the Communes were not ready. I was spending all my time talking, arguing, advocating and it was going nowhere. As a gesture of confidence-building and leadership, I had to break a circular argument plainly, for all too see. And I wanted it to involve UNAMIR, so that the confidence would spread there, as a first priority.

Of all the places we were falling down, the information battle was the worst. Every tiny rumour from the Communes was reverberating into the camps, carried overnight through the bush telegraph. A beating by an RPA soldier became a massacre. A shortage of beans became a famine, no matter about the maize and corn available in profusion; now hundreds were dying of starvation. It was all rubbish. Nobody had died of starvation in Rwanda for months and all the people knew it. But if the Interahamwe sent out this message, they would believe it, through fear, through lack of an alternative, or because that was what they wanted to believe. We had to defeat this ignorance. I chose the only weapon we had in our pitiful armoury - the truth.

We had to get inside the disinformation loop. I guessed that a rumour in a Commune returned to the camps within a 24-48 hour period. The target was therefore to get to the people with the truth before, or at worst, just after, the lie arrived. If we

206

sent Military Observer patrols to the target Communes at dawn to gather information from all sources, the RPA, the NGOs, the *Bourgmestre*, the people, they should be able to feed a report back to UNAMIR by radio, by 11 a.m. The next stage in the process was to turn this information into a news report, and send it down to the troops on the ground, to be read out at all the camps. My best estimate was this could be done by the following morning, just inside the disinformation loop.

On the ground, the people would come. They would see that we had something to say. They would listen, through our interpreters. We would tell the truth. If the RPA had shot an escaping prisoner in Ngenda, we would report it. We would not cover it up or tone it down. It would be a plain statement of fact, supported by whatever explanation we were given, but with no comment. We would let the people realise that we were telling the truth and then draw their own conclusions. So if they were concerned that the RPA were shooting prisoners, they would have something to make a judgement about. But if they heard that two hundred prisoners had been shot, we could say that we had talked to the NGOs, the *Bourgmestre* etc and our information was that it was one. If they chose to believe us they could; if not, we would be no worse off. If the RPA could be held responsible to the people through the 'press', as in a Western democracy, this would modify their behaviour. They could no longer get away with murder, if that was what was happening. We would be compromising their ability to act with a free hand, in the Home Communes.

I distributed the draft plan.

'How soon can you get this in action?' asked Mark Frohardt, sceptically.

'I can get it moving within UNAMIR within days, working on the ground within a week. With luck.'

'Well, if you can, that would be fantastic,' he admitted in his New England drawl.

*

I saluted smartly as I came to attention in front of his desk. Disdainfully, he motioned me to a seat. We both felt this was going to be tricky, only he didn't know quite how easy it was going to be for him.

'Brigadier, I've been thinking what you said about getting an African perspective on the problem and I wondered if I might trouble you for a few minutes?'

His eyebrows arched. He had not been expecting me in conciliatory and obsequious mode. Hopefully, nobody would find out either. I cringed inside as I remembered Brimelow's symbolic gesture.

'Yes, go ahead,' he invited gruffly.

'Firstly, Sir, I would like to explore your views on the motivation of the Hutu people. I think we have all heard the arguments but behind all those, deep down, I want to know why they won't go home.'

He sat very still for a few minutes, looking wistfully out of the window.

'I will tell you honestly that I do not understand them,' he admitted quietly. 'In Africa, if a person is dirty, they wash themselves. These people do not. They stay in the camps week after week and do not wash and do not wash their clothes. They have the cleanest water in Africa, brought to them by the NGOs, but they do not wash. I do not know why. In Africa, people work. They work all day and they love work. They love to produce, to be busy. But these people do not work. They sit outside their huts all day in the camps and do nothing. And in Africa, if somebody in our family dies, we weep. We weep all day and all night until there is no more weeping to be done. But these people do not weep. They have not wept for those who have died or wept for those whom their brothers have killed. I tell you honestly,' he transfixed me with his heavy, yellowed eyes, 'I do not understand these people.'

We talked quietly as the sun went down over Kigali and I learnt nothing about the African perspective on the Operation from him. But I learnt a great deal about the African perspective.

'So how was it?' Brimelow asked mischievously as we stood together at the Ballroom window, watching the dying embers of the Rwandese sunset.

'I don't like the taste,' I admitted, 'but I might get used to it.'

*

It had been another punishing day. I arrived home exhausted from the IOC and parked up the Jeep outside Britain House. I seriously doubted that I would survive the next seven weeks, when Sue was coming out to Kenya for a holiday, a real break together.

Kelvin was pottering around. After much behind-the-scenes manoeuvring, a lot of writing and a visit to the General, I had managed to keep the military team together in the IOC but it had not been easy. I resented Kelvin for bringing in an overhead which I could have lived without. If he only knew how much I was struggling, he probably would have let it ride, but nobody knew how much I was struggling. My public face was as upbeat as it could be. Deeper down, I thought it was now inevitable that we would fail.

The Government was still not in the lead. The confidence level in the people was low - they were not moving. The Communes were not ready on a scale and to a standard required. We were approaching deep moral issues on whether to turn off the food supplies. All the while I was fighting the impossible fight in UNAMIR, trying to keep them all on-side while pretending to everyone outside that the might and brilliance of UNAMIR was about to solve all their problems. Randolph might have cleared the deck for the benefit of

UNREO, but I would never get the General to support us again, unless I could invite him take it on in his role as acting SRSG, while the Ambassador was away. That task on its own was almost impossible. It was bleak, gloom, despair.

Britain House was no longer warm and welcoming in the evening, now that Yan had left. The two relative newcomers had had an unsettling effect. Mark Cuthbert-Brown and I had become closer, in response to this next invasion. Carl was very hard to get to know, a bit of a loner. Fraser was about to leave for the UK and, ever popular, he had gone on the party circuit that evening.

I had promised Kelvin a briefing on Op RETOUR, as I had now given it so many times before. But I had not expected to have to give it tonight and was dismayed by his request to run through it. But the PR game is like that. And I had still not given it to Carl.

I sat down with my battered blue folder, the one I had taken to Geneva, into the walnut-panelled office. Carl pulled up a chair. I was worn out, hungry and extremely unhappy and it must have shown in my presentation. But bit-by-bit, as I went through the rock-solid arguments which had propelled me into this Operation in the first place, it all seemed to fall back into place. They questioned me very closely, punishing my weary brain for over three solid hours, without a break, without a pause. They were as fascinated as I was by Rwanda, as willing to listen as Mark had been, as everybody had been, once it had been explained properly.

At about midnight, Carl thrust a gin and tonic into my hand. It was 50:50 and I gasped, really needing the hit. We opened a couple of tubes of crisps and ate them as a late supper, as we continued the debate into the wee hours, the atmosphere more relaxed. I looked at Kelvin and Carl and realised that something very special had happened in the past few hours, which had also affected Mark. In the process of giving up my soul, and in their receiving it, we had all become much closer.

210

And there was something more important from my perspective, which had taken place, and which Kelvin summed up with a very knowing twinkle.

'You know,' he said wisely, 'I think that this evening has been the best possible thing for you. Your faith was shaken, but in repeating it like the litany it is, you believe in your plan once more.'

*

I bounced into the Gang of Five, the following morning. I had asked Fraser to arrange a chair. It was at once much more relaxed. I hit them with it all. Already evidence of improvement, more people had gone home the previous day than at any time since the Busanze incident. The trend was demonstrably upwards. We had great new ideas on beating the disinformation battle, which would be working within days. We were studying ways of improving communications to the UNREO workers on the ground. Another NGO had decided to open an Open Relief Centre. All we had to do was push on until we could break through the crust. But it was happening, it was moving, let's get behind it.

The DFC did not destroy me. He talked instead about how he could use his contacts to find out a bit more on forthcoming RPA plans. The General asked when I thought the real breakthrough was going to take place. I answered evenly, giving them the sort of encouragement they should have been giving me.

I saw Kelvin afterwards. 'How did it go?' I queried.

'Almost too well,' he laughed. 'They're not used to the British officer in full flood. It's just too impressive.'

Good, I thought, let them be impressed. From now on, that's all they're going to be.

That afternoon, when the daily figures came in, the number of people who had gone home had just topped seven hundred.

It was the best we had done by over a hundred. Confidence and determination. These were the methods by which we would progress. Although I was completely worn out, there was nothing left but to go for it.

Carl grabbed me that evening. 'Look,' he explained gruffly, 'your time is short. You've got a lot to do. How would you like to have priority access to your own helicopter?'

It was an extraordinary thing for him to offer and I did not hesitate to snap it up. No more agonising about times in and out of Kigali, trying to juggle meetings with other schedules and activities. Now I was free to come and go as I pleased. Only the General and the SRSG had that kind of flexibility. It would make a big difference.

*

We circled the camp before landing at Gikongoro. I was picked up in an UNREO vehicle and whisked back up the hill on the ground. Cyanika was still very much alive. Although there were patches of ground clearly visible where before there had been a mass of blue tentage, the inroads we had made into the population still seemed slight. I walked the ground. There was the mound where 20,000 people were buried, still standing proud on the hillside. The stinking latrines were still stinking. Some 20-30 feet deep, it was impossible to guess what lay at the bottom. It seemed to be a favourite place to hide your murder victims in Rwanda.

The people were willing to listen. I pleaded with them to go home now and take the opportunity we were presenting to them. One yellow-eyed, middle-aged man wearing a suit and T-shirt, but no shoes, kept coming forward and waving his arm menacingly at my face, pointing, from a few inches away, as he shouted abuse. He was telling them that I was a liar. But they seemed to expect this behaviour and remained neutral and listened and talked.

212

This was a whistle-stop tour of the Operation. For the first time, I had met Tim Meisberger, UNREO's field officer in Gikongoro. He was a firebrand, a real maverick, I had been told. I knew nothing about that. All I could see was a dynamic and enthusiastic young American with a real passion for his work and determination to see it through. In Kigali, you would get the bleeding-hearts whingeing about how we must continue to feed the people and not use food as a weapon. Tim spoke the language of the IOC. If you don't use food as a benign weapon, the RPA will use its own variety, as an alternative. We had stopped feeding in Cyanika on 28 December, the day before D-Day. But Tim pointed out the heavy bags of food in each *blindée*. These people would not starve. Even if they were hungry, they could just move to another camp. I went out and saw what had to be done and what now needed to be done. And, unquestionably, because of that support we were getting from my military friends and from the people in UNREO who now were pulling together, like Mark and Tim and Barney, and the NGOs, I just knew it could be done.

*

Randolph was in Geneva; the SRSG was on leave. This left the way open for some new manoeuvres. With Mark Frohardt, I was hatching another plan for the General this time, to get the Government closely involved in the decision-making. So far, it had all been our running, from the bottom up. Ownership needed to be developed from the top down. I prepared a short position paper for the General, explaining the need for him to open discussions with the Government on some high level involvement.

He wrote back quickly: Yes, it was right that we should get the Government involved but he would need to discuss this with Randolph before he went any further. Mark phoned Randolph. Please tell the General that he can get on with the

213

discussions with the Government now and that you will pick it up on return, he asked. 'No,' relied Randolph. 'I do not want the General to have any discussions without me being there.' Back to square one.

Mark and I had a team talk.

'Right then,' we decided. 'Bottom up it is.'

*

Barney had arranged it, on a Saturday morning. We would brief the Minister for Rehabilitation, Justin Murara, in his own building, which also housed the IOC. I remembered him from our difficult discussions before Christmas. There was no building work going on; for the first time we had silence. Barney went through the humanitarian work in the camps. Mark talked about the issues affecting the Communes. I talked security and then we all talked politics. Justin received a Whitehall level of service. He promised to come at least once a week. I wondered what else he had to do, that we could not have more of his time; there was very little rebuilding and rehabilitation in Rwanda other than what was going on through the IOC. But at least once a week was better than anything we had had before.

*

I talked to Jan Arp. He was sceptical.

'Why do you need him?' he demanded. 'What will be his real contribution?' I explained that I wanted someone to work his way into the Government to make contact with officials and Ministers and hang in there like a limpet. It was essential - nobody else in Rwanda had the nouse and the knowledge to do it.

'All right,' he agreed, 'but Kelvin will have to explain this to the General and we just can't get an airfare - there is only one per individual per tour. You'll have to fund it from somewhere.'

'Alright,' said Kelvin, 'I'll see what I can do'.

He saw me the following evening. 'The General was suspicious,' he explained, 'but I told him that you needed your sounding board, that it was very difficult for you to think your way through all these problems without somebody close you can trust. I told him that you needed Yan like he needed the DFC.'

'And what did he say to that?' I spluttered.

'He said OK,' laughed Kelvin.

I talked to Randolph, recently returned from Geneva, after a late evening meeting. Randolph had not forgotten the determined visit which had led to the confrontation with the Secretary General. 'OK,' he agreed, 'but it'll have to be Economy.'

I visited his administrator, a bubbly Italian bombshell. 'Randolph has authorised the airfare for Yan Janiurek. Any chance you can get him an upgrade to Business Class?'

'What's he like,' she smiled coquettishly.

'Very handsome, young, dynamic and single,' I lied. 'Is there anything you would like from *Marks and Spencer*?'

\*

It was Monday morning. Millicent Mutuli, the UNREO press officer, had just come down to the IOC. She watched us all quietly for a few minutes, before she asked the question slowly, shouting out above the noise of the hammering.

'Have you heard the figures for today?' she yelled.

'No, sorry, Millicent, you'll have to wait until later, when they come in,' explained Barney patiently, at full volume, turning back to his work.

'Actually, Barney, I think you should get today's figures,' she said, deadpan. 'I think you'll find them quite interesting.'

215

Work stopped. Despite the noise, we could all sense that something was about to happen.

Barney called to Tim Meisberger on the radio. After three attempts, he managed to get through. He couldn't hear Tim in Gikongoro, above the noise of the hammering.

The Rwandese in the IOC shouted at the workers outside to be quiet. Suddenly the noise stopped. We could hear Barney's words clearly.

'Read those figures back. I say again, read those figures back,' he shouted, turning his back to us, jotting furiously. There was more static crackling.

'Roger out.' He turned to us, his face suffused.

'Ladies and gentlemen, unless there has been a terrible mistake, I can confirm that, today, the total of all people moved in Op RETOUR was 3,850.' There was a stunned silence. Our 'official capacity' was only 2000 per day; we had managed 1200 before, early the previous week. We knew that more would cram on the trucks, if need be, but this was extraordinary.

The room erupted. Like the eruption that had taken place at Mission Control Houston at the exact moment that Neil Armstrong had stepped onto the Moon. It had occupied our minds totally for as long as our numbed memories could recall, and now it had really happened, without any warning, so totally unexpected. There was cheering, hugging, hooting and hollering. We had finally broken through the crust.

When things had calmed down I wandered off to a remote part of the building, onto a concrete balcony which faced out over the steep blue hills of Rwanda. And without any shame or inhibition, I just cried my eyes out.

*

216

## Chapter 15

The Morning Brief was, relatively speaking, a pleasure. I waited for the Op RETOUR figures to come up and sat deadpan while they were read out. The DFC asked for them to be repeated. Yes, agreed Austen Yella, the figure was 3,850, bringing the total number of people moved by vehicle to 29,486.

Tirelessly, day on day, the occupants of Britain House had worked the Headquarters: Op RETOUR was the only chance to prevent a regional bonfire; bring home the IDPs, then the refugees and there would be some control over events; without this critical mass, there would be another bloodbath. Staff officers, who a few months before had become bored and listless with UN ineptitude, now quietly admitted that the Operation gave them real satisfaction as they saw it unfold and contributed to it. It motivated them – gave them a sense of common purpose - but is was not a good idea to be seen publicly to be too much of an enthusiast. Now, as the figures were announced, and a ripple ran around the room, I made eye contact with our supporters, feeling their pride, reinforcing their commitment. At grass roots, all of the effective people in UNAMIR were on our team. The rest just seemed to look on, speechless.

There was something even more telling in the briefing than that. From the moment the first staff officer started to give the information picture, right through to the final item on logistics, the only subject under discussion had been Op RETOUR. The Operation was, and was going to be, the 'only game in town'.

*

We were doing very well but one of the reasons was undoubtedly the fact that we were not feeding people in Cyanika. Voluntarily, *Care*, the NGO in Rukhondo, our next

217

major camp, now numbering 80,000, had agreed to carry out one last food distribution on 24 January. That would be it. Were we, they asked, happy with that? We were.

*

Barney and Mark were talking to a reporter in a 'quiet' corner of the IOC. I overheard Mark saying, quite plainly: 'This is the most successful humanitarian operation ever.' I cornered him afterwards.

'That's right,' he drawled with conviction. 'Nothing like this has ever happened before. It's way better than anything I've ever seen.'

In the same way as I was proud to be associated with this Operation, I lived in despair of it ever working well. It was an insight to believe that all the others, Somalia, Ethiopia, the Sudan and the rest, had been worse. By my polished British Army standards, we were a shambles.

*

There was a dozen of them. Journalists, TV crew, radio correspondents. All from Australia. They were visiting the Australian Medical Detachment and I had heard that the Commanding Officer, not a convert, had been very scathing about the Operation. The questioning hostility evident in the newsmen as they shuffled in, confirmed their antipathy. This was going to be a tough briefing.

After Andy Moore had given them an overview and Barney had described the IOC, I had my chance. It was pointless trying to undo the damage which had been done to us. I told them the plain truth. That we were labouring without the overt support of the Government. That the International Community had done little to help Rwanda and that what credibility we had as Westerners in Rwanda, we had built for ourselves. That we could not rely on political support in the future and had chosen, consciously, to demonstrate our commitment to help Rwanda by returning her citizens home in conditions of peace, safety and dignity in order to rebuild their lives. That we didn't care if others were critical of our endeavours or our methods because whoever you spoke to in Rwanda, whoever spoke the truth, would acknowledge that what we were doing was the right thing to do, and that was what motivated us. That we were already remarkably successful, that we would now go from strength to strength. That it was in their interests to watch us and support us because it was our intention to surmount all the obstacles in order to do the job. That we were grateful for the help of the Australian Medics in the camps and that Australians at home should be proud of what they were doing and that if they could do anything to raise our profile in Australia or persuade their Government to give aid direct to Kigali, rather than to those NGOs which still propped up the camps, they would be doing us and Rwanda a great service.

'How would you describe this Operation, in a nutshell?' asked a tough-looking, bearded journalist.

'This is quite simply the most successful integrated humanitarian operation ever,' I replied, surprising myself.

*

I gasped as the helicopter roared in over Cyanika. Where the previous week there had been many, now there were few. I met Tim Meisberger at the Landing Zone at Gikongoro and Colonel Dan Luyie of ZAMBATT. They were both in great form.

'It's really happening,' Tim promised. 'They're going home.' Dan was equally upbeat. For every one going home on the trucks, Dan felt that three or four were walking out, the vast majority going home too. Even with a conservative estimate, it seemed as though we were moving on a ratio of 3:1. I trusted him implicitly. His men were on the hillsides, patrolling through the night; if anyone knew what was really going on, it was the soldiers of Zambia. I was buoyed up by Dan's reports.

Up on the hill, the majority of *blindées* had gone. There were orderly queues of people waiting to be screened by the RPA soldiers, beside the church. The buses were marshalled in rows. It was all very civilised, very organised.

The RPA were being polite and helpful, our interpreter assured us. The RPA soldiers saluted me and looked respectful. It was an astonishing PR performance by them. They were being a lot more helpful to the people than many of the UN troops were. The people would open their bundles and show them what they were carrying. As well as the rolled-up sheeting of UNHCR blue plastic, each family had their meagre possessions and at least one big bag of food. It was what we already knew to be the case, but it was gratifying to see it demonstrated. After several months in the camp, these people had hoarded enough food to get by for at least a month. They would not starve, whatever the circumstances; they could walk for weeks with 20 kilos of food on their heads. And they could walk a very long way on 20 kilos.

There were not that many men. I asked the women where their husbands had gone. Some, they admitted, were in Zaire. Others had gone south to Kibeho, to escape the RPA, since they were afraid that they would be arrested and they wanted the women and children to go home first, to report back, through the bush telegraph. But others were following their husbands, who had already gone home and had now themselves sent word that it was safe. In all this information, the fact that we had read all these possibilities right, in roughly the right proportions, confirmed my feelings of good humour. We seemed to have learnt enough to put at least some of Rwanda into context, in just a few months.

I jumped up onto a UNHCR bus. The people were quiet. I spoke to them after the initial greetings in Kinyarwanda, and the line which we had all now used so many times:

'*Banyarwanda Nigihe Cyogutaha*' - 'People of Rwanda, it is time to go home.'

There was an audible sigh. I was a known person; they talked about me, examined me wherever I went, recognised me as a key representative of the International Community. Wherever I stopped to talk, a crowd would form. Now, through the interpreter, I reinforced our gratitude at how brave they were to be taking this major decision, but that it really was the right thing to do and that they should not be afraid. UN soldiers would meet them in their Communes. In many, there was an NGO available to help the *Bourgmestre*. That they should bring their problems to these people and that we would help them now and as long as we remained in Rwanda. That the killing was over and that they must learn to live in peace and reconciliation with their neighbours and that they should teach their children to love and not to hate.

When I had finished what had started to sound like a sermon, they clapped spontaneously and then crowded forward to shake my hands and to embrace my arms. As they had been in Cyanika for nearly six months, there were some earthy odours. There were tears and handshakes, and as I climbed down, they kept shouting out, shaking their hands together as a gesture of thanks.

I waved at them until the bus had disappeared off down the hill before I climbed onto the next one, and then the next, to confront again and again, the realities of our actions. In Kigali, it could be almost an intellectual exercise. Out here on the ground, the hopes and fears of all these people and the trust they had put in us was entirely tangible. I felt compelled to assume some direct responsibility for the risks they were taking in the cause of peace.

Some time later, I joined the others. We looked at the figures for the day, at the near-empty hillside. One by one, we all had our say. UNHCR, *Feed the Children*, the NGO that was now helping at Cyanika, UNREO and finally, me for UNAMIR.

221

Tomorrow, we would close Cyanika. And then the desperate existence of 30,000 Rwandese on this now barren hill would stop being a nightmare reality and become a distant memory.

*

I did not often go up to give a briefing for Op RETOUR; it was largely preferable to let the others do the talking. Since the improvements had started, I did not need to advocate the Operation - it spoke for itself. If I could not be given a hard time, then that was good for us. There was certainly some bitterness there and I did not want to fuel it.

But this morning, I felt I owed it to everybody who had been of help, and who had worked towards this milestone, to make a public announcement. When the humanitarian slot came up in the briefing, I walked out and told them that we were on our way now and that we needed everybody to push harder to achieve our goals. Today, I promised, something was going to happen which, a few weeks before, most people would have said was impossible. Despite the opposition and the difficulties which Op RETOUR had encountered, today we would close our first major camp. The closure would be peaceful and dignified and would be carried out with the full co-operation of the Government of Rwanda and the RPA. And today, we would now shift our focus onto Rukhondo, population 80,000.

*

Out in Rukhondo the trucks were already lining up. Second Lieutenant Innocent from ZAMBATT was organising the people. The Australian medics were carrying out health checks on the people before they mounted the trucks. Despite the unhelpfulness of some of their senior hierarchy, the Aussies were like good soldiers everywhere. Keen as mustard, stoical, cynical to the observer, and totally dedicated. I admired their deft handling of the people, their gentleness, their no-nonsense efficiency, their good humour. The Australian infantry who guarded them were mirror images of their British counterparts. One gap-toothed corporal had the children eating out of his hand with a series of magic tricks. Even the RPA were involved in the process, laughing and joking. It was hard not to be impressed with the UN and with Op RETOUR, out on the sunny hillside, with everything going so well.

Innocent was brilliant. Speaking to the people in a Swahili dialect which was similar to Kinyarwanda, he encouraged and cajoled them to go home, imparting the day's messages through our 'media' network. And when one or another shouted at him, to dispute the safety which he claimed, he would argue back, soon having the crowd with him, making them laugh, convincing them. Again, it was the best we could possibly offer. African troops, in tune with the people. Australians giving specialist support. The UN at its best.

But then Innocent and Dan Luyie showed us a low school building in the middle of the expanse of blue sheeting. Here, it was said, the RPA had an 'unofficial' prison and there were rumours of people being beaten and held without charge. Right in the middle of the camp, they were prepared to flaunt their contempt for the law, while outside they espoused a philosophy of 'hearts and minds'.

Next, a *blindée*. I had been invited in by the occupants. The stench was hard to bear. It was important to see at first hand how they lived. Bits of foam and rags made up the bed on one side and there were a few measly possessions, including a tin pot for cooking and the omnipresent machete. But as expected, in the corner of every *blindée* I inspected, was a sack of food. The family reserve. Or, from my perspective, the passport to the Home Commune.

Barney Mayhew and Chris Kaye from UNREO were up on the hill and joined me as I left one shelter. 'You'll never guess what just happened to us,' said Chris, amazed by his encounter.

223

'Up there was a group of blokes sitting around and when we asked them why they wouldn't go home, they replied as cheerfully as you like: 'We can't; we're murderers.''

*

'Have you talked to Yan?' I shouted over the awful line, the Nigerian corporal waiting behind me in the queue listening with great interest to every word.

'Yes, he's definitely coming,' Sue promised. 'The MOD are working on it now.'

'Well tell him to hurry up,' I shouted. 'We'll have them all home before he gets here.'

*

*Extract from a report from Tim Meisberger, UNREO Gikongoro, to the IOC, 1 February 1995:*

'I had a very good and long talk with the Judge at Masango who was the Camp Leader at Cyanika. There is a need to create a simple training or course for the people in the Gachachas. They are the ones that send people to prison and the way and under which circumstances they are working at the moment is questionable. If we can arrange something simple on this then this is info that the jungle telegraph will take back to the camps. This is something that the camp population is very concerned about and according to the Judge, this is what will make them come home. He thinks that a lot of the info is not needed as people have, below the gossip level, a good understanding of their Home Commune.'

*

I had been about to meet Randolph on a Sunday morning, before he had radioed to call it off. He had to go to Bujumbura at short notice. Things were hotting up in Burundi. As his helicopter clattered over the Belgian Village on the way south, it suddenly occurred to me that all my plans for the day had gone with that helicopter. After breakfast, I filled up a bucket of water and went outside to wash the Chinese Jeep. An UNREO vehicle stopped. It was Margaux.

'Anyone for tennis?' she shouted. 'The court is free but I've got nobody to play.'

The thought of playing tennis was as alien as taking time out to wash the Jeep. 'Oh yes,' I thought, 'I've got to play tennis.'

Afterwards, Kelvin, Mark Cuthbert-Brown and Carl joined us at the bar for a drink. And when Margaux had left, I asked Kelvin if he had ever gone twitching.

An hour later, I brought the Chinese Jeep to a standstill on the Byumba Road. The wetlands were alive with wildfowl, and right in front of us, standing on a pile of old rubble, was a hammerkopf – elegant, dark brown and intelligent, with a head shaped like a hammer. 'That,' I explained with all the sincerity of the novice twitcher, 'is my favourite bird.'

We were joined by some small children. Kelvin pulled out a smart Jermyn Street spotted handkerchief, tied it up into knots and turned it into a mouse, which then proceeded to run up his arm. At the end of this party piece, he asked one of the kids to pull the tail and the mouse turned back into a handkerchief. They loved it; he was a hit. He was doing naturally what Yan and I and now Mark had all done soon after arrival in Rwanda: Shown our strength of feeling for these poor people, after their terrible ordeal, by trying to communicate with them.

At home over a beer, we talked. I had not been so relaxed since my return to Rwanda from leave.

'I'll bet I know what you thought when we first met,' he said quietly.

'Oh what's that?' I replied, squirming a little.

225

'Who's this big cuckoo just come into my nest?' he smiled.

*

Fraser was leaving. In a ritual similar to that accorded to Kieran, we went up to the Club for a meal. Fraser ceremoniously handed over the starting handle of his Series 1 Land Rover to Mark Cuthbert-Brown. In the morning Mark, as the new owner, drove him to the airport and we followed in convoy, another cortege on its way to say farewell to one of our number. Fraser's impact had been significant as the General's right-hand man. He had achieved much and his shoes in the Headquarters would not be easy to fill. As we waved farewell to him, Sean and I reflected on our own position. In just a few weeks, we would walk up those same stairs and fly out of Rwanda forever. And while Sean, were it not for Lynne, would have happily jumped up and left on the same flight as Fraser, I did not want to go home at that moment, at all. I was doing my life's work.

*

On the way to the airport, on the next bright Sunday morning, the sound of singing carried over the whine of the Chinese Jeep's gearbox. A sizeable congregation was squeezed into a small hall, the people-pressure so great that many of the participants were hanging out of the open windows, still singing. I stopped the Jeep and walked back.

As I moved up to the open back door, the singing stopped. There must have been three hundred people squeezed into the hall. They all turned their heads to look at me.

'Come in, my friend' said the Pastor, from the front, and I was drawn in, pulling the blue beret from my head, as I had not expected to be and now could not avoid.

226

When I was sandwiched into the centre of the room, the service began again. Squashed in, I was forced to sway with them, to clap with them, to wear, self-consciously, the same smile they all directed at me. The Pastor said that there had been many bad things done in Rwanda but that the UN was now trying to help the Rwandese people. We prayed for peace and it felt as though I had now crossed another invisible line. As the days went by I was becoming more involved, more connected to the fabric, the soul of Rwanda. My role should have been one of objectivity, of rational analysis and clear decision-making. I could not allow these softer perceptions to cloud my thoughts.

*

We flew into the Southern Camps. At Ndago, the camp adjacent to Kibeho, we could not have been more surprised at the reception. Tens of thousands of people were there to greet us, their dark clothes, grubby with the months in the *blindées*. The occasional colourful headscarf and the flash of white teeth provided the only variety in an endless stretch of dark humanity ringing the football pitch. Perhaps the word had come that we were about to land by helicopter.

Mark Frohardt and Barney had been joined by Lazar, a senior official from the Ministry of Rehabilitation. On the military side, Mark Cuthbert-Brown had joined me. With the UNREO field officers and their interpreters, our entourage was at least impressive in size, although how we had walked into this crowd was a mystery. It became clear once we had entered the Camp chief's office and sat down, finding makeshift rough-hewn furniture to shuffle onto, that our visit was considered to be important for one very clear reason.

'I have assembled the Commune leaders,' explained the Chief through an interpreter, 'and told them about your plans. The people of six Communes will be leaving tomorrow.'

227

We were thrown into shock. We had thought of Ndago as being one of the last resorts for the Hutu, a final stand before they were consigned to hell or to Burundi. We had always assumed that the camp contained many hard-liners, and that dislodging their tight grip would be one of our final hurdles. And now here we were, being told that so many were about to go home.

'How many have you registered for departure?' queried Lazar.

'Maybe 15-20,000,' came the reply. It was unbelievable. All we had to do was say nothing and these people would be sent home, a fate for which they had been prepared psychologically, and prepared administratively. Most of them could walk home in less than one day. There was just one major hurdle to overcome - our consciences. We went into a huddle. The arguments flew thick and fast as we contemplated the gift we were being offered. To be fair, the Ministry representative was prepared to listen to a range of views. I thanked God that a stronger personality had not decided to join us that day, or there would have been no discussion at all. The faces of the IDPs were pressed hard against the window bars by the numbers pushing from behind. The building was completely surrounded, in silence, as we thrashed it out; they were unaware that their fates hung in the balance.

Mark Frohardt and I were of one mind, and that simplified the issue. The Operation was going well. One of our principles was that early operations must be successful. If we cast these people out, without first having prepared their Home Communes and without being in any position to guarantee their safety, they could come flowing back a few days later, in terror from the RPA, without the certainty of a food distribution in Ndago. We could not risk this group of 15,000 or 20,000 people wandering around Gikongoro Prefecture, possibly heading over the border into Burundi. They must stay until we came to them as part of our orderly, methodical plan, however poorly we could execute it.  If we could not provide conditions of peace, safety and dignity for them to go home, then we should not take the risk.   That it would have been taken anyway, had we not arrived that day in Ndago, was the most sobering thought.   In conditions of chaos, without proper control over the countryside, we risked these lives and all our hopes for these people, on the random throw of a dice.

*

On the following day, we were engaged once more in animated discussion, this time in the IOC.  The subject was food, which 'could not be used as a weapon'.  How many times had I been told that food could not be used as a weapon?  I was as sick of the trite phrase as I was of every piece of 'humanitarian' dogma.  What was morally right was not practically possible. As we had argued with Pascale on Christmas Eve, if we continued to feed the people, they would not go home.  If they did not go home voluntarily, then we would be faced with a much greater crisis as the RPA forced them out by violence. There had to be some compromises.

The Red Cross was the ultimate arbiter on this.  We could persuade the NGOs to stop feeding the people, but the Red Cross had the final responsibility to continue the feeding programmes and it was only if they were prepared to compromise that we could make some form of result possible. We had asked the Kigali representative to the IOC.

He listened carefully while Mark and I explained the issue. Before we could finish, the representative jumped in.

'There is no need for you to continue,' he explained.  'I am aware of the complexities of this situation and we are under great political pressure from the Government to stop feeding the people.  Very unhappily, we have agreed.'

Mark and I looked at each other in open-mouthed surprise. Nobody could ever anticipate the next twist or turn in the

229

Rwanda story. We had not wanted this result; it was the furthest from our minds.

'Well, we do not want you to stop feeding the people,' I explained, being rewarded with the same level of surprise. 'We believe there is a compromise which will be acceptable to all parties, but it does require your agreement and support. If we are to convince the Government, we have to present a united front.'

He listened as Mark explained that we needed a safety valve, that the Southern Camps, being the hardest nut to crack, should continue to be fed, while we closed the Northern Camps. People in fear for their lives could then go south until they registered in Kibeho and Ndago. Or those returning from their Home Communes, having had a bad experience, could also find somewhere to go that did not involve exodus to Burundi. Here was a morally defensible position which he could sell to the leaders of the organisation in Rome. Together, we could defend it to the Government. But if the Red Cross or the IOC showed any lack of solidarity, we knew that the Government and then the RPA could pounce on us. It was a dangerous game we played. Trust was one commodity in short supply. But with another unlikely private alliance, the result of yet another innovation by the IOC, coupled with the flexibility of one of the world's most prestigious humanitarian organisations, we had moved things along in the right direction, at little risk to life. Or so we hoped.

*

*Extract from a report from Tim Meisberger, UNREO Gikongoro, to the IOC, 9 February 1995:*

'On Monday, I visited Kamana and Munini. In each meeting, rough characters pushed themselves to the front of the crowd and shouted down everyone else. In Kamana they screamed that there was no security in Nyakizu that people who went there would be killed. I calmly informed the crowd that thousands of people had returned there with no problems, but the men with the murderous eyes continued to shout and make throat-cutting gestures. I scoffed at and ridiculed these men, trying my best to undermine their efforts to intimidate the crowd, but even with two Zambian soldiers at my back, I began to get nervous.'

'When there are no RPA troops in the camps, the Interahamwe dominates the people. Through massive campaigns of disinformation and intimidation, they ensure that the population fears for their lives. I asked the Prefect and the RPA Brigade Commander if they could station some troops in the camps and on Tuesday night they moved in. The people were afraid at first, not surprising after the stories they have heard, but as they grow used to their presence, and see they are not devils, I think it will have a calming effect. I believe that when there are RPA troops in the camps, Interahamwe rumours and intimidation are substantially reduced and people feel safe to leave. It will be interesting to see if the mood in those camps changes because of this, and if the departure rate goes up.'

'I feel that we should not be concentrating on a particular camp or area because it might tend to push people. Instead we should try to reduce all the camps at the same time. The increasing willingness of the Red Cross to stop food distribution in the camps, and perhaps the increasing impatience of the authorities with the situation, could produce a large movement in the next few weeks.'

*

The Southern Camps were the greatest next-stage problem. Where I had focused on the wider strategic issues throughout

231

my sleepless nights before Christmas, now the problem had narrowed down to the operational issue which faced us ever more. We were doing well in the North and I had great confidence that Rukhondo would dissolve even faster than Cyanika. The smaller camps were going too, the result of a relentless effort by the Zambians and because we sent trucks to them every day. If nobody got on the vehicles, they moved onto a larger target camp, but the people were being offered a chance to go home, every day. We knew that there was a general move southwards from the North, some of it still the reverberations of the RPA's clearances of the autumn. Soon there would be a hard-core of those who would not go home. It could be large, as many as 100,000-150,000 of the 350,000 we had started with. And how we were going to deal with them required a completely different approach. I needed to pre-empt all the permutations and ensure that we developed a plan which would actually work.

I stared up at the ceiling in my little room. There were creatures above. They could have been rats, or crows. I had tried to find how they could be getting in and out, but there was no sign of an entrance, although we had killed a rat a few days before, and another had been chased into my room and mysteriously vanished. Now, as the Southern Camps issue had me staring out of the window up at the moon all night long, the noise of these animals was driving me mad. Every time I tried to settle down, the scratching started again. At last, unable to take it any more, I sent a wave of pure mental anger up at them. Immediately there was silence. Later, as I started to doze, they began again. I sent the wave up again. Silence. Eventually I slept.

I met Brimelow in the morning. He looked worn out.

'Every month, during the full moon, I can't sleep,' he explained.

'Would you think I was mad if I said that there are creatures in my ceiling and that they seem to be affected by the moon too?' I asked.

He shook his head. He was really serious. 'And would you think I was mad if I told you that I could affect their behaviour with my mind,' I asked quietly, expecting him to explode in laughter.

'No mate,' he replied evenly, without a flicker of emotion. 'I'd say it was entirely possible.'

Now it was really true. Rwanda was mad. The people in UNAMIR were mad. The Agencies and NGOs were all mad. This was common knowledge. But now, without even noticing it happening, Alan Brimelow and I, Rwanda's most hard-bitten idealists, had gone mad too.

\*

Final proof of the general madness came the following day. Steve and Andy Moore were driving through Kigali in their pick-up truck. As they approached the main roundabout at the Church of the St Famille, they slowed to a halt to give way to oncoming traffic. From the bushes on the right, a man appeared, pointing a pistol directly at Steve's head. The Aussies were having a bad day and were engaging in a general moan, above the noise of the engine. Swept up in animated conversation, they only paused to shout one thing. 'Fuck off,' they yelled together. And the would-be ambusher, so surprised was he at their casual, angry indifference, that as they drove off, he turned tail and ran back into cover, to await a prey more likely to be impressed by his violent threat.

\*

# Chapter 16

Colonels Jan Arp and Kelvin Tutt wanted to visit the Operation. It was a fastball and I guessed the General had a hand in it. There was no time to plan, no opportunity to brief people on how they should play the visit. On the road out of Kigali, the fields were not as empty as they had been on my last trip overland, before Christmas. There was a striking increase in the number of people. At odd intervals, smoke betrayed the fires of the homecomers, as they cleared the vegetation from their plots. With a jolt, I realised that Op RETOUR was probably the major reason for this change. A good sign.

We began our grand tour in Gitarama. Lieutenant Colonel Hasnain, from Bangladesh, was adamant. The Open Relief Centres run by the *Lutheran World Federation* (LWF), a German NGO, existed on the map only. Visit one on the ground and you might find a stack of plastic sheeting, a sign proclaiming ownership, a single latrine. But there was no coordination, no place of administration, no support for the *Bourgmestre*. It was a sham. I was concerned but not surprised. Jan and Kelvin were supportive. They had heard the other side of the story only that morning in Kigali, at the NGO meeting where the LWF representative had promised that the Open Relief Centres were ready. It was an excellent illustration of the frustration and daily vexation which we faced and tried so hard to overcome.

Colonel Hasnain gave us a first real insight into a growing problem. The prisons were filling up fast. It had been so for several months but now, as we were moving tens of thousands home, so this pressure had increased. There were six thousand people in the Gitarama prison, designed for 150. I listened to his comments with increasing concern. We had hoped that the RPA would be sensible enough to let many people come home before they started to arrest what we assumed were the relatively few killers amongst them. Now, it was becoming clearer that they were not going to be so patient. Our whole plan was based initially on the concept of absorption - providing the means for the people in the Home Communes to re-establish themselves safely under UNAMIR security. By raising the arrest rate beyond our expectations, the RPA would disturb the absorption rate by increasing fear and decreasing the numbers prepared to leave the camps. While so many were being arrested, our confidence was also being eroded, increasing the moral pressure on us to stop encouraging people to go home. So the RPA could unhinge the Operation in the Home Communes by decreasing absorption and unravel our meltdown of the camps by using force. Jan and Kelvin could not appreciate this worry. They had no idea of the numerous delicate balances we needed to make this thing work. And I would not share my fears with anyone but Mark Frohardt.

We stopped briefly in Kigoma, an Open Relief Centre run by *Oxfam Quebec*. It was an illustration of perfect efficiency, marred only by the interpreter who asked Jan and Kelvin to come away from some recently dug ground - a mass grave, he explained. The accommodation was empty; the people had felt confident enough to go straight home on arrival. The NGO office was manned by bright, enthusiastic volunteers, next door to the *Bourgmestre*, beside the UNAMIR section post, where a dozen Mali UN soldiers looked serious and alert, close to the RPA post. The *Bourgmestre* was happy with the service and cooperation he had received from the NGO and UNAMIR and explained how well everything was going. As we were leaving, three busloads of IDPs from Rukhondo turned up, on cue. The people were apprehensive, but relaxed when they saw the UNAMIR soldiers and the top brass. They were all smiles. The children gurgled and cooed on their mothers' backs.

At Butare, we arrived at Tac Headquarters in time for the weekly NGO conference. Jan Arp said a few words before giving me the floor, introducing me as the 'father of Op RETOUR'. At every NGO meeting in Butare which I had attended, the sheer dedication and commitment of the people, ranging from the NGO workers, to the UNREO field officers and the staff at Tac Headquarters was humbling. Away from the cloying bureaucracy and politics in Kigali, they always seemed to be getting on with the job. They were doing brilliantly.

At dawn, I wished I had not had such a good night, drinking beer with the officers of Mali Company. Kelvin joined me at the gates, awaiting the transport. The people were coming up the hill past the National Museum of Rwanda, with enormous loads on their heads, moving towards the market.

'*Mnaramuzeeho,*' I shouted out cheerfully.

'*Mnaramuzee,*' they retorted, breaking into their wonderful white-teethed smiles as they always did when addressed in Kinyarwanda.

'*Amakurichi,*' some shouted.

'*Nimese, nimese chaani,*' I replied.

'What are you saying,' asked Kelvin. 'What's all this about?'

'Oh it's just a variation on the Good Morning theme,' I explained. '*Mnaramuzee* means 'What is the news from the mountains?' Surprisingly, the reply is 'What is the news from the mountains?''

'*Mnaramuzee,*' he shouted at the next unsuspecting load-carrier, toiling up the hill.

'*Mnaramuzee,*' cried the recipient, thrilled.

I watched Kelvin as he worked on his new-found greeting, quite delighted with the effect. In twenty minutes, he had generated several hundred Rwandese smiles.

We stopped in Cyanika, the better for Jan and Kelvin to marvel at what we had done. The latrines were being filled in; it had seemed to take a long time to organise but now it was happening. I stood on the hill and looked around at the devastation, stretching for acres in every direction. It was like Ypres, the mud churned up, the rubbish scattered around, a few bare stumps of trees remaining from what had been a wood. Though an eyesore, it was also our icon, the first tangible proof that the people could be encouraged to go home.

At Rukhondo, the tent city was dissolving. At least 50,000 had left. Colonel Dan Luyie was there again to meet us. The majority had walked out, he assured us, not south towards Kibeho but east towards home. Kelvin showed some children his famous mouse trick. We had several 'discussions' with the people, drawing a small crowd wherever we stopped. We would talk to people at random and they would largely agree that going home was the only option. Then they would be replaced by more vociferous types, Hutu extremists, if not actually Interahamwe. We needed to move quietly, speak forcefully, argue loudly and then move on, without causing a riot. Jan and Kelvin mastered the technique straight away. Neither had been in direct confrontation with the Hutu extremists before. To leave the Headquarters in Kigali and meet them face to face was an education for them. This was the sharp end of Op RETOUR.

On the way back to Kigali, we stopped at the Overnight Way Station at Butare. It was another textbook visit. The Station was organised to the nines, receiving families off the trucks and buses, and feeding, registering and issuing more rations and 'non-food items' (pots and pans etc) before they were moved onwards. For those who arrived too late to get home with several hours daylight ahead of them, there was tented accommodation. The whole thing was running like clockwork, moving the day's flow of over 1,200 people through without hiccup. Everywhere there were smiles, hands raised in greeting for the '*Mwiriway*' (Good Afternoon) which had now replaced Kelvin's '*Mnaramuzee*'. These people were glad to be going home, happy now to be in our hands, hopeful for the future.

As we pulled back into the IOC later that afternoon, I said my farewells to Kelvin and Jan. They were both excellent, professional officers, well balanced in their judgements, articulate and forceful. And they were both friends. Now they could also be allies, not just because they believed what they heard in Kigali, but because they had seen it on the ground. And it was working. By God, I pinched myself as I savoured the almost uncanny perfection with which the visit had gone, it really was working.

*

There was to be no magic solution to our press problem. We were not receiving international coverage and Randolph had not been able to produce some heavyweight media guru from New York, to fight our corner, as he had promised. We would have to start taking random initiatives, as we found them. I agreed to corner the British press.

I met the *Times* representative in a café in Kigali. Meeting people in a café in Kigali was obviously something he had done many times before. But I was deployed on operations and going out 'on the town' was not compatible with that up to now. He was polite and interested but wanted an angle.

'Come and see it,' I pleaded. 'Visit the IOC, go out on the ground, you will be amazed by what we have achieved. At least 60-70,000 have gone home. Probably more. This is the rebuilding programme, the rehabilitation programme, the reconciliation programme all rolled into one.'

Tom Walker was a good guy who had a strong 'feel' for Rwanda. But nothing ever appeared in the *Times*. His primary role was as media coordinator for *MSF*. *MSF* was hot-and-cold on Op RETOUR and did not overtly support us. Their French political connections and France's support of the former regime were two factors in this relationship. I guessed they would not be best pleased if Tom wrote an article praising our efforts.

Roger Hearing was the BBC's East Africa correspondent, flying in from Nairobi every now and again. I invited him to

239

the IOC and out onto the ground. I offered him a helicopter ride over the camps, including Cyanika. He was pleasant and positive but never took up the offer.

In a country as full of woe as was Rwanda, our tiny glimmer of hope did not burn brightly enough for the Western media. A few thousand bodies found newly butchered in the forest and there was a story. But a few tens of thousands going home in peace, safety and dignity? It was the kind of material which goes in at the end of the news, a little bit of light current affairs to balance out the horror and political chicanery of 'ordinary' news. But it would get no mileage out of Rwanda, which was only associated with killing and with camps. And so it was ignored.

I could rationalise this ambivalence but I could not stop being angry about it. The correspondents jetted in, visited the latest scene of carnage, wrote a few words, often very movingly, and were out again. They had no time for us. Most were just doing their jobs, for editors who were just as busy doing their jobs. And the unique cooperation, the striving, the fragile progress that we could demonstrate from the IOC was just not meat strong enough for their taste. Without their support, I feared that Op RETOUR would just wither and die, and with it would perish our hope for Rwanda.

*

Captain Stefan Grenier was about to depart, his tour of duty nearly over. When he turned up at the IOC on one of his final days, with a big package in the back of his vehicle, I could have hugged him. With Rwandese artists, he had put together a simple colour poster, showing the people going home, through all the stages of throwing off the Interahamwe yoke, registering, moving and being received by smiling RPA and UNAMIR soldiers in the Home Communes, before they began to till the land again. The message was completely clear, for an

240

illiterate population. He had produced 2,000 of these, ready for distribution throughout the camps. It was his parting gift, a tangible token of the reality of taking action, rather than just talking about it. I knew that with these, we could make further inroads into the psyche of the people.

In the corner of each poster was a crisp, black-and-white diagram. 'What's this?' I quizzed Stefan.

'It's a pictogram,' he explained. 'Picture language.'

It was a superb piece of inventive thinking. The father, followed by the mother, carrying a baby on her back and both of them walking with loads on their heads. The path to the round thatched hut bisected by an arrow which pointed to the open door. No matter which culture or nationality you were from, you could not fail to see this simple message as anything but the clearest of invitations: 'It is time to go home.'

While I discussed Stefan's outstanding contribution with Jan Arp, he agreed that we should have full-time professional support on the information front. 'I have a volunteer,' he promised. 'Just convince Colonel Moeen, the Chief Military Observer that you need him, and he's yours.' It took a few days of wheedling but eventually Major Alex Rusovski of the Russian Army reported for duty to me at the IOC. We had fought on opposing sides during the Cold War. It was an education to come face to face with a former GRU officer from the Psychological Warfare Directorate.

'My Colonel,' he exclaimed solemnly at my first briefing. 'I understand exactly what you wish me to achieve. But before I make any further plans, I need to know the answer to one simple question on the type of propaganda you want. Do you want me to tell lies, or tell the truth?'

'The truth will do fine, Alex,' I replied, sighing. 'Just to tell the whole truth will be a major propaganda victory for us.'

Out on the ground, UNREO's latest recruit, Charlie Main, an intrepid Brit, was having tremendous local effect. With a number of Zambian officers, he took it upon himself to put

241

together a tightly focussed local counter-propaganda operation. He would visit a few key Communes, gather detailed information and then tour the camps telling our side of the story. At one meeting in Ndago camp, he was asked to explain what had happened to one well-known man who had allegedly been shot by the RPA the night after he arrived home. Dutifully, Charlie travelled to the Commune in question and tracked down the house of the individual concerned, before driving back to the camp, and calling another meeting, all in the space of one day.

'I drove to the dead man's Commune,' he explained to the crowd, deliberately talking slowly through an interpreter. They were impressed.

'I went to the dead man's house.' There was an audible sigh.

'I knocked on the dead man's door,' he continued. The drama increased.

'The dead man opened it,' he continued, delighting in the shock effect of his words. 'And what's more, he was drunk on banana beer.' The crowd dissolved in laughter.

It was impossible to predict the effect of such information, coming from the Westerners, the only people they trusted. But that same night, we learnt, at least 20 families walked home, nearly all destined for the same Home Commune.

*

In his capacity as acting SRSG, the General was having a rough ride. He called me into his office to help sort out a minor political problem.

He had isolated himself behind a barrier of bureaucracy and bodyguards. It was no longer possible to stroll down to his office, stick your head around Fraser's door and be waved in to see him. Now he was protected. I had to give up my pistol at the top of the stairs before I was escorted to see him. Whoever was advising him on personal security had clearly no idea of

242

how this impacted on the staff. If you felt your General thought that you might shoot him, were you supposed to be more open in your opinions, or less?

'What do you know about Mark Frohardt?' he demanded.

'He's the best senior operator throughout the Agencies. I trust him totally. He's hard but extremely competent.' I replied truthfully.

'Well if you hadn't said that, he would have been toast,' replied the General.

Mark had been stitched up. As Randolph was away again, he had been left as Acting Humanitarian Coordinator for Rwanda; Charles Petrie was in Burundi. Mark had drafted a letter to the Government for Agency discussion. Someone had carefully removed the word 'Draft' by photocopying it and then had circulated it to all the UN Agency Heads, claiming that Mark was deliberately trying to take over the Operation on behalf of UNREO. No matter that he was going through proper channels. No matter either that he was being ultra-cautious. Somebody senior wanted rid of him. The General made sure that he would survive, but it was a close thing. And Mark was their best man. What would have happened to the humanitarian push, I wondered, if they had taken him out?

*

I had stopped working on my computer, to stretch. Beyond the IOC, the rolling hills of Rwanda stood empty, blue and humid in the after-rain haze. There was something on the telephone wire running across the back of the compound. I focussed my binoculars. It was big, bigger than I had first thought. As I watched, it moved, swooping low and back up effortlessly, to land perfectly on the wire a hundred metres further along, just one wing-beat required to provide the necessary kinetic energy. Tucking in its wings, it hunched again, observing.

I leafed through my new book. It must be an....augur buzzard. ...very rare. It stayed for an hour, while I worked away, each visitor to the office inspecting it closely and then confirmed the identity from the white markings on the chest. There was no better break from the unrelenting pressure of work than to spot an augur buzzard. I missed Yan.

*

It had been a struggle but at last, the first real Task Force meeting was to take place. Justin Murara, the Minister, was driving it, a commitment which was central to the whole process. He had promised to devote every Monday afternoon henceforth to the meetings. Mark Frohardt and I pulled the thing together. We cleared an agenda with Justin which covered the structure, progress to date and several key issues including feeding in the Southern Camps. We expected senior representatives from the Ministries of Defence (the RPA), Justice, and Information as well as the Heads of all the UN Agencies, or their Deputies.

The result was mixed. The Ministry of Defence sent a junior Captain. Our own Lieutenant Andre, currently deputising for Lieutenant Cameron, was clearly more senior, more experienced and better connected. The others produced third or fourth tier civil servants, unwilling to describe their exact roles. Justin was clearly vexed. On the UN side, the Agencies sent high-level people.

In the end, it was inconclusive. There was general agreement that the Operation was going extremely well (and the lack of public Government support for it was tacitly acknowledged too) but no definitive statements were made. One clear factor seemed to be that the Government was not really functioning properly – to bring together the meeting had actually been a major effort. So these players were not senior enough to recommend policy with ministerial authority and

244

Justin demanded higher-level representation at the next meeting. The Red Cross received broad and unspecified support to continue feeding in the Southern Camps, although the RPA officer objected in principle. The Red Cross people thanked us afterwards for our loyalty. But at least, in the endless battle with bureaucrats and vested interests, we reasoned later, we had actually made a small gain.

*

I had now drafted the paper on the Southern Camps. When the agonising and the debate were over, it came down to a pretty straightforward solution. We should continue to encourage people to go home, turning off the food supply in the camps as we went, until a number of Southern Camps were left, where food was still available. The RPA could decide which camps to leave open, and whether to have one large camp or several smaller ones, based on their own security fears. The effort would then be increased in this nucleus, until the point was reached when no more people would go home. This might leave up to 50-100,000 people still in camps, probably the hard core and certainly those who thought they had the most to fear, if they returned to their Home Communes. At a certain point, we would make this a turnstile system, allowing those who wanted to leave the opportunity to do so, but not allowing them back in. There had to be some point at which we did not continue to pander to everyone's needs and this, for me, was it. For those who were then left, the Government and the RPA would have every right to investigate each individual. If they were given the all-clear, they could go home, possibly with a pass in hand. If not, they would be arrested and face the due process of law, but under the strict eye of the International Community. I was sure the bridges we had built with the Red Cross would be vital in this plan. They would do the feeding and they would monitor the legal process. For those who were

245

murderers, the opportunity to leave for Burundi or Zaire was fast approaching, and this would loosen the Interahamwe grip on the camps. For those with a clear conscience, the chance to take their courage in hand would finally arrive.

\*

*Extract from an interview with Major General Paul Kagame, Vice President and Minister for Defence, on Radio Rwanda, on 16 February 1995:*

'There is now a disease called 'reconciliation' or 'dialogue'. Is that dialogue between who and who? The killers and the victims? I personally understand dialogue and reconciliation as talks between people of different ethnic groups and different ideologies or different religions. What sort of dialogue is to be held between the Rwandese?'

'These foreign people should not interfere in our internal affairs. We do not want them to give us instructions, we just want them to give us aid, unconditional aid.'

'They are hypocrites. They say that if you do not do that, you will not have money. We have been refugees for 30 years and they did not care about us, I tell you the truth, they like some refugees and hate others. They did not save people from massacres; they brought planes and soldiers to evacuate their own people and left us people who they saw being massacred.'

'We believe that all refugees are not criminals but most criminals are among them. We want all refugees to return home but still we have the responsibility to punish criminals. The right to be repatriated does not exclude the right to punish criminals.'

'But still, can we forgive those who have no remorse, who do not repent? People like, I heard it was in Karera, are even boasting for having massacred many people.'

*

I had been summoned to appear at breakfast. The General had moved his entourage out of the house in the Belgian Village and down to a convent complex just off the Byumba road. I arrived at 6 a.m., parking the Chinese Jeep ostentatiously outside the front door. The buildings were modern, smart, spacious and rather swish for a convent. The nuns had all left. Instead, the General had established his staff and a number of clerks and bodyguards. It was a bit too heavyweight. Even the SRSG lived in his modest house in the Village and Randolph shared a basic, rented house in a suburb in Kigali.

I met the party I was to escort, over breakfast. The spread was unbelievable - bacon, eggs, sausages, waffles, pancakes and maple syrup. The 'whole nine yards' as a Canadian would have said. The General probably had no idea how his staff lived or what our diet consisted of. We subsisted on food parcels from home, supplemented by local staples, so this was an unexpected treat. In between mouthfuls, I discussed our visit with the Canadian visitors: A number of civil servants, the ambassador from Uganda, who also covered Rwanda, and the Secretary of State for Foreign Affairs, Mrs Stewart. As soon as the morning mist had cleared, we flew out to Kibeho.

The people were up too, no doubt having breakfasted on something less gluttonous. They lined the route up past the church and the school. I gave them the two handed greeting. *'Mnaramuzeeho,'* I shouted. *'Mnaramuzee'* returned several thousand voices.

They gathered around us and I encouraged members of the party to talk to them, to ask them why they wouldn't go home, warning them not to get too involved. Dan Luyie appeared and

247

I chatted with him, getting an up to date briefing from the ground. In his view, things were going well. More and more people were walking home. Very few were moving into Kibeho/Ndago.

Mrs Stewart was an experienced humanitarian. She had worked for a major NGO in a previous appointment. As the meetings continued, I pulled her aside. 'Look just outside the immediate circle,' I told her, 'and tell me what you see.'

She inspected the crowd. 'There's a ring of young men. They look very hostile,' she replied.

'These are the extremists, the hard core,' I explained, 'probably Interahamwe. They move in on every meeting and threaten the people by their intimidating presence. Would you speak the truth to a Westerner if you knew that you could be macheted later in your *blindée*, as an example to encourage the others?'

Dan Luyie walked quietly over to an RPA officer and had a brief word. A few minutes later, two RPA soldiers walked nonchalantly through the area of the crowd where the young men were concentrated. Almost imperceptibly, they melted away.

'Will they speak now?' she asked quietly, conscious of the dynamic she had just witnessed.

'Some will speak anyway,' I answered. 'They will speak out against oppression and murder, whatever the risks. They will always speak the truth.'

'It is people like that who make this all worthwhile,' she said quietly.

'It is people like that who prove that reconciliation can take place. We must protect and encourage them,' I agreed.

We flew back over the wasteland of Cyanika and onto Rukhondo, now nearly empty, but with distinct pockets of people still covered in the blue plastic *blindées*. These were the Commune groups which would not move easily. In each one, you could trace a series of events, real or imagined, which

248

spoke of poor security at home. With Charlie and his team, we could whittle away at these. And when the food ran out, many would just go home anyway. We had promised them rations there and, for many, it was just the actual process of making a decision.

We landed at the convent and the visitors agreed that they would have liked to tour the whole Operation. There was not enough time.

'And what message should I carry back with me?' Mrs Stewart asked.

'It's very simple. Canada must help the Government of Rwanda, so that it can deliver the peaceful reconciliation and justice that we all desire.'

*

# Chapter 17

I dreaded the Morning Briefs now. It was not enough that Op RETOUR had taken over UNAMIR. It was not even enough that I kept a very low profile for fear of angering enemies. The General now seemed to get some pleasure from publicly criticising the Operation. After the humanitarian brief was over, he would frequently mumble something scathing. Those at the front would hear, while those at the back would not even know he had spoken. But Kelvin or Jan Arp would gesture at me, rolling their eyes, and I would come to the front to ask the General to repeat his question.

Invariably, it was some impossible query. 'Why haven't you got a better handle on what's happening in these Communes?' or 'Why haven't more people gone home?' Everyone knew we were under-resourced, doing wonders with very little. Our inadequacies, which were the subject of every discussion I had with any influential official, needed to be shored up with support, not illuminated for public criticism. They were in any case, the inadequacies of the entire humanitarian and military structure, not the failings of one officer. The General seemed to take some perverse pleasure in displaying me in a cleft stick. It would have been normal military etiquette for him to have summoned me to his office or to the Gang of Five, if he felt there was a problem which was within my control. Instead, I now endured a daily ritual of public humiliation which made me seethe with anger. It was equally embarrassing for those officers who could see what was happening, the DFC included.

As I finished one particularly bruising session, and the General left, I clearly heard a strong Australian voice say loudly: 'Waste of fucking time and money.' Mark Cuthbert-Brown confirmed later that it had been Colonel Wayne Ramsey, Australian Contingent Commander and Force Medical Officer. I did not value his professional military opinion in the

251

slightest. But in this derogatory and unnecessary comment, pandering to the General's evident dissatisfaction and given loudly in front of junior officers, against the credo of the combat soldier, I sensed at last the forces that must have boiled within the Gang of Five before Op HOPE. No wonder we were having such a rough ride.

*

Carl's eccentricities were now well established. His culinary skills were probably the most limited of us all - his only repertoire a vegetable stew, prepared by adding Oxo cubes and water to sliced-up vegetables, lighting the stove and withdrawing for three hours. He was learning to play the flute, a task in which he felt no shame in our inclusion. A private visit to his Toyota would have helped our relationship. But he was not short on opinions about Rwanda and his verbal cut and thrust would liven up our regular debates.

*

We were eating breakfast when Madame Sadaka Ogata came on the BBC World Service to talk about Rwanda. We heard her with growing disbelief. The international listener would have imagined that Op RETOUR was a UNHCR success story. She spoke of how well her people on the ground were doing, how so many people had been encouraged to go home and helped on arrival in their Home Communes. And how the refugees in Zaire and Tanzania would soon be of prime concern.

We could not have foreseen a public battle between UNHCR and UNREO over the ownership of Op RETOUR. It did have its advantages - it might draw attention to our struggles. But Mark Frohardt, Barney Mayhew and Randolph Kent from the 'upstart' Agency, UNREO, were my team-mates now and I did not want them to be put down as the result of another political squabble. The infighting between the Agencies was worsening as the days went by and we moved ahead, driving the Operation from the bottom. I hoped it would all work out for us, but having seen the assassination attempt on Mark already, I feared deeply for us if it should not.

\*

The prisons continued to fill. Mark Cuthbert-Brown, in his capacity as UNAMIR Provost Marshal, visited them regularly and kept us informed of developments. In Kigali, there was just one square metre for each prisoner. They were sleeping in rotation. Sanitation was appalling and many groups just stood like cattle in their own ordure, adding to their discomfort with every passing day. In Butare, Mark's regular visits to his 44 Op HOPE arrestees kept them alive and well provided for. He had established such a rapport with their guards and with the officials that they were almost apologetic, when he visited one day, to explain that one of the prisoners had escaped. They feared that he would be disappointed not to see the man.

At home in Britain House, we cheered. 'I hope they all escape,' said Carl.

\*

The SRSG returned, after nearly a month away. We met in the hallway of the Amahoro Hotel but he seemed unfocussed at first. I could imagine the whirlwind return, the mounds of paper, the sea of faces, the briefings, the pressure and the stress. Still I was disappointed that he was not aching for an update on Op RETOUR. In his office I spoke to him strongly, with conviction. His focus seemed to come back. 'I think it is going very well,' he agreed. 'I would like to visit the camps on the ground.'

I hoped that at last we might get the political energy we needed. Without support being provided to the Government by the International Community, our gains could easily evaporate. But reward their commitment with real funds for restructuring, and we could make huge inroads. The SRSG really was the main chance. No progress had been made on this in his absence. The political showboat was drifting and it needed the captain at the helm once more, going full stream ahead. We could not maintain command of the ship from the engine room.

We were, I knew, relying on him too much. If he failed to deliver, we would all be sunk. We had to develop an alternative plan as well, to improve our chances of political support.

*

The helicopter banked steeply before running in and flaring up for the landing. It was all very combat. Once in a while the civilian pilots from *Canadian Helicopters* did a little tactical flying - for us and them, great fun. With Mark Cuthbert-Brown and Barney, I had travelled to Sake to check out the situation in one of the furthest-flung Communes.

We met the *Bourgmestre*. He was sour. 'This no good man,' explained our interpreter. Some were excellent. Inevitably, with the power and privilege which came with the job, some were not.

Our first stop was on the outskirts of the village. There was no Open Relief Centre but an NGO had nonetheless set up a large plastic domed shelter, which was occupied by a dozen IDPs. They had arrived the day before and were evasive when I asked them why they had not completed the journey to their homes.

'We fear that bad men might come and kill us on the walk,' they explained.

'How far is it?' I queried.

'About twelve kilometres.'

Our Ghanaian platoon commander stepped forward, without prompting. 'Tomorrow I shall bring a section here with vehicles,' he promised. 'We will transport these people home and we will stay with them until they feel safe.' It was a brilliant response, textbook UN professionalism. We drove further into the countryside, buoyed up by the initiative and determination of our troops. With support like this on the ground, the Operation was at least being given a chance.

A little way on, a good-looking, strong woman, about 30 years old, was walking down to the lake, carrying a huge load on her head. We stopped and I asked her to give us an outline of how conditions were in Sake. She had come from Cyanika, she explained, and had been well looked after. She did not fear bad men. There was much food in the ground and it was nearly all edible.

This was certainly news. We had been briefed by numerous 'experts' and had assumed that after months of neglect, most of the crops would have gone to seed or rotted. Here, in a brief encounter, was another myth exploded. I thought it likely that if we had explored this idea further, we would probably have discovered that the whole of Rwanda was still well stocked and that the crisis feeding in the camps, before people went home, was largely unnecessary. The waste, the awful waste of all this aid, foreign dollars needed instead to rebuild the country.

It began to rain and we moved into a small empty hut. We were too far south for mines to be a danger.

'Would you ask this lady if I might have my photograph taken with her?' I asked the interpreter, as Mark took my camera and composed the shot.

Without any hesitation, she came over towards me and turning around, moved up against me, pressed her bottom right into my groin. 'I only wanted a photograph,' I explained laughing and backing away. She pressed up to me again, as if this was what was expected of her. I could feel the warmth of her buttocks through my thin tropical combat trousers. I had to turn away, still smiling, but blushing a beetroot red. Mark and Barney wasted no time in winding me up.

'My goodness, you are attractive to women,' jibed Barney.

'There's no limit to what you won't do in the cause of peace and reconciliation,' bantered Mark.

Our next stop was at a small hut complex. Another handsome girl came to the door, hastily re-arranging her clothes. Her husband was still in Rukhondo but he would be coming home soon, she explained. 'And who,' we enquired, 'was the young man?'

'This is a friend of my brother's,' she explained without hesitation, but with a certain haughty defiance. 'He is looking after me while my husband is away.'

The strapping youth in the doorway looked uncomfortable. It was clear that knowledgeable though we were becoming on the customs and traditions of Rwanda, there was a still a lot to learn.

She changed the subject. Her mother had been taken two nights before and was being held in the Commune jail. She had done nothing but people were spreading rumours that she was involved in the killings. Mark started to take notes. He questioned her closely. Even if her story were only half-true, it was probably a case of Tutsi returnees, acting as vigilantes, and taking the lead in the distribution of justice.

On the way back to the helicopter, we stopped to ask directions to the jail. A low, rough building, it was in amongst the other Commune constructions, a single barefoot civilian carrying an AK-47, its only guard. The prisoners were a pathetic bunch. Nearly all old and frightened but, surprisingly, allowed to wander freely about the area. There was no wire.

Mark asked to see the lady in question and she appeared, clearly in fear that we had come to wreak some further injustice on her. Her story accorded so precisely with that of her daughter that we all instinctively believed her. Mark promised to bring her name to the attention of the Prosecutor in Kibungo, whom he knew.

Through her tears, her gratitude was overwhelming. 'I could have been here for the rest of my life,' she wailed. 'How did you manage to find me?'

'We're the UN. We're here to help the people of Rwanda,' said Mark.

'And we've got Mark Cuthbert-Brown on our side,' I smiled to myself.

We took a circuit of the Commune before a low banking pass over the jail. Mark and I waved from the window as she stood in the dirt, surrounded by her friends who had been given new hope too by our fleeting visit.

We landed in the early evening, strolled to the Chinese Jeep and were home in time for a cold beer at sunset. Several new pieces had been slotted into the jigsaw of Rwanda by our afternoon's work and I felt a much-needed surge of optimism. We amused Kelvin and Carl with tales from Sake, particularly those close encounters of the amorous kind, before the day's soldiering was done. And for once, it had been a good day's soldiering.

*

It was unauthorised, risky, contrary to all the rules and if they had found out about it, my bosses would have gone ballistic. I would certainly have been sacked, sent home in disgrace. But with four weeks to go in Rwanda, there was no longer any point in holding back. My genuine respect for the RPA's fighting skills was matched on the other side by the reputation I had developed with senior RPA officers, for my evident determination to do the best for Rwanda. There was enough common ground within this, to try to achieve something. Good contacts, quiet operators, had now arranged this opportunity to work up something new, to cut through the red tape.

I left my pistol at the entrance to the Ministry of Defence. It was against all regulations to give up your weapon, under these circumstances, but it was the only way to get in. I was whisked up stairs and along corridors to the stark office. There I put my case for the peaceful resolution of the Southern Camps - a partnership between the RPA and the UN, brokered by the Red Cross. They would get what they wanted - the people home and the criminals behind bars. We would get what we wanted - peaceful repatriation. Then we hoped that we would get what we both wanted - foreign aid and assistance to restructure, enable rehabilitation and reconciliation.

This was agreed.

I picked up the pistol at the gate and realised how much my heart was still racing from the gravity of the encounter. I had just talked to the moderate element in the RPA, the soldiers-turned-statesmen. The problem was that nobody knew quite how the internal politics in the Ministry were going to go. The hawks were up against the doves and I had only spoken to the doves.

\*

The Monday evening Sabena flight from Brussels was on time. It was still extraordinary to contemplate people leaving a thriving, bustling, well-lit Western city and disembarking, ten hours later, at Kigali International Airport. Mark Cuthbert-Brown and I waited by the door, inspecting the numerous bullet holes which scarred the building.

His beret was no better than when we had last seen him depart, nearly two months before. If anything, he had more kit than last time.

'What kept you?' had to be the first words from my lips.

'Oh, I hope I'm not late,' he lisped in mock James Bond. 'I've been sent to save the world. Where is she?'

258

*

That next afternoon, Yan started to make me feel more human again. We had to get out of the IOC. His head was reeling from trying to absorb the thousands of changes of the last two months, the new personalities, the activities on the ground, the political changes. The General's negative attitude and the DFC's increasing support were dimensions which nobody could have predicted. By 2 o'clock, he was frazzled and we jumped into the Jeep and headed out on the Byumba road, our destination the Kigali Overnight Way Station, which I had not yet had time to visit. On the way out of town, he told me about his escape.

First there were the signals messages, sent initially by Kelvin as Senior British Officer and then supported by the UN 'system', including Randolph. I could imagine the disbelief this correspondence would have caused in the Ministry of Defence. It was a story out of *Boy's Own*: Rwanda desperately needs this particular RAF Squadron Leader to help direct and coordinate the rehabilitation of that country. Get him here as fast as possible - one airline ticket enclosed!

Yan told me about how eventually, after the shock waves had subsided amongst the bureaucrats, he had been summoned to his boss's office. It was a sweet moment, he enthused, when you are busy planning a rather boring exercise in Norway, to be told that you are indispensable and have to leave immediately for Africa.

Now as we bombed along the road, waving our '*Mwiriways*' at the people, Yan was back in his element and I felt I could really start to be objective again. Without a sounding board, it was almost impossible, at least for me, to form long-term plans consistently. I needed that balance.

The Overnight Way Station was an excellent facility, this time run largely by the Government, with some NGO help. We moved through the groups of families, becoming more and more disconcerted as we heard that some had been there for several weeks. They could not go home, they said, because Tutsi returnees around Ngenda had taken their homes and they feared there would be bloodshed if they appeared and asked for their land back. We moved and talked. Out on the ground and listening to their fears, the people buoyed me up and gave me further determination. And now with Yan to help along the banter, we soon had them laughing and joking, at ease with us. In between questions, he would fire shots out of the side of his mouth at me: 'Didn't expect that answer, did you?' 'Never knew that did you, Colonel Know-All?' He was my conscience, and if there were ever the slightest hint of confidence in my search for accurate information, he quickly humbled it.

Before we left, we were invited by the official in charge to visit another compound, just across the dusty road, in a similar school complex. I parked the Jeep in the centre of the compound and, hesitatingly at first, the people emerged from within the buildings. These were Tutsis, returnees from 1959.

'And why have you not gone home?' I enquired.

'Because our land is near Gisenyi. The people there have taken our land and the bad men from Goma will come at night and kill us if we go back.'

In a reversal so common in Rwanda, these people were afraid of the Hutu who had established themselves in the West, in exactly the way in which the people in the compound across the way feared the Tutsi from the South. That was it. Complex, difficult, impossible? But our expert advice, from the Rwandese, was that it was possible. And that these two communities could live peacefully side-by-side as they waited for history to take its course, was another source of encouragement.

Debating it hotly in the Jeep on the way home, Yan turned over all the stones again, with a fresh mind. He agreed - there was no alternative but forward.

260

Every time I flew over the bridge at Busoro, I started to get cross. The bridge had been blown during the war. If it had been re-established months earlier, as surely was feasible, we could have halved the journey time from Gikongoro to Ngenda and Kibungo. Instead, we had to stage the people through that Overnight Way Station at Kigali, costing unnecessary time and effort and reducing the efficiency of the transport system in the South East by 50%. Now finally, the Indian Engineers, under Colonel Singh, were to re-establish the link. Yan had taken on the project as one of his first and just as he reported his success gleefully at the IOC, we received a message from UNAMIR to deflate us. There was some quarrying to be done and civilian workers would be required. The task had been costed at $300 but UNAMIR would not pay the cash – it had no direct budget for construction. Before we could even think of organising a solution, Barney had opened his wallet and peeled off $300. It was done and dusted in the blink of an eye. And two weeks later, when the bridge opened to the music of the Indian Gurkha Band, there was a special glow of satisfaction from all of us. It should have been called Barney Bridge.

*

At very short notice, I was invited to Goma. Steve Smith, the NGO coordinator, wanted the operational view of Op RETOUR and how it was to be extended into Zaire and the refugees. I was desperately keen to move this next phase ahead. Jan Arp and Kelvin both considered the risks of me going over the border in civilian clothes, against the benefits to the Operation. That took about 30 seconds. I was free to go where we had all been desperate to go for months. Since my first fleeting glance at the hell of Goma from the helicopter during October, it had held a dark fascination for me. In those teeming camps were the core perpetrators of the genocide, still armed to the teeth, defiant, unmoving and surrounded by a million soft bodies to protect them.

Steve picked me up an hour before dawn, with two NGO workers on board. In civilian clothes, sitting in the front of an *Oxfam* Land Rover, I had not felt so vulnerable before. At the first RPA checkpoint we were searched. Our bags were emptied. There was little ceremony and very few smiles. In the Chinese Jeep, I was normally waved through after a few words in Kinyarwanda and the ubiquitous head-nod. Now, I was getting a taste of the NGO view of the RPA.

The conversation swung from topic to topic. The incidence of AIDS in the Goma camps had increased recently in the under-fives. The speculation was that sex with children was one way to ensure that the disease could be avoided. It was an unthinkable statistic, a single point of reference for Goma which confirmed its reputation as hell-on-earth.

At the border in Gisenyi, we encountered a small problem. I had no entry visa for Rwanda. The UNAMIR pass was normally sufficient, in and out of Kigali, and my passport had never been stamped and authenticated. Very quietly, Steve explained the situation to the Rwandese side, and I slipped across the border. While we waited to be processed on the Zairean side, the building next door, the Zaire Army arrived. I had heard much about these men and their reputation for extortion and violence. Now, as they leapt from their jeeps, their arrogance and swagger betrayed their intent.

'They will hassle us,' promised Steve 'and try to get money out of us.' But while they pushed through the other Western NGO people, and through the waiting locals moving in both directions, they kept well away from us. I watched them intently and they watched me back. They knew and they knew that I knew that they knew. And so our little party was left untouched.

'We must take you with us every time we come,' my companions joked as we pulled out. I gave a hard smile to the soldiers and they smiled back, shiftily, conscious of their behaviour, embarrassed. It is a funny old thing, but in every country in the world, a soldier can always spot a soldier.

A meeting had been arranged for all the main NGOs in Goma. There was no UNREO, no UNAMIR, no real UN support. Instead, under Steve's leadership, they had all banded together. A Californian businessman, he had put his various enterprises to one side and moved to Rwanda to do this job. We met in a small building on the edge of the town. There were some preliminaries. I was introduced as a UN official, working with the Ministry of Rehabilitation. Apart from the security angle, Steve felt there might be an anti-military problem. I could see why they would not trust a soldier, but that always made me angry. It was a case in point that some could be trusted.

I talked for nearly three hours, with many interruptions. They were transfixed by the idea of Op RETOUR, astounded by its success. The sweep of political, material and humanitarian issues which it covered in one package, was again pored over, analysed, kicked around. And once again, it was not found wanting. We had thought of everything, although we could not solve everything. We were ahead on the problems and we knew that our solution supported our drive towards success, against time and against the odds.

'And when will we be getting Op RETOUR?' they demanded.

'As soon as we build sufficient momentum with the IDPs to convince people that it is the right way ahead,' I promised.

'You don't need to convince us,' growled a muscular, bearded Italian. 'It's the only way ahead.'

As I was saying my farewells, a pretty young girl from *MSF* came up to say goodbye. 'Thank you for coming here today,' she said with a surprising, serious intensity. 'You have given us hope.'

My *quid pro quo* for the presentation was a visit to the camps. Bruce Mclean, the head of one NGO, took me to Mugunga, the largest, most concentrated crush of humanity in Zaire. Beneath the towering volcanoes, just on the other side of the *Parc des Volcans* and Dian Fossey's gorillas, 250,000 people squatted down in their own mess. In a few square kilometres, on the bare volcanic earth, a town had been set up. Shops, garages, even brothels - the basic commercial requirements of an African town, all made of corrugated iron and blue UNHCR plastic sheeting. Bruce explained just how bad things were. There was no discipline, no law and order, save that of the Interahamwe. They had no respect for the NGOs; they knew that they had to be fed, given medicine, or the world would know about it. And so they treated the NGOs like dirt, refusing to cooperate, undermining all the positive programmes they were trying to establish, occasionally becoming brutally physical. At night, the NGOs left, for the comparative safety of Goma. And then the rule of the mob really reigned. Bruce pointed out a dozen places where he had witnessed machete massacres, hangings, burnings. The pressure of these awful working relationships was so great that the NGO people fell into two categories: Those who could not take the pressure and left after a few months and those who were tough enough to carry on, at great cost to their humanity and mental stability. In the faces of those I had spent the morning with, were all these problems. They were just ordinary people doing their jobs, I reasoned, but there really was an element of the saint in anyone who continued to operate in these conditions. Their desperation and their no-nonsense support of Op RETOUR were not only rooted in idealism. They were hanging on for it.

'And what would happen,' I asked Bruce, pointing up at the Virunga volcanoes, 'if we were to set up a Welcome Centre just

264

over that hill inside Rwanda, defended by the RPA and with UNAMIR and NGO support?'

He thought about it for a few minutes. 'There would be deaths,' he predicted quietly, 'but the momentum would increase despite the threats. Already the overnight movement is starting to build. Within days, thousands would cross and then there would be a flood.'

My route home was to be an even more unusual one than the route in. Michael, a German doctor working for *International Rescue,* was driving a truck back to Kigali and I would be his co-driver.

I amazed him by how badly I could mangle his language.

'You think my German's bad, you should hear my Kinyarwanda,' I promised.

The vehicle was an old Army 8-tonner, donated by the British Foreign Office and he cursed British engineering jokingly as he crunched the gears. We were stopped at the border, this time by the RPA, who were accusing NGOs of importing weapons into the interior. We were searched thoroughly, even though I was again recognised for my military connections.

Michael and I had several hours to talk on the way back to Kigali. I explained what I was doing. He questioned me at great length about the Operation. As darkness fell, I had to admit my worst fears.

'I leave the Army shortly. My wife and family need me back. I have a good job waiting for me in an investment bank. But I worry that others will not push this as hard as I have because I have been committed to it from the beginning.'

'It seems to me,' he said very deliberately, 'that you do not have any choices at all. You are engaged in something extraordinary and you have to complete it.'

\*

265

Randolph and I finished another meeting and we turned to a topic which had been nagging me since I had first talked it over with Sue.

'I can probably get you a one year UN contract,' he promised, 'if you will stay. You're guaranteed to carry on the same role, in civilian clothes.'

'I'll think about it,' I promised. 'Sue is coming out to Africa in two weeks and then I'll decide, if that's OK.'

*

We had just arrived home at 11 p.m. when a horrible screaming started out in the night. Yan grabbed his binoculars and we ran outside. Kelvin, Carl and Mark watched from the doorstep. Across the valley, there was a terrible din. A woman was clearly in awful pain. We surveyed the area and thought we saw shapes moving on a track. But there was nothing we could do. With hundreds of metres to traverse across thick vegetation, almost certainly sown with landmines, and with us armed only with pistols, it made no sense to venture out. When the screaming had stopped, we went inside, deeply frustrated by our inability to intervene. On the following morning, as we surveyed the scene in daylight, it suddenly occurred to me what had happened.

'Look over there, matey,' I pointed. In our concern, we had forgotten that the hospital was just across the valley. The sound that had carried on the night air was more than likely a woman giving birth.

*

# Chapter 18

'So how many people have we persuaded to go home?' demanded Yan.

I explained the complexity of the calculation problem, how UNREO was now placing the tracking of IDPs as its number one priority. We had so little information flowing back from the countryside that it was really impossible to know exactly what was going on. We had a good idea how many were in the camps in Gikongoro Prefecture and a fair idea how many were being added to them, through the NGOs, the Red Cross and the UNREO Field Officers, backed up by information provided by UNAMIR and the Government. We had a good idea how many were in prison and the scale of the increase there. But there was a massive void in our connectivity to the Communes and the sub-Communes and the individual houses, so that in the end, we could only be very vague.

The RPA had forced out a camp population which had almost entirely moved east and south, below the line of the road from Gitarama to Kibuye, before Op RETOUR began. Few of these had gone home. Few, it would seem, had gone to Zaire. Almost none had crossed the border into Burundi and the rumour there was that the RPA or the Tutsi Army were dealing harshly with anyone who tried. It was a reasonably safe bet that the vast majority of the IDPs, between 300,000 and 350,000, had been in Gikongoro when the Operation had started. Of these, we had 'closed' or melted down camps which had contained 175,000 and reduced numbers in several more. That was one end of the scale. At the other end, we had transported 40,000 by vehicle, even though some of these journeys were by the 'tourists', those who went home on reconnaissance or to go shopping in Butare, and then subsequently returned on foot to the camps. I guessed at least 25-30,000 were genuine; the rest, at maximum, were tourists. This was the other end of the scale. In the middle, to help us

267

cover the huge gap between 25,000 and 175,000 plus, there were two yardsticks. The first was that the prevailing information on the ground was that for every one going home by vehicle, three or four were walking. That would put the minimum figure at 75-100,000. The other was that there had been very little increase in the size of the Southern Camps, by all the available estimates including the feeding figures, hearsay from the people and eyeballing on the ground or by helicopter. There were certainly no more than 120,000 left in the Southern Camps, suggesting that 180-230,000 had gone somewhere else. I agonised over these figures and their implications for us almost hourly. My gut feeling was that when faced with the inevitability of their camps closing, or the rumour that their Commune was filling up fast, most people were just going home.

'On the balance of all this,' I explained to Yan, 'I reckon we've moved at least 100,000 but it could be 200,000 or even 250,000.'

'And how many do we need to move?'

We had to reach the critical mass, the change in perceptions, the belief that it was now better to be home than in a camp. It had to be so obvious that the innocent refugees started to slip out in numbers, for fear that they would lose their claim in the Home Communes.

'I don't know,' I admitted quietly, 'but I think we're pretty close now, if not actually there.'

'But that's brilliant,' he exploded. 'Why don't we tell the world? The money would come flowing in.'

'It doesn't make any difference,' I promised. 'They just don't want to know. But if we fall down badly and there's a bloodbath in the Southern Camps, the media will be here by the planeload.'

\*

With typical madness, just as we arrived home, he challenged me to a game of tennis. It was 11 p.m. but the court, behind Britain House, had some malfunctioning floodlights. For the first two games, I ran him ragged. Then he suggested a change.

'Let's swap ends,' he shouted across the net. 'The light's better on your side.' Grudgingly, I agreed. He was up to something. It became clear after the first couple of points. The clay court was slippery and wet where I now skidded and slid and dry where he moved neatly about.

'Time to change again,' I shouted, after two games which went to him.

'No, I'm fine here,' he yelled back.

Two nights later, I threw the Jeep at the dirt track to the Belgian Village at speed. Yan was behind in his Toyota. I switched off my headlights. He hesitated and then did the same. I increased speed and watched in the darkness as he fell further behind. I burnt him off completely. He was intensely competitive and never bottled out of a challenge but I was able to park outside Britain House a good few minutes before him. He arrived, shaken and stirred from the experience of driving down the pitted, steep-sided track in the dark.

'What kept you?' I asked innocently, as he smouldered quietly. 'All those carrots you pilots eat don't seem to work against us artillery types.' He was not to know that I had a lazy eye and could see well at night, and I was not about to tell him.

*

The entourage filled two helicopters. As the dust settled in Kibeho, 12 of us ran out from under the spinning blades. At last, the SRSG and the General were going to visit the Operation together.

At the registration point for Op RETOUR, there was little happening. Few people were leaving although we persisted in offering them the chance. Half a dozen UNAMIR trucks were

269

lined up ready to depart, the dark void under each canopy containing a sea of darker faces, showing only white eyes and teeth in the gloom. The SRSG was bouncy, energetic, inquiring. He interrogated the passengers on each truck and he listened carefully to the answers. One group was definitely 'tourists' on their way to the market in Butare. The incidence of 'tourism' was higher out of Kibeho and Ndago than elsewhere. Most people were not ready to leave. The hard core was well entrenched. But the majority this morning, a few hundred, were genuine and were showing immense courage by leaving in broad daylight, under the sneers and threats of the young men, the Interahamwe. The SRSG was very positive and encouraging, the consummate politician, saying all the right things. I was relieved and pleased.

But the General was unhappy. As we rejoined his group, he started to give me a hard time, in front of the bodyguards, the UN workers, even the RPA.

'I have spoken to these people,' he said very disparagingly, gesturing at the trucks, 'and most of them are tourists.'

'A small number are tourists, General,' I agreed. 'But we've moved very few from this camp and we're well aware that the intimidation levels here are very high.' It sounded lame, I knew. He was putting me on the defensive.

'Give me one good reason why I should use my trucks on this,' he demanded.

'Because many of them are genuinely going home. I have spoken to them too,' said the SRSG strongly. I could not believe my ears. The SRSG was prepared to go into bat for us against the General.

The General knew as well as I did that he had no other earthly purpose for those trucks. If they could only be used to sustain UNAMIR, then UNAMIR genuinely had no mission in Rwanda.

We moved off among the people. The SRSG did the talking. The General and his team stayed in the margins. The

General smoked, kicked the dirt, spoke with his bodyguards. He was sending a clear message: He was only there because he had to be. It was a painful, charged atmosphere.

'Yan,' I hissed. 'For God's sake can't you keep him amused? He's going off quickly.'

'I can't,' he grimaced. 'I've tried everything, even *Blackadder*. He's just Mr Morose.'

'Try again,' I insisted, 'or we'll lose it.'

Out of the corner of my eye I watched Yan's valiant efforts to keep the General interested in the visit. The body language said it all: Bugger off!

But the SRSG was on form, refreshed from his leave, raring to go.

'It is time for you all to go home,' he told an expectant crowd by the church. 'Please, pick up your possessions and get on the trucks.'

'But we will all be killed by the RPA,' they shouted back and I watched the Interahamwe militiamen moving in to threaten the crowd and whip up some anger.

'You will not be killed,' the SRSG retorted, full of certainty. 'The UN will look after you. Blue beret soldiers will be there to protect you.'

I blanched. Even at my most enthusiastic, I had never guaranteed their safety. It was one thing to encourage, acknowledging some risk; another to promise safe passage. But in all the mealy-mouthing and slippery tricks I had witnessed in Rwanda, no one had ever had the courage to say this. And for the top man to feel so passionately about it was extraordinary. He was probably wrong, was making the UN vulnerable, but I just had to admire him for his sincerity.

The General appeared by his side, suddenly animated by the promises being made by the SRSG. Within minutes, he too was talking to the crowd, arguing the case for reconciliation, driving home the message. Now, at last, he was acting positively.

271

'How did you do it?' I questioned Yan out of the corner of my mouth.

'I told him that if he didn't get his arse over here and start doing his job, he'd never fly in one of my helicopters again,' smirked Yan.

The tour was successful, although the General soon lost interest again. At every stop, it became clear that I was the only one who had a sufficient grasp of the detail of the Operation to be able to give all the answers. That was why I was there. As soon as some UN Commander or NGO official needed support, he would turn to me. I responded as neutrally as I could with the right answer but inexorably was drawn into a more detailed discussion. Every time I ended up coming forward from the back row to explain a point or illustrate something on the map, I saw the General's eyes hood over.

At the end, Yan came up. 'I was watching him throughout,' he said grimly. 'He hates you. I think you're a right old sad geezer sometimes myself,' he continued, in order to cheer me up, 'but he just hates you.'

On the way back to Kigali, we flew over the village of Kaduha, where the RPA had killed so many IDPs when they had emptied the camp in November. Now, it was said, an RPA officer had forced the Hutu residents of the village to exhume a mass grave and display to the world the results of the Interahamwe handiwork; perhaps some of these people had been involved in the killing. The SRSG and General wanted to see for themselves. We circled the church twice before the General spotted the bodies from his window seat and then we went around again to see more clearly. At first it looked as though trestle tables had been erected in the sunlight but when we looked more closely, we could make out the simple wooden framework across which had been laid the bodies of hundreds of people. Their grey limbs, occasionally covered by some darkly coloured material, lay stick-like across the frames, like cordwood left out to dry in the afternoon air. As soon as our

272

minds had registered what we saw, we each turned away. In the desperation of the camps and the constant striving of those of us involved in the Operation, these pitiful near-skeletons, thrusting their arms skywards at us, with their half-imagined open mouths, turned the cry for reconciliation into a scream for revenge. And if I started to think about that too much, I knew I would lose faith.

*

Yan and I joined Lillian Wong in her hilltop house in time to watch the sun go down over the city. Up to now, I had not shrugged off my loyalty to the UN and was still undeniably inhibited in my reporting of the events on Op RETOUR. I did not want to let the Foreign Office feel that there was too much fracturing of the resolve and commitment of the UN, for fear that the aid, still not forthcoming from most countries, might dry up entirely from the UK. With Lillian representing us in Kigali and Baroness Lynda Chalker fighting our cause in London, we had come so far in our efforts to establish good relations with the Government.

But now, with only two weeks to go before my time as a soldier was over, there just seemed little point in portraying things as better than they were. While Yan listened soberly on the other end of the sofa, I told her that I thought that we had brought this thing about as far as we could without top level support and that if the flame of hope we were trying to fan from the tiny ember we had created did not soon burn brightly, it would surely die. And as we debated the consequences of that, a cold chill ran through the room. If we could not support the cause of peace and justice and give the Government encouragement to return the IDPs and then the refugees, and then invite them to work with us tirelessly to minimise the disruption and pain and grief that we knew would be caused by the return, there was nothing but a grim future for Rwanda.

None of us cared if the killers lived in exile forever. But we all fervently hoped that the innocent would be given the chance to return and then be left unmolested to rebuild their lives, with those who had remained and those who had returned from previous exiles.

Lillian had a marvellous understanding of the whole jigsaw puzzle. There was only one other non-Rwandese in the country I had met who had the same depth of knowledge - the DFC.

As we drove to the Village under the starry sky, I talked to Yan about my leave. In less than 24 hours time, I would meet Sue in Nairobi and we would spend a week on safari. The worlds were too far apart for me to make any real sense of it all. With Lillian, the endless possibilities of the future soon narrowed down to the few practicalities which we had agreed. But in my meeting with Sue lay the real destiny, the whole breadth of our lives to be laid out. And I just could not square this circle at all.

'What's up with you?' demanded Yan. 'You look like you're half asleep.'

'My brain is all scrambled up by this Rwanda stuff,' I mumbled. 'I'm just trying to work out what to do with the rest of my life.'

Our Australian friends and colleagues were leaving, a few weeks ahead of us in their six-month rotation. But before we could go to the Australia House farewell party, there was a mountain of work to be done. Yan had been back in-country for ten days, on a pretty steep learning curve. Now it was time for me to hand over to him. For a week, he would try to run with this Operation, picking things up as he went. The politics, the grief, the frustration were nothing short of terrible and I had only just managed to hang on for dear life. I knew it would be an awful week for him but there was nothing I could do, except cancel my leave. With only a week left after that, it hardly seemed sensible. Besides, there was absolutely nobody else in the whole world that I would have trusted it to.

At Australia House, I searched among the milling guests, but everyone told me the same. He didn't want to party; he just wanted to leave quietly; he had gone out. I was bitterly disappointed not to say goodbye to Alan Brimelow.

Charlie Main arrived at the party from Gikongoro and pulled Yan and me aside.

'Bad news, I'm afraid,' he explained quietly. As we absorbed his news, Barney appeared and then Margaux. For the other UNAMIR people there and for the other UN workers and the NGOs, we were probably just that group of sad characters who had no idea how to enjoy ourselves. We were always talking work.

Charlie brought enough bad news to sober the whole party. He had visited several Commune lockups and small prisons in the past few days. In his view, there was no doubt that there was a growing, widespread brutality. Many prisoners, incarcerated without charge or trial had been systematically beaten in order to wring a confession out of them. It was well known, Charlie explained, that many of the RPA were turning nasty and that returnees were helping to establish a vigilante presence - the 1959ers - denouncing any male IDP who dared to return. It was not widespread, he added, but it was certainly happening in and around Butare. There was no doubt about it.

'What shall I do?' demanded Yan as we turned it over in the early hours. My plane was due to leave at 8 a.m. He was very unhappy.

'It's a brewing crisis and we have met hundreds of them. If you think the evidence is strong enough,' I said quietly, 'you must bring it to a halt.'

I was not trying to abandon him. But I was definitely leaving him in charge.

*

275

For one week, out on the Masai Mara, in the Aberdares and finally at the Mount Kenya Safari Club, Sue and I lived as we had never lived before. At the Club, the tennis net was stretched along the Equator. Each shot went from the Northern to the Southern Hemisphere. 'Your tennis has improved,' called Sue from the North.

'A little bit of practice in Kigali, dear,' I explained noncommittally, from the South.

In the background, behind this wonderful time of our lives, lay the spectre of Rwanda and the terrible choice I had to make. In deciding to leave the Army, in order to give stability to my family, I had promised to put down roots. Part of that was the job in the bank, a chance to live a more routine life. Now I was opening up the idea of throwing it all away by staying in Africa to drive Op RETOUR. It may have been my life's work but my life was not just for me; it was for Sue and for Rory and Patrick as well. A one-year contract, even if it did materialise, was not enough to move the family to Rwanda, to Nairobi or even to Geneva, with any degree of certainty. It was a huge risk and I knew it would involve separation, long hours, unbearable stresses, all things I could abide but my family could not.

We talked late most nights. In the end, as the great heronry at the Club settled down under the maroon corona of the sunset around Mount Kenya, I recognised the pressure I had put us all under by deciding to leave the Army. We had just come through a year of uncertainty, of questioning fundamentals, of seeking a new career while keeping a very busy one going in a parallel world in which no one could know of my intent. In that year, the house search, the school search, the job search, the great looming culture shock of leaving my first vocation. And then six months in Rwanda, for my own reasons, one last chance to get my boots muddy, to achieve something lasting, that I could be proud of. I looked into my wife's deep brown eyes and it became clear that all this had not come without cost. And to cap it all, I was now offering up an open-ended stretch that started with a year of separation. It really could not continue like this. It had to be the one or the other. I was either going to be driven, pressing on in the face of adversity, here in Africa. Or I was going to be a husband and a father.

*

Catapulted, thrown back into the cauldron, no time to think about it all.

The Morning Brief was different. The officers of UNAMIR were enthusiastic and energetic. There was much hand-waving over the map. People spoke more clearly and loudly than usual. Questions to which everyone knew the answers were asked in an innocent fashion and answered with untypical accuracy. Senior officers showed determination and commitment. Action points flowed. Fine judgement, deep compassion, heavy responsibility manfully shouldered. This was the impression given. While I watched it all with grim amusement, Yan whispering a series of hilarious cynical remarks in my ear, I realised that there would be one major advantage. I would not be called up for a public humiliation on why Rwanda had not been sorted out yet. If you listened to the brief, it was clear that Rwanda was well in hand.

It would all have been remarkable had not the BBC been there. The TV crew had been in-country for a few days. Yan had explained how he had ambushed them as soon as they had appeared. 'Come and visit the most successful integrated humanitarian operation of all time,' he had told them. 'It's amazing.'

After much procrastination, when he had worn them down with his charm, they eventually agreed. 'We'll visit the camps on Sunday,' they announced.

'Unfortunately nothing happens in the camps on Sundays,' explained Yan. 'The rest of the Operation is running. You can visit the Ministry, the IOC, the Open Relief Centres in the

Communes, the Overnight Way Stations. On Sunday, most of the humanitarian staff have a day of rest. And we've found that a day of reflection enables more people to decide to go home. I'm sorry. How about another day?'

They had got annoyed, he explained. They did not want to negotiate.

As soon as the brief was over, I moved up to the young woman who seemed to be in charge.

I introduced myself, receiving no reply. I pressed on. 'Yan Janiurek told me that you wanted to visit the camps and I just wanted to let you know that we can get you to Kibeho today. I'm taking the Task Force, including a Government Minister, out by helicopter and you'd be welcome to come along. There and back in a couple of hours.'

'I've told your people already,' she replied, not looking up from packing her briefcase. 'We have other priorities. You've missed your chance.'

I followed her out of the room, putting the case as we walked. That it was a unique opportunity, a real exclusive, how helpful it would be for Rwanda and for the Operation. All the arguments I had used before to others members of her profession, to no effect. We climbed the stairs in the hotel, heading for the SRSG's office, presumably her next interview.

She broke her aloof silence. 'Look I've told you. We've got other things planned. We're not interested.'

I watched her back as she walked up ahead of me to the next level, her long hair lank against her thin print dress which swayed as she moved, her dusty feet showing white where the straps on her scruffy sandals had rubbed through the grime and suddenly it seemed to me that it was time to stop being polite.

'Well I've got an exclusive for you,' I shouted at her as loud as I could. In the corridor, people stopped and stared. She kept moving. 'How about 'World's most prestigious broadcasting corporation loses its manners?''

278

I met Yan at the bottom of the stairs. 'What did she say?' he demanded.

'Same as she said last week, matey,' I replied. 'Bugger off!'

*

As the helicopters departed and the noise and dust subsided, I realised that something was wrong. The people were lining the hill below the church in Kibeho. That was quite normal for a helicopter visit; there was precious little excitement in the camps. But the numbers overlooking the landing area were far greater than normal. And the crowd was silent. I did not give them a greeting. And moving down the track towards us was a group of UNAMIR soldiers, with a number of civilians and behind them, a large group of RPA. Something was seriously wrong.

Charlie Main from UNREO was the first to arrive. There were a dozen of us from the Task Force, including Justin Murara, the Minister. The other Ministries had sent ever more important delegates to our meetings. And the RPA had sent a senior Captain. It had all been improving but I wondered what body blow we were about to receive as Charlie and the Zambian Major stepped up to us.

Charlie did the talking. There had been a serious incident the night before and there was now big trouble. At the UNAMIR post, a grenade had been thrown and then the RPA had opened fire, first in the air, and then at the crowd. There were several casualties. The occupants of one *blindée*, a man, woman and their baby, had been killed. There was much unrest. The people were demanding that UNAMIR take action against the RPA.

I looked at my watch. It was only 9.45 a.m. The Morning Brief had started at 8 a.m. and now we had flown into this. I had been back from leave for less than two hours and already the pressure was ferocious. The BBC had certainly missed an exclusive.

'Let's look upon this as an opportunity,' I argued strongly. 'The only organisation that is working across all the boundaries of Rwanda is us. We have arrived at a crucial moment. Let's take some positive action now and show these people that we really do have their interests at heart and that we want them to return in peace and dignity. Justin, will you show your concern in public? It would have a tremendous effect on the people.'

There was much shuffling of feet but the public position we were in required some action and so reluctantly, led by Justin, the large group moved up over the hill to the UNAMIR post, opening the vast crowd as we went.

At the platoon headquarters, there was a grenade burst-mark just outside the sandbags. It was impossible to say from which direction it had come. The RPA commander was adamant it had been thrown from the crowd. Some of them, hearing his words, started to shout out that he was lying. Quietly, the Zambian Major told me that they believed it had been thrown or dropped by the RPA. The unrest was breaking through the crowd like a wave. It was very dangerous. But I was convinced that this was an opportunity not to be denied. For us, it would be a PR coup if we could show the Government's concern. The bodies were in the back of a UN truck. I asked the soldiers to pull back the tarpaulin. In the dark shadows lay three bloody bundles of rags. The white soles of the mother and father's feet were clearly visible. The baby, who had been shot with the same bullet as the mother whilst on her back, was now lying a few feet away on the wooden floor of the truck.

'Tell them that there will be an investigation, Justin,' I pleaded, drawing him towards the tailgate. 'Come over here and look at the bodies now and say that the Government will find out who did this and bring the perpetrators to justice.' I watched him intently, as the RPA watched him intently, as the people in their thousands watched him intently.

280

But he waved at the people and turned away. I walked quickly up to him. 'You have to do this,' I pleaded. 'It will change everything. In one moment, we can defeat the power of the Interahamwe in Kibeho. You have to give justice if you want to achieve reconciliation.'

He hesitated briefly and then quickly walked over, looked at the bodies and then moved away, parting the crowd. He had done as much as he dared, while the RPA watched him. If he had criticised them, it would not have gone well for him in Kigali. But even then, I sensed that this flunked opportunity was a defining moment for us. If we had shown more determination, Kibeho might soon have gone the way of so many other camps under Op RETOUR.

We followed him up the hill to the *MSF* post. The crowd, silent again, parted as we walked. I looked into their faces. The blank, sullen expressions gave it all away. We were just not welcome.

At the hospital, I was asked to give up my weapon. Reluctantly, I handed it over to Major Mark McKay, a newly arrived Australian who was now working with us in the IOC, replacing Andy Moore. With Justin and the other Task Force people, I went inside.

There was certainly one shot; there might have been more. Suddenly, the people were running, screaming, diving for cover. I ran for the hospital entrance. After nearly six months without any bullets flying, now with just a few days to go, I had given up my pistol at the vital moment. Just my luck to die unarmed, having carried the bloody thing around for months, I thought, the adrenaline slowing everything down to the numb half-reality of an emergency. Everywhere, children were screaming and crying. I watched a young child being thrown out of harm's way by his mother, only to crumple into a wall and fall senseless and bleeding to the ground. It was a stampede. I joined Mark who had taken cover under a low wall and took my pistol back with relief. Gradually, the noise died

281

down. There was some shouting, much crying. We climbed out and walked around. One of the Zambian soldiers came up. 'It was the RPA,' he shouted. 'They opened fire.'

We were really losing control of the situation and yet Justin became determined to press on. He could not have criticised the RPA but as part of our visit to the camp and the hospital, he was scheduled to address the crowd and he intended to continue. As I took my place on the concrete rostrum with the others, well above the heads of the crowd, now returned, I thought we must be going mad. Things had never been so bad. The tension was palpable and here we were exposing ourselves as perfect targets. But if it was hard to continue, it was equally hard to bottle out. We were surrounded now by the majority population of the camp, at least 60-70-80,000 people. If they had wanted to, so close were they now pressed, they could have torn us all, UN soldiers and RPA included, into the tiniest shreds. You only had to remember the mass graves of Rwanda.

Bravely, defiantly, Justin spoke. They listened; he had quietened them down. After about ten minutes, all in Kinyarwanda, the situation seemed better. My eyes were swivelling in my head, trying to pick out any signs of brewing trouble. The flap on my pistol holster was undone, an unconscious drill, more for comfort than for any practical reason.

A movement started in the crowd. At first it was imperceptible but then it grew into a distinct wave, a change of perspective, like the sea breaking on the beach, caught out of the corner of the eye. Then suddenly they were all running, all moving away, all getting as far as they could away from us. That dissipation of so many people was a deep rustling, like dried leaves blowing into a street corner on a cold winter's day in England. Within it, there were sounds of individuals, of children shouting and their parents chiding but the fading away was accomplished without any real, strong voice. They blew away, running down the hill in all directions, leaving us up on

282

the rostrum without any cover. Over the microphone, Justin's tones were excited as he tried to get them back, tried to find out what was happening. I thought I knew. Now, exposed on the hill, we would be attacked.

I stayed on the rostrum with Justin and some of the others, Barney, Charlie, the RPA Captain. There was nowhere to run; we could be shot easily. We told Justin to get down. He continued to shout through the microphone. Nobody was listening. The UNAMIR troops took up firing positions. The RPA cocked their weapons.

Gradually, slowly, the people drifted back. Sombre, frightened, on edge. It was electric. We tried to look relaxed. Our people behaved properly with confidence and authority. There was no sign of panic. Soon the word spread. It was the extremists, the Interahamwe. They had demonstrated their power by organising the people to run and now were sending them back.

When the majority of the crowd had returned, Justin resumed, engaging several of the people in his questioning. They too had a turn at the microphone. It was all very democratic and impressive. It went some way towards reconciliation, although it was already too late. The visit had been bad for us, had shown our vulnerability, had demonstrated our lack of cohesion. The RPA had just caused another public relations disaster. Unfortunately, the Task Force had been associated with it.

We left by vehicle, thousands of stony faces watching us. There was no politeness, just pure hostility.

At Runyinya, we stopped *en route* to Butare and Tac Headquarters. We had come to visit the Commune jail. We moved around in one large group being led by the *Bourgmestre*, who explained what was happening. As we went from room to room, meeting the prisoners, the RPA Captain slipped away.

Eventually, we entered a room with a dozen frightened-looking men sitting on the ground, their backs to the wall. One

283

old man jumped up. Through the interpreter, he denied that he had killed anybody, said that he was a victim of a land dispute with another family. We listened to him with a deep concern. The real killers were only a few kilometres away and it seemed unlikely that those with blood on their hands would have returned. It was within nightly raiding distance of the Southern Camps and the RPA kept a heavy presence in the area.

The RPA Captain entered. 'These men are all killers,' he announced arrogantly. 'This man has killed,' he said, pointing at the old man. 'And this person has killed five people himself,' he went on, pointing to a younger man sitting on the floor. Immediately he got up and waited expectantly. Yes, he agreed under questioning, he had killed many people.

There was something odd about the certainty of the RPA Captain. It suddenly became clear that he had been in the room before us and singled these men out as murderers. What threat he had placed them under in order to get them to confess to us, I could not tell. It was all too improbable. We were being duped.

As we continued the tour, I pulled back until I was level with the RPA officer. 'Could I have a word please?' I enquired. I stepped off to the side, along a high wall, away from the others. 'I don't believe your accusations,' I told him bluntly. 'What you just did was disgraceful. How can we all bring justice to Rwanda if you lie like this?'

His face broke into an evil grin. 'You people want criminals. We will give you criminals. What will the UN do about any criminals we give you? You will do nothing. We don't need you and your Human Rights. We will bring our own justice.' He stalked off, leaving me feeling empty, distraught that after all our work, we still had so little credibility with some of the RPA.

At Butare, Colonel Osae-Addae stormed out to meet us. 'Why are you here?' he demanded. 'I know nothing about this visit.'

I tried to explain that that we had a Government Minister with us, that the visit had been properly arranged and all the rest of it but he just kept berating me for the lack of forewarning. I was having a bad day. And in Kigali, I was seriously out of touch with another major problem which Yan was dealing with. I had had enough of this painful progress and called up a helicopter. Meetings had been set up with the Prefect. The others could go to them. They looked mute as I gave my leave and ran down the hill and underneath the spinning blades. But there really wasn't any time left to deal with the finer points.

*

# Chapter 19

They were in the Ops Room, arguing, deciding what to do. Austen Yella, Carl Dixon and Yan. I could tell as I came in that they had not expected me, and my sudden arrival had caused some tension. I had only been away a week but I had quickly become an alien on my own turf.

'What's happening, mates?' I enquired airily. 'Everything OK?'

Everything was not OK. At first they were evasive.

'We've decided to stop the Operation,' Yan eventually said. I wanted to explode. I did not normally involve either Austen or Carl in the decision-making process and it did not seem to have anything to do with them at all. But the problem ran deeper than that. In just one week I would be gone and Austen and Carl and all the others would be left to carry the flag. I did not want to destroy their confidence, their commitment. It was a very hard moment. I might only be in Rwanda for one more week but I still wanted to call the shots.

'Perhaps you could explain why you've come to this conclusion,' I said warily, noncommittally.

Yan went through it. There was evidence that the RPA were up to no good in the Communes. Reports of killings were on the increase. Confidence was waning. The Southern Camps were crystallising, becoming harder. UNAMIR should not be associated with such a dubious future.

I heard them out but I was deeply unhappy. And I was struggling. In a week much had changed and although I was still deeply connected to the framework, there was no guarantee that I had kept abreast of all the tiny details which were needed to exercise this level of fine judgement. Once again I cursed myself for going on leave. I argued the counter-arguments, but not strongly. I was tired, stressed and miserable, and I needed time to think.

But I did give them a little bit of a punch. 'We'll look at all the angles and then we'll decide,' I promised. 'But we will not take unilateral action from UNAMIR. Not without involving all our hard-won allies in Kigali.' And I left them with a clear message: I'm not done yet.

I might have been tired, but still I could not sleep. I was just too deeply immersed to lose one precious hour of my involvement in this extraordinary business on its final stretch. In the quiet of the early dawn, I came back to the surface. Deep down inside, the mental keel which had so far guided me in some unseen groove, once more engaged itself. I was back on track. Relaxed, certain, determined.

I bounced into breakfast and told Kelvin. 'I've worked it all out,' I promised. 'I know what we have to do.' He listened, dubious at first but becoming more convinced. Eventually, he was converted.

Yan, Carl and Mark arrived, followed shortly by Sean. The conversation spilled over onto them. They became involved. Carl was furious. Yan was beside himself.

'You can't do this,' they yelled. Loud, deep passion, welling up from inside us all. It came out with an unstoppable force and suddenly we were all shouting, all demanding. All our hopes, all our fears, coming together in one great expulsion of stridency, of insistence, of hearing our passionate beliefs being crushed by the other's arguments. At first it was me versus Yan and Carl, the one who had been away against those who had been running with it over the previous week. Then Kelvin joined in and then Mark and then Sean. They all supported me. In Britain House, we finished off as we had started this thing. With open debate, honest argument and no quarter given.

They were subdued. Carl threw in the towel. 'You've called it right for six months,' he accepted. 'I'll have to give you this one too.'

There was only Yan. Silently, we packed our kit and went out to the Chinese Jeep. It was pouring with rain. The seats of the Jeep were sodden. The footwells had an inch of water in them. I cranked the motor and headed out for the IOC. I had just got off the dirt road and started to speed up on the tarmac, when it started.

'Why did you bring me out here?' he demanded. 'What good have I done? I've just got in the way; I haven't done anything useful. I couldn't even stand in for you when you were on leave. I didn't even get that right.'

It hurt me far more than a direct confrontation. I could have handled that, could have found the words to win the argument. But I could not win an argument in which he was bent on self-inflicted pain.

'It's not true,' I shouted back over the wind and the roar of the engine. 'You've been brilliant. You've brought everything into perspective. I was really wasted when you arrived. Frankly, I couldn't have carried on much longer.'

Then I told him about the pain and the anger and the humiliation of this enterprise. How it had eaten at my very core. How I had lost a great chunk of my youth and my love of life and my ability to consider the future beyond the next hourly crisis. About how my family had really started to fade from my consciousness, so wrapped up was I in Rwanda. I told it to him then and I did not hold back. Finally I told him about the guilt. How I had started all this without the sure knowledge that it could be finished. How our failure to get the three million on the move was going to have knock-on effects forever in this region. And that I felt it was my fault, my failure, my lack of determination, my weakness. Me not being clever enough. Me not outmanoeuvring all those who stood in our way.

'And when you came, you helped me to cope with all that. Only now, you're experiencing it yourself.'

And as we talked it out, the rain, or the tears, streaming down our faces, and our voices being carried on the wind, I knew then, with a great sense of relief, that it really was all over.

*

We had a meeting about the prisons. We were trying to find novel ways of getting people out on bail. The overcrowding was appalling. The RPA was unlikely to bend; it would have to be something very lateral. An Australian lawyer, Major Craig McConaghy, had rolled his sleeves up and was helping the Human Rights effort, providing new insight and energy. His solution was to provide an ID card system for all prisoners, properly controlled and understood throughout Rwanda. If they had ID cards, he argued, they could be recognised and accounted for in their Home Communes. I did not say much.

Afterwards, Yan sidled up. 'So what do you think of this idea?' he asked. 'You were strangely silent.'

'I thought it was weak, actually,' I admitted. I gave him the counter-arguments. How the system would expose the innocent to abuse by the denouncers and the land-grabbers in the Communes. How giving the wrong people control over such a system would be far worse than the chaos there was now. And so on.

'But why didn't you say all this?' he questioned. 'They will do loads of work before they start to understand the complexities of it. You could have saved them huge amounts of time.'

'Because we have to stop,' I explained resignedly. 'They're the next generation. They have to overcome the obstacles and learn the ropes. They're bursting with enthusiasm and alive to all the possibilities. Rwanda needs them like they are. Not with our tired old pessimism to defeat them before they start. It's all that energy, all that determination that's needed. Let it flow. They'll probably think of brilliant new ways to get around these obstacles. But let's not tell them it can't be done.'

'All right,' he accepted eventually. And we left the IOC as free men.

*

Now we had the report, it was difficult to know what to do with it. *Oxfam* had commissioned a study in the camps mainly concentrating on the remaining hard-core of Kibeho and Ndago. Their findings were absolutely incontrovertible. The main reason that people would not go home was the security situation. The most complete element of that unsurprising strand was the hardest-hitting. The people had lost their faith in UNAMIR to protect them. Op HOPE had convinced them that we were on the side of the RPA and not to be trusted. There was no real point in saying, 'I told you so.' Despite its weaknesses, UNAMIR had contributed far more to Op RETOUR than might have been the case. We wanted them to continue their commitment. It was no time to throw teddy bears.

'I think we should be magnanimous,' pronounced Yan. 'Let's give the report quietly to a few key players so that the lesson isn't lost. But let's not rake over the old coals.'

*

'You will be aware that there is a good deal of resistance to this recommendation, gentlemen, but in my view, Operation RETOUR must continue.'

The Gang of Five were quiet. I outlined the reasoning. There was evidence that the RPA was getting much tougher in the Communes. The distilled deduction from that was that if we were concerned that the people might be threatened, we should not encourage them to go home. But there was a difference between not encouraging them to go home and halting our contribution to the Operation. And if we did not

291

continue to lead this process, the RPA would get even tougher in the camps, and would kill those who we had a duty to protect. Everybody was relying on us; the UN Agencies, the NGOs, the Government, even the RPA. Our withdrawal of support would crumble the numerous unique alliances that had been built around the Operation. In the discord and disharmony that would arise, Rwanda would be split again and chaos would ensue. If we were to do that, we might as well go home. Worse, we would not be able to show our UN face in the next or any humanitarian disaster. The military had put this thing together. If we allowed it to fall asunder, we would be vilified, publicly pilloried, with every justification. We had provided Rwanda with the only piece of common ground she had and while we continued to engage in the process, others would too. But do not stop investing in Rwanda. Whatever happened, our trucks must be there every day. Our assistance must be available. Our security, such as we could provide, must be provided.

The General was not happy. But he went around the room. The new Chief of Staff from India, Colonel Shiva, was on side. I had got to him the day before. Kelvin, my stalwart champion, agreed. Jan Arp, excellent bloke, agreed. The new Australian medic, Colonel Warfe, agreed. Then came the DFC. He too agreed, and strongly. Finally, it was the General.

'Very well, Tom,' he assented, without much enthusiasm. 'We accept your recommendation. UNAMIR will continue to support Operation RETOUR. That is all'

I saluted and marched out, still very much the stranger in that claustrophobic room but on very good terms with its occupants, individually, outside it. All its occupants except one.

*

I was involved in personal administration, getting ready for the flight home. Everywhere I carried my various sheets of scruffy UN paperwork, I received the same reaction: 'But you can't be leaving.' 'We heard you were staying in the Army.' 'I thought you were going to work for UNREO.' It went on, adding to the guilt, particularly when someone would say something a bit deeper: 'It will stop as soon as you leave. You're the only one driving it along.' It was all very kind and very well meant. But it was making it all too bloody painful.

I wrote 40 thank-you letters to everyone who had helped, including the SRSG and the General.

Yan, Sean and I were having a combined farewell at the bar, scene of so many riotous evenings in the early days, but now more tame as our six-month generation moved out. We went through and agreed a list. The General was not on it. It was my single act of defiance on departure. I might have had to endure the humiliation but that did not mean he could then get an automatic invitation.

*

The DFC and I talked for a long time. Randolph had told me that he had waited for a helicopter with him one afternoon and they had got talking. The DFC's wife of over 30 years had died just a year before. He had come to Rwanda shortly afterwards and the war had started a few months later. I saw then, as Randolph described it, that he was still grieving for her, would always be grieving for her. He had had all that to contend with. And then I had become a thorn in his flesh as well. I had questioned his judgement. Now, I felt humbled by his equilibrium.

'You have to have dreams,' he mused as we said our farewells. 'You brought your dream to life here in Rwanda and it turned to a reality. It is dreams which make us human, which

293

change the world. You have had a fine dream.' Coming from him, it was the best compliment I could have received.

The General was very reasonable. There was little humour left in him. Rwanda had squeezed him dry. We talked about my future in the bank, and we left it at that.

The SRSG was excellent. We kicked the big ideas around for half an hour. 'And will you write a book about your remarkable experiences?' he asked obliquely, I assumed, inviting positive comment.

'Well Ambassador, I think I will,' I exclaimed. It had not occurred to me before.

I ran down the stairs, jumped behind an unmanned computer to write the action points of our meeting and got them back to the SRSG exactly 12 minutes later. All of the action points were for him.

*

At the final Saturday Morning Brief, I stood up when my time came. I had thought about saying something significant and it was expected. The room was full. I told them about the reason for it, once again, why we had had to do it, why we still needed to do it. I explained, once again, that we had had to go early, before we were prepared. I pointed out that we were critically underesourced and then I told them what we had done.

For the first time ever, we had brought together the UN Agencies, the NGOs, the host Government and the military in a common cause, under common leadership for a single purpose. In 1945, Europe had had the Marshall Plan. In 1994 and 1995, Rwanda had had Op RETOUR. From UNAMIR, we had led, driven, coordinated and contributed the bulk of the energy and our commitment had been key to unifying the others and in raising their contributions. Some Agencies and NGOs had behaved magnificently; others had fallen well short. We still had no formal structures in most Communes, but somehow, it was working. At least 100,000 had gone home; it could be as many as 250,000; more would follow. The refugees were now slipping over the border from Zaire in ever-increasing numbers – 1,200 the previous day. I urged them to use their skills wisely to keep it all going. I urged them to record the event, to prove what could be achieved. I urged them to keep their hope alive.

'And finally,' I announced, moving up close to them, reaching out to connect with them, 'many people have said over the past few months that this has been my Operation. That has never been true. It has never been *my* Operation; it has always been *our* Operation. But from Monday morning, it will no longer be *our* Operation; it will be *your* Operation. And with it and all your other endeavours in Rwanda, I wish you the best of luck.'

\*

The party was a hoot. It was truly international, including Agency, NGO, Government and RPA people as well as our own. There were speeches. Kelvin said two typically perceptive things: That I had got Rwanda under my fingernails and that, in his view, more than anyone else he had met, I had loved her people. I was presented with a wooden carving of the Op RETOUR pictogram, the wonderful icon which Stefan Grenier's team had designed. It was a brilliant gift, the result of a lot of thought by Kelvin and the boys. I was really choked. Randolph stepped up to take the stage. He was kind enough to suggest that our new-found civil-military unity had prevented the disaster of Somalia repeating itself. His views were seriously impressive; I couldn't wait to see the 'mahddel'.

His gutsy reproach to the Secretary General had changed my opinions and I had found him easier and easier to like. In the same way as my views on the DFC had changed, so they had of Randolph. In a strange way, these two had caused my most significant education in Rwanda. That was one side of the experience which had the quality of permanent enrichment about it.

For myself, I had little to say. It was my last speech in the Army, but I could not really feel that awesome sense of disconnect. My horizons were far too short to take that in. It seemed to me right then that I should thank these people for their help above all else. The team from Britain House - Kelvin, Sean, Carl and the irrepressible Yan; Mark Frohardt, Barney Mayhew, Margaux Van de Fliert, Charlie Main, all the UNREO people, World Food Programme, Human Rights, UNICEF, and so it went on. Standing on the steep, grassy bank, under the starry sky of Africa, as I looked out over their smiling upturned faces and as I waffled on through a few wisecracks, I was absolutely certain of one thing. I would not know friendship, forged in such adversity, again.

*

The last morning was the beginning of the best day, marred only by my inevitable farewell to the Chinese Jeep, an icon of Op RETOUR around Kigali, if ever there was one. I had hatched a cunning plan to spirit the Jeep out of Rwanda in a container, since it had already been written off, and had negotiated a cash contribution to UNAMIR for its scrap value. But somehow inevitably, the wrong chassis number had been entered into the computer, the paperwork had not been authorised, and there was simply no time to unravel this ineptitude or repeat the process. The Jeep would just have to be another casualty of the UN bureaucratic system.

Before the party the previous night, I had finally cleared the last piece of work I had intended to do. Now, Sunday was free. At dawn we drove in convoy to Lillian's house. Lillian climbed in the front of the Chinese Jeep. Kelvin and Carl were in the back. Behind us in the Land Rover, Yan drove a bevvy of Unriettes - Margaux, Betty,

296

Anita. We passed a barn owl watching us from a low wall, seven hammerkopf, many raptors. And we came out onto the Ruhengeri ridge at Tare just as the sun splashed its first rays of the day onto the volcanoes. We drank champagne, scrounged and saved for this moment. It was nothing short of magical.

Breakfast. And then out to the airport for a helicopter ride to Gisenyi. At the hotel on the lake, we drank coffee, and walked about, marvelling at the beauty of the place, the trees full of weavers, the shore lined with cormorants. And after lunch we climbed into the helicopter once more. The others moved over to give me the best seat and the pilot came on the intercom. 'Where would you like to go?' he asked.

'One last spin by the volcanoes and then home, high up so I can see the whole country,' I begged.

I looked down at the green calderas and then beyond into Zaire where the beast lay. The beast that we had not subdued and now could not be subdued until major changes had occurred. Past the gorillas and then on down the most beautiful ridge in the world. Cutting south, we approached Kigali from Gitarama. As I looked down at the tiny fields and the houses and the smoke and the splashes of colour, through the volume of emotion, I could then see real change, as I had not been able to in the maintenance, the delivery of the thing. There were people in the fields in numbers. They stopped and waved as we flew over. I waved back, conscious that they could not see me. But all over Rwanda, as I looked at her for the last time, it was clear that she was starting to come back to life. Perhaps, after all, we really had made a difference.

*

297

## Chapter 20

I first heard the news on Radio 4, as I was getting ready to leave the house. I tried to listen again as I sat on the train and then at lunchtime, I left my desk and went to the *Currys* shop around the corner, so that I could watch the news on one of the display TVs. At work, I was distracted and extremely upset. They probably thought I was weird. The first two weeks in the bank had not been easy in the transition. I was trying to cope with overwhelming change and grief. My father-in-law had died just days after my return. The bank was about to be taken over by a foreign competitor; everyone's future was in question. Now the void was really opening up.

One of my colleagues picked it up in the afternoon. 'Is it true?' she asked. 'Could they have killed so many people in the camp?'

'I suppose it is,' I replied noncommittally. I did not want to discuss it with these people, warm though they were. I did not want any of it to come out.

We were moving house, from Uxbridge to High Wycombe. It was the ninth move in our marriage. We were combining it with a death in the family and a new job. These are supposed to be the three most stressful events in life. The fourth is divorce. That did not seem very far away either.

These were the darkest days. I was trying to unpack in the new house at the weekend when Barney's clear, clipped tones came over the radio, from the IOC. Yes, he said sombrely, it looked as though up to 5,000 people might have been killed. There may have been some shooting from the crowd but it was impossible to say. A full investigation was taking place. Earlier reports had said 8,000 had died.

I was awake all night. I hugged Sue and the children very hard in the morning. As the 7.24 train pulled into the station, I stepped up to the platform edge. I watched the front of the train, saw the driver's face. Got ready.

It came and it went and my feet stayed where they were. The process of recovery began then. I counted my blessings all the way into London.

\*

Sean married Lynne in a glitzy all-American razzmatazz, transplanted from New York and superimposed on Tyne-and-Wear. Dinner at Lumley Castle the previous day, an English country churchyard and the reception in a stately home. The occupants of Britain House were there, in their uniforms, clanking with bits of paraphernalia. I was in a suit. 'Don't come near us, you bloody civvy,' they joshed.

Mark Cuthbert-Brown had been at Kibeho when the massacre had occurred. The RPA and the NGOs, including the Red Cross, had been preparing the camp for closure. There had been a crude exit plan but as soon as the hard-core militias, now cornered, tried to break out, surrounded by soft bodies, the RPA had opened fire with automatic weapons, rocket-propelled grenades and even mortars. It seemed to Mark to be more the local actions of the RPA than any obvious Government policy, but it had resulted in the deaths of 1,200-1,500 people, and not, according to Mark's best estimate, the 8,000 originally reported. Twelve hundred deaths could be explained away by an act of atrocious indiscipline; 8,000 could only be the result of premeditated murder. The debate on this figure still rages but the evidence is long gone. There were many reports of RPA convoys carrying dead bodies to be buried in the Nyungwe Forest, before the press, suddenly interested after months of indifference, had arrived.

The UN troops had received strict orders, straight from UN Headquarters in New York. UNAMIR troops were not to open fire under any circumstances. I recalled the carefully drafted Rules of Engagement which Alan Brimelow and I had pored over for many long nights. There was no doubt about it. It was the duty of every UNAMIR soldier to open fire in defence of unarmed Rwandese civilians. Clearly, when it had come to the crunch, the UN had failed to protect the citizens of Rwanda, for the second time in one year.

Nonetheless, despite these restrictions, there had been many selfless acts of heroism by UNAMIR troops, in some cases stepping between the RPA and the people. Mark, who had spent the most traumatic night of his life in Kibeho, received the Queen's Commendation for Brave Conduct. To a champion of justice and decency, it could not have been better awarded.

\*

I became a BBC 'expert' on Rwanda. I was asked what could be done about Goma and the killers. If there is ever to be peace in the region, I argued, the International Community must purchase an unpopulated piece of Zaire, away from the border with Rwanda and allow them to live in some form of nation-state, stripped of the protection of the innocent. They would be isolated and hated at first but at least they might establish a community which was not based on violence and oppression. We must try to love them, I pleaded, since if we do not, there will never be any hope for their children.

\*

Just after Yan left the RAF, we gathered the Britain House people together again in our new home - Yan, Kelvin, Fraser and Mark. Yan and Jane were about to go on the trip of the lifetime - a journey around the world. It was awkward with the wives. Our talk of Rwanda quickly faded. They did not want to hear us describe it. Ironically, the subject that had bonded us all so closely, now back home, kept us far apart. And every veteran will say the same.

At the end of the year, a letter came. It was from the local Brigade Commander, congratulating me on the award of the MBE. I was surprised and, almost defiantly, felt no need of the recognition. As I told Kelvin, my rewards I had already had and would continue to enjoy in some marvellous memories. But it was a great honour and, at last, public acknowledgement of the success of Op RETOUR, an award for Yan and Barney and Mark and the others as much as it was for me. Quite the best thing was the numerous letters I received from old friends, retired former schoolmasters, and loads of mates from the Army. But I could not share it at work. A merchant bank is no place to expose such a colourful past.

I dusted off my uniform, took a day off and went up to the Palace. The Queen was very well briefed and She made me blush. When asked what She said, I can give only one answer: 'Did you borrow a thinner man's uniform?'

As I walked across the forecourt of Buckingham Palace with my mother and Sue and her mother, the guard came up to attention and presented arms. I had been a civilian for nearly a year but it was at that point, as I returned the salute with a crisp and instinctive 'Carry on, please,' that I really left the Army.

*

The momentum of Op RETOUR slowed down after Kibeho. The General withdrew military support to the IOC on the very next day. It was the only thing that held all these precarious alliances together and he deliberately smashed it apart. I can still neither understand nor forgive that response. When the country most needed it, the UN, which had established some joined-up thinking, actually took it away.

In retrospect, I do feel better about the whole experience. Kibeho confirmed the major role we had played in levering out nearly a quarter of a million Hutu IDPs from under the bayonets of the RPA. But I still feel the guilt of the lives lost unnecessarily. I know the security operation was botched and that the RPA behaved atrociously, but I still have a nagging feeling that if I had delayed my departure for just two or three more months, it might not have happened. I would have insisted on a level of detailed planning which would have exposed the risks to the RPA and guided them towards a more deliberate solution. But if Kibeho had closed successfully, then we would have pushed on to Zaire and maybe Goma would have produced an even more vicious bloodbath. There are too many scenarios and it is pointless to agonise for long.

History has moved it all on. In 1996, the rebel forces of Laurent Kabila attacked Zaire, eventually taking the country (returning its name to Congo), quite clearly with the assistance of the RPA. The people in Goma and Bukavu flooded back, released from their shackles, fearful of the RPA but still determined to bring their lives back towards normality. Others, inevitably the most guilty, fled into the forests of Congo and were hunted down by the RPA over many months. Some are still there, living a nomadic existence. But as I now write, the regional bonfire which we had tried so hard to smother continues to flicker and flame. Five years on, it is estimated that a further 900,000 people have died. Kabila was killed in January 2001, not before he had turned on Rwanda and joined forces with the Interahamwe. Zimbabwe, under President Mugabe, with help from Angola, Namibia, Chad, Libya and the Sudan, now supports this faction against Uganda, Rwanda and Burundi. The huge country of Congo is divided between these forces, each side seeking control of the gold, diamond and precious mineral mines.

How could any degree of political ambition or personal greed involve an alliance with the Interahamwe?

Those who played politics or sat on the fence rather than give their wholehearted support to Op RETOUR, must now

303

examine their consciences. We had developed the detail for the IDP phase and the broad strategy for the refugees. Beyond that, our aspiration was that the restoration of Rwanda without violence would lead inevitably to a stabilisation of the region. We had also articulated contingency plans to modify the process, in the light of political change. Despite its inadequacies, would our makeshift strategic plan to steal the innocent from the guilty have resulted in the loss of 900,000 lives and the prospect of further unending grief for this region? Surely an imperfect regional strategy would have been better than the anarchy which has since ensued?

The West continues largely to ignore Rwanda, has failed to deliver the promises of 1994 and 1995. If nearly 2 million people can die in such a short time, without exciting any lasting interest from the rest of the world, is it any wonder that we have so little credibility in Africa? Geography and economics certainly have something to do with it, but if the victims had been white, as they were in Bosnia and Kosovo, it would have been a different story.

Despite all the experiences of Op RETOUR, there is still no strategic planning and implementation organisation at the UN. The term 'IOC' does not figure in any humanitarian planning manual. We are back where we started in 1994.

In Rwanda, many have been imprisoned or tried for the genocide. Now, it is said, it is becoming more and more difficult to separate out the innocent from the guilty. But there is definitely some semblance of justice and reconciliation and I know we were the catalyst for that. Perhaps by my own values, we were weak in several areas. Judged by our results, however, Op RETOUR was a success. By the standards of Africa and of the UN, the Operation was, in retrospect, nothing short of a triumph.

\*

304

I will go back. Not now while it still hurts, while a report in the press or a clip of video on the news can open it all up again in seconds. But later, when I have done a few other things and travelled a few more roads and I can put it all into perspective, I will go back. I will take Sue and Rory and Patrick and we will climb the Ruhengeri ridge at dawn.

And then, just as the volcanoes light up for another African day, and the valley-mist burns off in the welcome warmth of the sun, I shall show them the most wonderful thing that I have ever seen. Deep down in the dark folds of the continent, the tiny splashes of colour that speak of life returned where once there was only death. Of peace and hope. And a land never to be forgotten. The land of a Thousand Hills.

*